Also by Richard Timothy Conroy

Our Man in Belize
The Indian Exhibition
Mr. Smithson's Bones
Old Ways in the New World

OUR MAN IN VIENNA

A Memoir

RICHARD TIMOTHY CONROY

With Illustrations by the Author

Thomas Dunne Books
St. Martin's Press ≈ New York

THOMAS DUNNE BOOKS.
An imprint of St. Martin's Press.

www.stmartins.com

The photograph of Richard Timothy Conroy and his family, March 17, 1963, is reprinted by permission of The Knoxville News-Sentinel Company.

Book design by Diane Hobbing of Snap-Haus Graphics

Library of Congress Cataloging-in-Publication Data

Conroy, Richard Timothy.
    Our man in Vienna : a memoir / Richard Timothy Conroy.—1st ed.
        p. cm.
    ISBN 0-312-26493-3
    1. Conroy, Richard Timothy. 2. Diplomats—United States—Biography. 3. Diplomats—Austria—Vienna—Biography. 4. United States. Foreign Service—Biography. 5. Vienna (Austria)—Social life and customs—20th century. I. Title.

E840.8. C663 A3 2000
327.730436'092—dc 21
[B]
                                                        00-026188

First Edition: August 2000

10 9 8 7 6 5 4 3 2 1

To Franz Bader and Otto Natzler
and all the other Viennese who,
in taking refuge in America,
gave us more than we gave them,
and to my wife, Sarah,
who rightly considers herself Viennese by experience

■ ■ ■ ■ ■ ■ ■ ■ ■ ■ ■ ■ ■ ■ ■ ■ ■

CONTENTS

P R E F A C E

Life and Death
in Vienna

This is the second (and most likely the last) volume of my memoirs of the Foreign Service. The first, *Our Man in Belize*, tells of life in a place once "described" by Aldous Huxley as one of the ends of the earth. Vienna, on the other hand, has for centuries been one of the centers. A very different place.

Most people who write such remembrances of diplomatic life seem to have lived on another planet than the one with which I am most familiar. Good for them; better for me. They have stared down the enemy and made him flinch. They have caused national boundaries to move, governments to rise or fall, and have sent cables directly to the President, bypassing those nosy and obstructive people in the State Department. (The most famous of these was probably one Ambassador Galbraith was said to have sent from New Delhi directly to President Kennedy suggesting that U.S. aid to India was somewhat like a gastric manifestation in the wind.)

I, on the other hand, have mostly been on the receiving end, and seldom have I been, as they used to say, "mentioned in dispatches." (Bit of trivia: Foreign Service dispatches were discontinued July 1, 1962. I don't know why.)

To be honest, letters from my superiors and various grateful citizens to Washington commending me were probably more or less balanced by letters of condemnation. There was that former assistant attorney general who— But forget him, I think he must have had an ulcer or something. I like to think that during my fifteen years in the service, letters or no, I did some important good for some unimportant people.

It was due to me that a Viennese hooker and an American of questionable moral character were able to enjoy blissful retirement together in America. I did keep a nice Jewish lady from Brooklyn from being sliced up like salami in Budapest. And of course I sprung the Polish-American schoolteacher from jail after he was bitten by the prostitute. And one should not forget that American teenager from the private school in Switzerland who was living in an abandoned palace with two Swedes, a German, and an Englishman named Charlie—

But enough about that, for now. My greatest failures may have been that I was unable to save a rather sweet (albeit murderous) Texas housewife from Iraqi vengeance, or a nice (though glittery) Alabama girl from being rubbed out by the mob. Readers won't know about the Texan, but that will all be explained. Readers (and watchers) may remember the flashy Alabama lady when she testified before the Kefauver crime committee. When asked why she lived high and never paid income tax, Virginia Hill replied she never worked a day in her life, that men just gave her money. "You can't keep them from it." Though the respite was not forever, she was fortunate to be away from home when her housemate, Bugsy Siegel, was assassinated in her living room. He had a gold latchkey in the pocket of his bathrobe. "Why not?" Miss Hill later commented. "It is a big house."

They, the ladies, both died on my watch, and had I handled their cases differently— Well, nothing I can do about it now.

All this, and much more, is what this memoir is about.

I believe it is impossible to write a memoir without referring to real people, unless it is an account of the author's years waiting for rescue on an otherwise uninhabited island. So, quite a large number of people play a part in this memoir.

I have rechristened most of them. However, there are a few exceptions. I can't imagine writing about Virginia Hill without mentioning her name, and the names of some of those with whom she was associated. For a great many years her every move and word were reported by the press, and TV covered her appearance before the Kefauver crime committee. So, no precedent is being shattered here. And the poor woman is now more than thirty years dead.

Going against the advice of my friends, I have retained my own name and that of my wife. No point in hiding it, in Washington people would be bound to find us out.

I also mention Simon Wiesenthal and several Jews of my acquaintance who escaped Austria and who contributed much to their adopted America. That is a story that can't be told too often.

As far as the rest of you are concerned, living or dead, I have given you new names (with a few exceptions, naturally). You may deny that you ever met me and I will support your denial. You can claim that your former self (if that really was you) was misperceived, misunderstood, or whatever else. Undoubtedly.

Memoirs are just that. What the author remembers. They are

always subjective, often ill informed—just like life, in fact. They are one person's opinion. They are not history.

Of course history is not history, either, it is just something better researched (usually) than its poor cousin, the memoir. A good history contains the opinions of many people, a consensus, maybe. If the opinions of many people are wrong, history becomes myth. If the memoirist's opinion is wrong, then it becomes just a comment upon the author. Quaint, perhaps, but nothing more than that.

I hope this account will reveal something about a Vienna in the early sixties, as it emerged from those first postwar years when Austria hung balanced between East and West. And how this affected the people who came through my hands at the American embassy.

In an odd way, I became prepared for my Viennese experience some years after leaving Austria, when I became a client of art dealer and bookseller Franz Bader. Franz had fled Vienna in 1939, two jumps ahead of the Nazi "final solution," and had become established in Washington as a dealer in paintings, sculptures, and prints. During my time abroad I had begun to presume myself an artist and, upon my return to Washington, Franz was too courteous to disabuse me of it, thus establishing our association that was to continue some twenty-five years, until Franz died in the early nineties. Neither Franz nor I ever made much money from my paintings (hardly any, actually) but I gained from Franz something much more valuable. That was a clearer understanding of the often baffling Vienna I had left behind.

For help in writing this book, I am also immeasurably indebted to several women, who, I hasten to add, are in no way responsible for any errors or omissions that I may have made.

They gave me good advice, but I may still have got it wrong. One of these is Virginia Devine, who knows far more about Vienna (and probably about anything else) than I. Another is my wife, a journalist for half a century, who is my conscience when I am tempted to be egregiously self-serving, and who kept her temper when, after she had done a magazine article on the embassy in Vienna, she was told by the ambassador's wife, "You can't possibly print that."

I must also mention Sabine Yanul, who continues today the Franz Bader Bookstore, a bookselling tradition begun when the late Franz Bader was apprenticed to the trade in Vienna's First District during the last days of the old Austro-Hungarian Empire and rose to become proprietor of the Wallishausser Bookshop before the Nazis came marching into Vienna. It was Sabine who for this book set me straight on what I thought I remembered of the lyrics of Bertolt Brecht.

Because it still bugs me, I have appended, as a final chapter, a description of an awful thirty days that came at the end of my Austrian assignment. I had just returned to the United States when a well-meaning friend in the State Department arranged for me to be detailed for a month to escort around the United States a high official from an oil sheikhdom in the Middle East. The country has to remain hidden under a pseudonym. Nobody wants another war in the Middle East.

OUR MAN IN VIENNA

The author, his wife, Sarah Booth Conroy, and their two small daughters on the eve of their departure for Vienna

P R O L O G U E

Belize, Just Before Christmas 1962

Vienna, as I viewed it from the tiny Central American town of Belize, was incomprehensible, but not, to me, exactly unimaginable. I imagined it as an enchanted city, a place of palaces and monumental buildings, with cuisine to be savored and remembered, and music—music everywhere. Vienna, a wondrous place surely blessed by the spirits of Mozart, of Beethoven, of Haydn. And Schubert, too, I supposed, though I'd never much liked *lieder*.

I flexed my fingers. They looked normal except for the gray mud under the nails from Hurricane Hattie. But out of shape. My piano was lying dead in my living room. Beside my piano, a box full of loose felts, hammers, and other pieces of the piano action that had become unglued after the great hurricane and tidal surge a year ago. Perhaps—just maybe—we could give my Chickering a decent burial in Belize and buy another piano in Vienna. A shiver (rare in Belize, for climatological reasons) of anticipation ran down my spine.

Too much to hope—no, too much to expect but not too much to hope for, I thought as I read once more my travel orders. Maybe I was really going to Vientiane and the name, Vienna, was some cruel trick of the eye. The effect of capricious light from the walls of my mold-stained office. Mold the same color as the mud or maybe a bit darker. I angled the piece of paper, better to gather the light from the window, from that part of it not filled by the huge air conditioner that was grinding away, wringing water out of the atmosphere.

No, my orders definitely said Vienna. Something was wrong in Washington; the Department of State was sending me to heaven. Perhaps they'd been told I was dead. I got to my feet. As had happened regularly for the past year, my swivel chair once again crashed backward, the casters having rotted loose in the pedestal. No, I was pretty well sure I wasn't dead. Couldn't be any rot in heaven and the other place would be without any hope. I had hope for sure.

My feet kicking up tiny puffs of gray dust from the now powdered but still indelible sewage that had inundated the consulate during the previous year's hurricane, I walked out into the hall and toward the office of my boss, the consul.

He heard me coming and grabbed papers up from his desk, pretending to work. I ignored his subterfuge. It no longer bothered me; I would be the same way when I became the boss. If ever. "Sir, I'm going to Vienna," I said and waved my orders at him. He peered at me over his glasses.

"As?"

"Visa officer, it says."

"They still hate you in Washington."

"Why do you say that?" A rhetorical question, the answer being well known, but my boss took it seriously.

"It figures. Pruitt never turned in your efficiency report when he left here."

Pruitt had been my boss in Belize up until six months before. We didn't exactly hit it off. "Are you going to give me a report when I leave, sir?"

"I'll have to think about it."

I turned and was almost out the door when he yelled after me, "You might rather I didn't."

1

The Sergeant

He sat glaring at me. I knew that look from somewhere. He drew on his cigarette while I searched my memory, mentally airbrushing out the flag behind his desk and the State Department–issue mug shot of J. F. Kennedy, and everything else in the room, leaving only the grim, death's head and those eyes, boring through my outer layers, searching for my wormlike soul.

No luck. Something familiar, but not quite the same. I set to work. Mentally, I revolved his head ninety degrees. A trick I had, left over from my first job when I was a structural steel detailer. You never know when such things are going to come in handy. He exhaled thin blue smoke. A dragon breathing fire.

His head now in profile (in my mind), I began inserting background details, ones that seemed to be missing. Sketched in a window, just to the left. Wasn't really there, in that windowless office, reason told me, but it ought to be. I outlined a body. Thin. That much was right, I was sure of it.

The Vienna Rathaus (City Hall)

Dressed in—hmmm—the dark blue suit was wrong, too diplomatic. Let's give him nondescript pants and a tweed jacket. An old one. Brown. Salt and pepper. And the body needed a bow tie. Couldn't quite make out the color, but a dark tie, nothing flashy. The tweeds didn't seem to hang right. The body should be doing something. A pose of some sort. Back bent forward, elbow on something.

That's it, foot on a radiator, yes, I remembered that, elbow on knee. And chin in hand. And the scowl topping it off. I blinked and it was all gone, all my additions, but the scowl remained, it was the dominant feature of the consul general, the man who sat in front of me. I averted my eyes, looking around the room. There was a real radiator but it was off to the other side. The wrong side. And, yes, there was no window at all. Hmmm.

But I was on the right track. I looked out my imaginary window, the one I had drawn on the blank wall. Outside was a river, a familiar one. All at once I knew where I was. He must have seen the astonishment in my face, for he froze, his cigarette halfway to his lips for another drag.

"Baylor," I said, more to myself than to him. The image that had sharpened in my memory was that of my English teacher. One day, during the dark times of the Second World War, he had come into the classroom, black straight hair cut long for the times, and eyes hollow under almost Romanesque arched brows. He had scowled in just that way at me and two dozen other students in gray uniforms, then he had walked, a gaunt, stick figure, over to the window that looked out over the Tennessee River, just a few miles downstream from Moccasin Bend. He had put one brogan-shod foot up on the radiator, propped an elbow on his knee, supported his chin in his hand, and stared out of the window as the minutes bled out of the hour allocated for junior English.

Fifteen, maybe twenty minutes went by; the class hardly breathed. Then, with a slap he brought his foot back to the floor, turned and looked at us, scowl still in place. "Vegetables," he announced, having found a category into which we all seemed to fit. Then he gathered up his papers from his desk and strode from the classroom. We sat, frozen, for another half an hour until the bell rang.

"Did you say Baylor?" Consul General Philander Trudgeon asked.

The image vanished and I moved forward twenty years and crossed an ocean. "Uh—It's nothing. I was just reminded of something, sort of."

"You said Baylor." Trudgeon swiveled his chair around. With his back to me, he pulled a large, paperbound book from his bookcase. He turned partway back, presenting himself in profile, this time without my helpful imagination. The hair was different, I decided. Gray instead of black. A long, thin arm stretched out and groped for his spectacles. He put them on, perched near the end of his long, thin nose. He opened the book and hunted through the pages.

I could see it was the stud book. Stud book was the popular name for the State Department's Biographic Register. It contained capsule information about Foreign Service officers, myself included. Trudgeon found the passage he wanted and frowned as he began to read. I rated only about six lines, but it did say where I was from.

"So you went to Baylor School, did you?"

"Yes, sir," I admitted.

"You know that song?"

"Song, sir? Which one do you mean?" I supposed there must have been a school song, but it was so unmemorable I couldn't now recall it.

"You know the one, the one that begins, 'Underneath Mission Ridge . . .' "

I grinned. For the first time since I had arrived at my new assignment. "You mean the one about that other school, the one on the other side of town?"

"Yeah."

" 'Underneath Mission Ridge stands a school of folly; where three hundred sons of bitches call themselves McCallie. They are slippery slimy bastards; they are full of—' " I left off, unsure how he would react to scatology.

The death's head broke out in a smile of pure pleasure. "Yeah," he repeated. "Did you like Baylor?"

"Not very much," I admitted.

"Neither did I. Have you been upstairs?"

"Not yet. I suppose I better go on up and report to Mr. Lehar."

"He'll keep. Sit down for a few minutes."

It was a star-crossed meeting, as it turned out, but more about that, later.

• • •

Trudgeon's office was on one side of the building lobby and across from it was the passport and citizenship section, dealing with Americans and their problems. Upstairs was the visa section, where I was being assigned, initially, processing requests of foreigners to visit or to immigrate to the United States. On upper floors were the regional office of the U.S. Immigration and Naturalization Service, and the U.S. Public Health Service.

The building was a large one, prewar, but I don't know by how many years. It faced onto Friedrich Schmidt Platz, named for the architect who was responsible for the heavy stone nineteenth-century Rathaus, or city hall, that loomed over an adjacent side of the square.

Within the embassy, we usually referred to our building as the Rathaus, too. Inaccurate, but easier than saying Number 2 Friedrich Schmidt Platz. Upstairs in our Rathaus, and entered from around the corner at number 7, Rathausstrasse, were apartments for some of the embassy staff and for some of the people in our mission to the International Atomic Energy Agency.

In the cellar of our building was our embassy commissary. It was now a convenience but had once, just after the war, been a necessity for our people stationed in what was then a very hungry Vienna. Now, in 1963, except for such necessities as duty-free whiskey and tobacco, and such peculiar American requirements as jars of baby food, the commissary was superfluous.

There was a time when the State Department, in a premature effort to promote California wines, made the commissary quit handling European wine and stock our domestic product. It was a short-lived experiment. The ambassador's wife was overheard in the commissary saying to another embassy wife, "My dear, California wine is not even good for cooking." Not strictly accurate, of course, but devastating to the State Department's trade promotion effort.

More to the point was a small privately owned bar in the building, a few steps below street level, which was rumored to be supplied with potables from our commissary through some subterranean means. I never knew the truth of that and was disinclined to find out. Austrians needed their whiskey, too.

• • •

After leaving Trudgeon's office, I went upstairs to report to the chief of the visa section, consul Frank Lehar, a fairly senior man, bound to make consul general, someday. For myself, I was still a vice consul, somewhat overage or what some call "long in the tooth," a horse-trading term, I understand. I might someday make consul if they didn't run me off first.

"Sit down," said Lehar's strong, resonant voice, pitched somewhere between the upper limits of a baritone and the lower reach of a tenor. A good bit of nose in it, I remember thinking. The sort of voice that would stand out well against a mezzo.

"Yes, sir," I said and sat, conscious that with my postnasal drip, nobody could hear me beyond the orchestra pit. Lehar. Good name, I decided.

"Been to see the old man, I suppose."

"Ambassador Kitteldorfer? No, at the embassy I've just spoken to the people in Admin."

"Trudgeon."

"Oh. Oh!" Then it occurred to me that since I was more than an hour late, Lehar had probably called down to Trudgeon's secretary asking about me. The phone had rung several times while I was there. "Consul General Trudgeon. Yes, I had a nice meeting with him." I looked Lehar over for some sign whether I should have said it was a nice meeting. I could have been more neutral.

"What did you think of him?"

Right. I should have left out the nice. "He must be near retirement," I said. Lehar relaxed a notch. Without saying anything bad about Trudgeon, I had suggested that he looked to be rather old for somebody who hadn't yet made it to career minister rank. Bumping up against mandatory retirement for the lower grade.

"Did he say anything about me?"

Ummm. A loyalty test. Tread carefully. "He asked if I'd been in to see you yet."

"You hadn't."

Quite true. "I hadn't."

Lehar shifted in his chair. "Somebody is bound to tell you this, so you might as well hear it from me. We don't get along."

"I'm sorry— Different styles—" I fumbled for something to say. I was familiar with the concept of not getting along with one's chief. "Well, no assignment—"

"He has never invited me to his house."

I dropped the 'is forever' part of what I was going to say. "Maybe he hasn't gotten around—"

"In four years? Well, more than three, anyway."

"Maybe he doesn't entertain many from the embassy. I can recall some parties I would rather have skipped—"

Lehar suddenly reached for a file. Mine, probably. For the moment, the inquisition was apparently over. I had no doubt it would return one way or another. Lehar opened the folder and hunted through the papers. "You've had some visa experience." A statement; certainly not a question.

"Yes, sir. Zurich and Belize."

"Ummm."

I wasn't sure what that meant so I kept quiet. I suspected that 'Ummm' was a superior officer's way of saying that a third assignment, one after another, as visa officer was no recommendation. The low road to oblivion, maybe.

"There are six officers in the consulate. Counting the consul general."

"I see." What he said was clear enough but I wasn't sure what he was driving at.

"But two are new minted."

"Oh." Must be rotational officers, out on their first assignment, trying out in different offices.

"That means you are the fourth man and the other two don't count."

"Oh. I see. Well, I'm used to that. I was on the bottom in Belize, too." I was beginning to understand that Vienna was not all the step up that it had seemed months ago when I got my travel orders in Belize. Maybe my chief back there had been right; they still hated me in Washington.

Abruptly, Lehar got up out of his chair. "You'll want to meet the staff and have a look at where you'll be working."

• • •

Later, I looked at the small group of customers waiting patiently to see me and then, to put off the inevitable, I walked over to the window and put my foot on the radiator. Elbow on knee, chin in hand. Uncomfortable, but then I wasn't as thin as my old English teacher—It came to me, Mr. Hitt, that was his name. I scowled, anyway, for practice. I wondered if Hitt was still alive. Likely; what's twenty years? Like Mr. Hitt, I stared out of the window. No view of the Tennessee River, just the dark gray Rathaus. Not only was I not Mr. Hitt, but this wasn't Baylor, either. And certainly not Belize. Nothing in Belize remotely like the Rathaus.

This must really be Vienna. I looked for the Danube. No sign of it. Window in the right direction but too many buildings in the way, I supposed. Looked a bit to the right. Couldn't see the famous Ferris wheel either. Groped for the German word— Reisenrad, that's it. Maybe my German would come back, but it was appalling how much I had forgotten since my time in Zurich.

Stood on tiptoes. No sign of the Reisenrad, buildings in the way of that, too, though the Prater park must be over in that direction, somewhere. Looked for men dressed in overcoats, standing in doorways. Thought I saw one. Occurred to me that most of what I thought I knew about Vienna came from the movies. Maybe a little bit from operettas and such, but that wasn't very much up to date. A *Fiaker* ambled down the street, the clip-clopping of the horse hooves quite audible through my closed second-floor window. Rosalinde, disguised as a Hungarian countess, on her way to Prince Orlofsky's party? No, wrong time of day, but maybe operettas weren't entirely dead, after all.

The Sergeant ∗ 13

As I turned from the window, prepared to get down to work, my eye was caught by a long, dark blue car parked by the side of the Rathaus. Italian, by the look of it. A Lancia, maybe. The lower parts of a man protruded from its open hood. Something familiar about him. I squinted to see him better. No improvement. I searched my memory for associations. No luck. Couldn't be Harry Lime hanging out of the car; too thin. Maybe Harry was still around but he wouldn't be my problem. After all, as Lehar said, I was only the fourth man in the consulate. I breathed in the fresh Austrian air and decided that even if I was only number four, it beat being on the bottom in Belize.

• • •

The best evidence that I had moved here from Belize was negative: the whole city of Vienna was not crowding into the visa section, waiting to try their stories on the new visa vice consul. When I took over the consulate's visa operations in Belize, it was only a few hours before the word had spread around the city that a new, and perhaps more gullible, "visa mon" had arrived. Smiling local people swarmed into the office to try me out. But Vienna had hardly noticed my coming at all. I thought.

The day proceeded as I should have expected. The people wanting to go to America were almost all qualified. People with jobs, families, and homes to come back to. People with enough money to make the trip to America and stay in a hotel instead of in somebody's servants' quarters. People who could pay for a restaurant meal and not have to wash dishes or bus tables for it. Tourists and business travelers, you might say. Real ones.

Little remarkable about these people except that some Austrians brought in more documentation than I would have expected, and many seemed to think it peculiar that they were asked to swear to the truth of the statements they had made on their applications. Cultural differences, I supposed.

"Mr. Conroy—"

There had been a lull in the stream of applicants and I was fiddling around, taking inventory of the previous occupant's leavings in my desk, thinking about perhaps dumping everything out and starting over, when one of the visa clerks, Gerhard Huber, appeared at my door. "May I come in?" he asked and when I nodded, he took it as an invitation to close the door. "There is a man outside. He wants a business visa."

"I take it there's something wrong?"

"He is in the lookout book."

The lookout book was a compendium of visa refusals, worldwide, including people the Immigration Service had turned away at the port of entry. Good, I thought, I'm finally being noticed by the incorrigibles, the ones who made the job interesting.

"Am I to tell him to go away?"

"No, if he wants to apply again, give him an application form. I'll look at it."

On paper, Mr. Foltin certainly looked qualified. He was a wholesale grocer and an Austrian from Burgenland. The easternmost Austrian province of Burgenland, lying next to the Hungarian border, was once part of Hungary until the breakup of the Austro-Hungarian Dual Monarchy at the end of the First World War. After the Second World War, Burgenland was in the Russian occupation zone until the Soviets and the other allied forces withdrew from Austria following the signing of the State Treaty in 1955.

The visa refusal was shown as having been issued in Vienna; we might still have some files. I went over to the large safe in the corner of my office to have a look.

When I was in Zurich several years earlier, a whirlwind—maybe tornado is the proper term—had come through in the persons of a high consular official with the rank of career minister and his sidekick, a woman whose name I have successfully repressed and now cannot recall. I will refer to her as Miss Borgia, which about sums up my feelings about her. While the minister distracted the attention of our consul general, Miss Borgia, cloaked in his authority, raped our visa refusal files, throwing out everything more than ninety days old, despite our protests that the Swiss would no longer make such information as police records available to us. Her contention was that once the refusal had been made, it would stand forever in our lookout book and need never be questioned again. Her confidence in the rightness of some lowly vice consul's visa decisions would have been quite gratifying in particular had it not been so horrifying in general. If you get what I mean.

Had the minister and his assistant gotten as far as Vienna before the plague had been stopped? I pulled open a drawer in the office safe to see. And as Howard Carter said upon breaking the seal on Tutankhamen's tomb, I saw things, wonderful things. Four big drawers in the safe, packed tight as a tick. At random, I eased out an envelope, being careful not to tear it in the process. Inside were photographs, views of the bodies of a man and two women hanging out of the open door of a car, a prewar Fiat, from the look of it. Like a Topolino, but bigger. Black-and-white photos, but the bodies were covered with dark splotches that must have been blood. The victims appeared to be beyond caring.

Another file, a bundle, really, was fat with facts, describing the political shenanigans of Herr Gellert, an Austrian engineer with a penchant for joining things—the Nazi Party, the Communist Party, and others I didn't recognize. I extracted the most recent piece of paper. The man was now in Indonesia, working for Sukarno, it said. Nothing for us in Vienna to worry about anymore, but better keep it anyway. I forced the file back into the drawer.

It looked as though there was going to be reading enough for a long winter. I counted the months—wintertime would come again in six months, no, seven. If the records burners came back, I would forget the safe combination. Perhaps that was how my predecessor saved all this—this— I pulled some more files. There were some cables from the Department of State and other consulates, but mostly it was CIC stuff, the military's Counter Intelligence Corps files, and dating from the occupation period. We had apparently learned something from the Germans—keep records on everything and everybody.

And here it was, the file on Mr. Foltin, thin, hardly anything in it. I took it out, closed the safe, returned to my desk and opened up the folder. The bulk of the material was made up of evaluations, all relating to something interesting: the photograph of a man in a Red Army uniform. According to the evaluation papers, this was Mr. Foltin and the uniform was that of a sergeant in the Red Army of the Soviet Union. I can no longer recollect the details, but the unit was identified and our counterintelligence people seemed to have no doubt of its authenticity. I turned the photo over and there was a date and some other numbers, meaningless to me. The notes were written by a European, judging from the day preceding the month, the small cross on the figure 7, and the figure 1 with the downward swooping serif. 23/5/1947. Hmmm.

"Show Mr. Foltin in," I asked Gerhard.

The man who presented himself looked ordinary enough. Fifty years old, maybe. Fairly typical Austrian type if there is such. Had been eating well in recent years. Drinking well, too, judging from a certain redness of his nose. I held up the photograph for comparison. The same man, probably. Any difference was accounted for by the almost sixteen years that had elapsed, assuming the date on the photo was correct. "Please sit down, Mr. Foltin," Communist agent, war criminal, or whatever you might be. "We have refused you a visa before."

"Yes. But I thought I try again."

"Why?"

"You are new Konsul. May be you change mind."

"That makes sense." I appreciated the promotion to consul, however much premature. "Do you know why you were refused before? How many times, is it, twice?"

He thought for a moment. "Is three times," he decided. "Also I come here more times but they tell me go away."

"Do you know why you have been refused?"

"No. They never say. Maybe I not have much money. Now I have more." Mr. Foltin pulled out a bank letter listing his assets. I looked it over. Pretty good, translating schillings into dollars. But you never know about these things. In my experience, money can make a quick visit to the bank, just long enough for a letter like this, and then most of it hurries back to rich Uncle Otto or maybe to a loan shark. Even a cash register temporarily out of balance. But this letter looked better than most. It was for a business account and showed an average balance over several years.

"Has anyone ever said anything about security problems?"

"For that I bring you the letter from my bank. I have good

security." He smiled, showing a gold tooth. If he needed more money he could pawn that.

"No, I mean about political things. Did anybody ever say you were an agent for the Russians?"

"Russians?" Mr. Foltin's mouth dropped open. "No! I am Catholic. *Volkspartei*. I never was Communist!"

"How do you explain this?" I turned the photo so he could see it.

He gasped. "*Wie*— How— How you get that?"

"Is that you?"

"Yes— Yes, but that is not what you think."

"I think it is a picture of you in the uniform of a Red Army sergeant."

"Yes, it is, but I am not in the Red Army. Not ever."

"You were in a play. You know—like in the Burgtheater." I tried not to be sarcastic. I failed.

Mr. Foltin put on an earnest expression. I prepared myself for the con. No nationality appears to have a monopoly on the con. Visa applicants seem to come by it naturally. Mr. Foltin sidled up to my desk, dragging the heavy, government-issue chair with him. "You do not know how it was in Wien after the war," he said.

"No, I suppose I don't," I agreed, not quite knowing what to expect.

"Was *Hungersnot* in Wien." (In German this word is not pronounced the way you might think. It is more like Hoongersnote, but with a soft "g.") He paused for me, a well-fed American, to reflect upon what he had said.

"Hunger?"

"No, more hunger."

"Famine?"

"Yes. That is it."

"Oh."

"Ungarn—Hungary—was, before the war, our, how you say it—" He groped for the right expression, then smiled. "Bread box."

"I think we would call it the bread basket. I don't know exactly why."

"Yes, exactly so!" He looked me straight in the eyes. "Always bread basket, before the First War, too. In Austria we never have food enough. And before the Second War, I also was business man. As a young man. In small way, you know. That is before the Germans invade us."

"Before *Anschluss*," I suggested. Anschluss wasn't quite what you would call an invasion. The Austrians were waving more flags than bayonets.

"I have this business, buy *Lebensmittel* in Hungary and bring it to Wien to sell."

I knew about Lebensmittel, foodstuffs. It was pronounced more or less, laybens-mittel. My wife had gotten confused with the pronunciation in Switzerland and called it (phonetically) leebens-mittel, which might be translated as love-stuff, had there been such a word. Much amusement for the Swiss.

I was smiling (inappropriately, Mr. Foltin must have thought) as he continued, "It is good business and when the Germans come, is even better, but they make me join *Wehrmacht*. *Glücklicher-weise*—I am what you call lucky and do not go to fight in Russia, but I am *endlich*, supply sergeant. Then come the Russians here in Wien and the war is finished. And in all Wien there is nothing to eat and nothing to burn in the *Ziegelofen*. You know, to keep warm. More worse even than during war. Then next winter it is not so bad because there is the food from the UNRRA, but is only the one year. Then again very bad until begins the Marshall Plan. That is 1948. *Herbst* 1946 *bis Frühling* 1948, that is worst time. I mean to say, from Autumn 19——"

"I understood you."

"So when I am out of army, I go again into business."

"Bringing Lebensmittel from Hungary?"

"Yes. Is no problem in Hungary. Those Hungarians, they cannot eat so much food as they have because, you see, they are used to much export, during the war, even, when it go to Germany. But now there is new problem. It is the Russians."

"Explain it to me." I saw what he was getting at, but I wanted his version. One learns in this business not to put words in the mouth of the visa applicant, because if they are smart, they soon have you the same as talking to yourself.

"Russians occupy Hungary but I can manage there because the Hungarians, they wish sell and we wish buy. Problem is the Russian zone in Austria. Russians control everything from the Hungarian *Grenze* to the First *Bezirk* of Wien. Nothing can move in Russian Zone without a permit. *Gar nichts.*"

"Did you try to get a permit?" The distances between the Hungarian border and the First District of Vienna could not be much over forty miles, but there had been a considerable Soviet army encamped in that small area.

Mr. Foltin rounded his eyes and said "Yes——" drawn out to indicate that he had tried every trick of the trade. "But is impossible. Or is impossible for so small businessman as me. Not so hard travel to Hungary, but I can bring nothing back. I think Russians, they want Wien to go hungry so we say to them, 'Welcome, come in and take over.' Again like Anschluss."

It was certainly true that for a long time, ten years, the Soviets were poised for a takeover of Austria and only after it became apparent that the Western Allies would not abandon Austria did they agree to the State Treaty ending the occupation. But the Soviets exacted a price—Austrian neutrality and the promise of considerable reparations from Austria including oil shipments to the Soviet Union. Expensive freedom, but worth every schilling.

"So I have this idea," continued Mr. Foltin. "I find a so big *flasche Schnapps* and I make friend with a Russian army sergeant who is not so very—*klug?*"

"Clever."

"Yes, he is not so clever, that one, but he like the Schnapps and he does not take the Schnapps away from me. I cannot stop him if he take it, but then I must get more Schnapps and find another Russian. Not so easy. He has to be same size as me."

"But the first one you tried didn't give you any problem?"

"No problem but he drinks so much I think *flasche* not big enough and maybe I not find more on that night."

"You had to get him drunk enough so you could take off his uniform?" I asked, doubtfully. There I was, putting words in the applicant's mouth. I knew better.

"No, have not that much Schnapps. We drink and I tell him how wonderful is the Red Army. I also tell him my girl, she won't—you know—" Mr. Foltin managed a salacious laugh.

It sounded pretty genuine to me. "You told the sergeant she wouldn't sleep with you."

"Exactly so. She would not, as you say, sleep with me because I am only Austrian. It is different if she think I am in Red Army. So he let me put on his uniform and take my photograph."

"You are lucky he didn't decide just to sleep with your girl."

"Not problem. My girl, she hates the Russians and sleep with me all the time. Red Army want her, I just show him some other girl. Many *dumm* girls like uniform, any kind. American also."

I let that one go by. "Okay, now we have this picture of you in the Red Army uniform. Now what?"

"I make the copies and when I go to Hungary, I buy everything my wagon can carry. *Knüppelvoll.* When I come back to *grenze*, I don't show the permit. No, I show picture and say I am Red Army intelligence and—my cover, you call it?—is selling Lebensmittel."

"Did it work?"

"I not go to prison. Sure, it work until now. Not work for go to States." He looked ruefully at the photo.

"Well, don't give up hope, maybe we can get you mustered out of the Red Army."

2

Spooks

*I*t was the next morning before I had a lull in the stream of applicants and could think about my Red Army sergeant. Once more I went through the thin file. Nothing of substance except that photo. Rather good, I thought, for a copy made under difficult circumstances. I was certain our copy had originated with military intelligence. Whether ours, the British, or the French, I wasn't sure. Probably not American, judging from the handwriting on the back.

The question of its being genuine seemed to be resolved. Mr. Foltin had owned up to it. So it wasn't a spoiler, a photo rigged up to discredit Foltin for some obscure reason. I concluded that the only thing to do was to put our own people to work checking him out.

I called Gerhard Huber into my office and closed the door after him. "Sit down, Gerhard, I want to ask you something." Huber took on that guarded look of someone about to be asked something embarrassing or compromising. Going over in his mind, I supposed, which particular one of his sins was being called to account. Huber was a strapping young man, probably a few years younger than I. Women seemed to find him attractive, and one of my staff, a lady of Hungarian extraction, often perched like an exotic bird on his desk.

"I need to get in touch with someone in our CIA," I said.

"Your CIA?" Huber relaxed a notch, simple suspicion replacing his complex uneasiness.

"Yes."

"And you're asking me?"

"Of course. I never met a local employee who didn't know everything that we were supposed to be keeping secret." I should explain that local employees are usually citizens of the country where we are assigned abroad, and though they are often trusted,

Zurich, Switzerland, where the author served earlier

up to a point, they are never cleared for our deepest, darkest secrets.

Huber smiled. He performed one of those little rituals such persons use to fill time while they decide how to proceed. He pinched the crease in one of his trouser legs and pulled it so it would not flatten out as it went over his knee. Then, needing more time, he adjusted the amount of shirt cuff showing below his jacket sleeve. He made up his mind. "Well, one can't help hearing things. The embassy isn't such a big place, you know." He recalled a bit of his uneasiness by shifting in his chair. "But of course we would never breathe a word outside of the office. I venture to say—"

"That doesn't concern me at all. I just need a current background check on Mr. Foltin. It's been many years since we had anything new."

"But the lookout book—"

"—is all based on information from the first few years after the war."

"Then you should see Mr. Soper. That's Eddie Soper. Or if he is not available, you could try Paul Warren. All those people have offices on a floor by themselves at the embassy. We never go up there."

"Thanks." I would go and see the spooks in the main embassy building at my first opportunity. I'm not sure how the name "spooks" ever got started, but even many of the CIA station people used the word, seemingly regarding it as not being derogatory.

My visit to CIA a couple of mornings later began rather badly. For one thing it was a cold, drizzly day for April and I wore my black Swiss loden cape. Getting in or out of a cape gracefully requires turning with a maneuver not unlike a matador's pirouette that causes the garment to swirl rather dramatically. And this I did as I arrived on the spooks' floor, setting down my briefcase and choosing the center of the reception area, where my wet cape could swing freely and nothing important would be splattered as I stepped out of it.

A passing young man with a rather shapeless face stared at me for an instant and ran down the stairs. Putting my cape over my arm, bending for my briefcase, still gracefully, I hoped, I strode down the hall looking for Soper's name on a door. The receptionist came running after me, yelling for me to stop. The commotion brought people out of the offices and I found myself announcing to the entire CIA Vienna station that I was here to see Mr. Soper.

"You are supposed to call upstairs from main reception on the first floor," Soper chided me.

"I didn't see the sign."

"Everybody is just supposed to know that. Except for the Austrians, of course, and we instruct them when they ask for an appointment."

"Oh."

As Soper was leading me into his office, it occurred to him that some explanation was necessary. "You see, there are some people who come up here who don't want to be seen by anybody else. You know what I mean."

"Yes," I agreed, though it seemed unnecessarily paranoid. "So that's why— A young man positively ran down the stairs when I arrived."

"Pudding faced?"

"That's him. I mean, he."

"Baby Ruth."

"Is that really his name?"

"Of course not; it's just what we call him. Now, what can we do for you?"

"There's this Austrian—" I explained about Mr. Foltin and extracted his file from my briefcase. I repeated what Foltin had told me.

Soper was amused; he hadn't seen the picture before. "By God, you can't trust anybody."

"No, I suppose not, but I believe his story. It just isn't plausible that he's with Soviet intelligence. Why would he still be peddling fruits and vegetables sixteen years later?"

"No, I give you that. What you can't trust is a Soviet border guard. Our people must have gotten to somebody. I wonder how they did it? Pushed the right button, I suppose. Maybe one of the Jews who fled the Nazis into Russia and got conscripted by the Reds. Or maybe a Ukrainian who wasn't properly grateful for Stalin. Could be anybody."

"Since Mr. Foltin doesn't deny it, maybe you could poke around a bit to see if there's any current reason to doubt his story."

"I'd like to oblige you, but we're really not supposed to do background checks for visa applicants. Makes us too visible, and it isn't our business. The best we could do would be to query the Interior Ministry about him, but since he's an Austrian, even a clean bill of health from them wouldn't count for much against what's in your file."

"There's another way of looking at it."

"There usually is," Soper agreed. His pleasant expression melted.

"If he really is with Soviet intelligence and is still operating in Vienna, then you've either got a slick agent or a sleeper you

Spooks ▪ *29*

don't know about. I would imagine either would be CIA business."

Soper looked thoughtful. "I would imagine you're right."

• • •

I came away from the spooks' nest feeling uncertain about them. Soper seemed reasonable enough, but the panic triggered by my unsanctioned trip down the hall did not bode well. In the past, I had reservations about CIA people, except for my Belize assignment, where there were none, or if there were any, they were under such deep cover the consulate didn't know about them.

At our consulate general in Zurich, my first post abroad, I was also assigned as a visa officer. And Zurich had its own sizable cell of spooks. Two or three, anyway, that we knew about, unless you counted our very own Mata Hari, who made it four. I was told, as soon as I arrived, that each one of the CIA people had a nominal assignment to one of the sections of the consulate general. This one might be a commercial officer or that one might be a passport officer, that sort of thing.

Soon, I was invited to a cocktail party and an Italian consul came up to me and we talked about this and that. Then when he had me answering his questions nicely, he asked about one of the American staff, someone I'll call Groucho. Well, I knew very well Groucho was a spook, but I couldn't very well admit it. And I hadn't yet been told what Groucho's cover was. So I thought: Groucho is a person of considerable "presence" so surely he wouldn't put up with being thought of as a visa or a citizenship officer. And since we already had a consul general, Groucho couldn't very well be that. "He's an economic officer," I announced, certain that nothing else was possible because all the political officers were at the embassy in Bern.

Monday morning, back at the office, I checked just to make sure. Well, it turned out Groucho was a visa officer, a vice consul just like me. So I decided I'd better confess before something even worse (I couldn't imagine what) happened. "I blew your cover, Groucho," I blurted. Then I told him all about it.

Groucho thought it was hilarious. The Italian, he explained, was a member of the Italian equivalent of the CIA and he knew exactly what Groucho was. He was just playing games with me. Machiavellian, I decided. Or maybe something simpler, like *gatto e topolino*. Topolino, mouse. That's what the Fiat was called, the one in the picture in my safe in Vienna. The picture with the bullet-riddled bodies. A blood-soaked Fiat Topolino. Nothing funny about that.

I suppose I ought to explain about our very own Mata Hari, the one back in Zurich. Her name was really Lilith, probably evidence of her mother's severe bout with postpartum depression. Our Lilith preyed not upon children as the name might suggest, but upon the husbands on the consulate staff. She worked her way down the corridor that led from the spooks' nest to the rest of the consulate general. Lilith paused at my office only long enough to be sure she wasn't passing up anything important and proceeded on to another section peopled with officers of higher grade and greater promise. Even now, forty years later, my wife's usual cheery countenance takes on a dark and hostile mien when she thinks about Lilith. I assure her Lilith was just what you have to expect of a female spook, trying to keep in practice.

• • •

In Vienna on this particular day, years after Zurich, I was returning from my meeting with Soper at the main embassy building and I stopped off at Laterndl for lunch. Decided not to pay extra for a cloth napkin. Ordered *champignon gebacken* with that wonderful (and caloric) sauce like a good tartar, had a big bowl of meaty goulash soup, and topped everything off with *palatschinken* with *Marillen Konserve* and *Schlag* bubbling through the pores in the crepes. Left the restaurant several pounds heavier and quite a few schillings lighter. But happy.

As I approached the consulate, I saw, down the street and beside the Rathaus (the real one, the city hall), the long dark blue car I had seen from my office window on my first day. As before, there was a man protruding from the open hood. If the car was devouring the man, it seemed to be slow about it. I went to see.

A Lancia Flamina, and the man was thin. I burped; I had eaten my apricot crepes too fast, a greedy habit of mine. The man jumped and bumped his head. He rubbed it, considering whether to swear. Evidently he decided not. "Oh, it's you. Know anything about these damned things?"

"Cars?"

"Italian cars. The engine misses when you step down on it."

"Plugs."

"Changed them already."

"Wrong heat range, maybe."

"What kind of car you got?"

"American."

"Humpf." Consul General Trudgeon turned back to his engine.

"I better get back to work."

A muffled "Humpf" came from under the hood.

• • •

Lehar was still out to lunch (literally) when I got back to the visa office. The locals gave me disapproving looks and I swear that

Christa Jaeger, the senior visa clerk, came close to me and sniffed for signs I had stopped off for a drink or something. "Mr. Conroy," she said, "there was a man after you left for—for wherever— He wanted to see you."

"For a visa? Mr. Lehar could have handled it."

"He didn't say. I even offered him an application form, but he didn't want it. He just wanted to see you." Christa smirked. She couldn't imagine how I could be of use to anybody. Even my German was pretty terrible.

It takes a while for the locals to forget how wonderful your predecessor was and to become equally loyal to you. It almost seems as though they hold it against you for running off the departed. Of course in this case I suppose my predecessor really was something; he was later appointed as American ambassador to Moscow. Oh, well. "Did he leave his name?"

"I asked, but he wouldn't say. He just sat there, peeking over the top of a newspaper at everybody who came up the steps from the lobby. He was very nervous. I think he is here from East Europe. I could tell by his trousers."

"His pants?"

"The legs do not taper; just come straight down."

I had not noticed, but now that Christa mentioned it, clothes from Communist countries did look different.

"He left this note for you." Frau Christa handed me a much folded piece of paper.

I smoothed it out on my desk. *"Wait not possible. Try come again. Then you must immediately speak. Very dangerous."* No signature, but European handwriting, certainly. I looked at the words. A man with limited English or a man nervous and in a hurry, I could not tell.

• • •

The weekend was memorable, I'm sorry to have to say. The leased Bechstein grand piano was delivered to our apartment and Nanny, the hopelessly neurotic Hungarian children's nurse, arrived almost at the same moment. A conjunction of neuroses defying containment. My poor wife. Doubly poor wife. She had just slipped on ice when taking the daughters to nursery school and had broken her leg. One of her two, perhaps I should say.

First the piano. Pianos have three legs and seldom break them. Nevertheless, my Chickering had died a lingering and horrible death in Belize a year earlier and since then I had been climbing the walls, pulse irregular, drumming my fingers on the steering wheel of the car, doing finger exercises on my dinner plate, tapping out three against two rhythms with my fork and knife, all the usual manifestations of withdrawal. All key-boarded up, you might say.

Upon arrival in Vienna, happenstantially one of the great musical cities of the world, I had leased a Bechstein. Large, old, affordable, but as it turned out, ill chosen. A piano that in its youth might have been capable of Brahms and Beethoven, but in its dotage certainly unsuitable for Mozart, Scarlatti, and the others who matter. It seemed so unlike the instrument I had selected at the shop that I wondered if they had switched it in its bassinet before making delivery.

In the ordinary course of things, almost as important as a piano for a well-ordered household, is a nanny, *haustochter, au pair,* or whatever you wish to call the person who keeps the children out of the jam pot. Generally speaking, an embassy will have a revolving cadre of such persons, passed on from one to another of the families assigned for two, three, or four years to the embassy.

A Haustochter (to use the local term, which translates as

"daughter of the house") is supposed to be treated much as would be an older daughter with responsibility for looking after younger siblings. A rather nineteenth-century concept, I suspect. But it was a suitable occupation for a young woman just out of school, with no ambition for further education, not yet ready for marriage, with a wish to learn English, and harboring a burning desire to get away from the restrictions of her own home to the presumed anarchy of an American household.

We had such a wench in Zurich, the daughter of a Scandinavian plywood manufacturer. She took the job so she "could learn English," which she already spoke perfectly, and so she could climb out of her bedroom window at night to meet Italian men who had come to Switzerland either to take higher-paying jobs or to meet Scandinavian girls. Perhaps both. We were slow catching on, and wondered why our heating bills were so high. Then our neighbor told us that our au pair would leave the window open when she went out every night.

At this point I should mention that Swiss law in those days made the householder responsible for any love children produced by such girls under age twenty. I don't quite know what the official assumption was. Perhaps it was all right if the girl was twenty to—you know. And if the wife didn't find out. Of course if children resulted, it wasn't going to be easy to keep the wife from noticing. "Dear, are you absolutely certain there's supposed to be four in the nursery?"

But back to Vienna. Nanny was certainly over twenty. Perhaps not quite threefold. I don't remember how we got her. She may have had a real name but it has been removed from my memory. She lasted only a few days and we paid her a bonus to depart and never come back. A hard lesson that nannies and haustochters are not necessarily interchangeable.

Despite her Hungarian origins, Nanny's English was perfect even though the things she said were weird; she claimed to have nannied in England, a country that teaches its children to speak beautifully while subjecting them to other things best not here discussed.

When Nanny first arrived, she went around to all of our candelabra and carefully counted the arms. We had quite a lot of such things, wooden ones from Guatemala, several made of wrought iron, some of brass. We tended to collect the things, especially after having lived several months in Belize without electricity.

My wife caught on first. Nanny was trying to figure out if we were Jewish. None of our candelabra had seven arms, though, and Nanny seemed satisfied for the moment.

Religion apart, Nanny's dietary rules were mystifying. "I cannot eat that," Nanny declared each time we confronted her with mealtime. "A person cannot eat anything they have not learned to eat by the time they are seven years old."

"Is that a rule?" asked my wife in wonderment.

"Everybody knows that."

As the first day, a Saturday, proceeded, and as I sat at the Bechstein hating it more by the minute, matters deteriorated between my wife and Nanny, with the children standing by in wonderment. Any sort of irregularity, on the part of the children, or our rather irregular household, precipitated Nanny's neurotic outbursts. It came to a head when a tremendous crash shook the house, audible to me even at the monster piano. Nanny, as it turned out, had become so nervous that she had managed to push a tray of our best hereditary (my wife's mother's) china off of a table. Nippon china does not bounce on a hardwood floor, we discovered.

Well, I won't try to recover the suppressed details, but Nanny lasted not even a week and I struggled with the Bechstein for three years.

On Monday, my wife started looking for a replacement for Nanny, this time a proper Haustochter. I went back to work. My fingers hurt. The action of the Bechstein was too heavy.

In the afternoon, Gerhard Huber came into my office and sidled up to my desk. "There is a gentleman to see you."

"For a visa?"

"He does not wish to say. He was here also on Friday. When you were—over at the embassy."

The man was indeed nervous. I looked at his yellowed fingers. He smoked a lot, and right down to the end of his cigarettes. Eastern European, certainly. They all seem to smoke like that. They and the Chinese. But he didn't look to be Chinese. "You are consul?" he asked.

"Vice consul, actually." Suspicion came all over him, dropping like a window shade with a broken spring in the roller. At my obvious age (somewhere in my thirties; I won't say where) to be still a vice consul, it had to be a cover. Groucho at my first post came again to mind. Perhaps I should have explained how I had made my chief in Belize so mad he had held up my efficiency report for two years, effectively halting my progress through the hierarchy. But that would have made my visitor even more wary—a cover story, just what you would expect.

"I wish to see passport."

"Passport? You mean, my passport?" He nodded, or rather he jerked his head up and down. Well, why not? I got up, fished it out of the safe, and handed it to him. He examined it minutely, holding it up to the light. I was reminded of the story they used to tell about Mother Shipley. Ruth Shipley was for many years director of the State Department's Passport Office. She was famous for keeping her many clerks at very low civil service grades, which also made her beloved of the stingy Congress. She therefore enjoyed a certain degree of independence from the State Department, and indeed, even from President Roosevelt, as it turned out.

Then came the war and Roosevelt put William Donovan in charge of the Office of Strategic Services (forerunner of the CIA), for the purpose of reestablishing the American intelligence activities that had been abandoned some years before as being ungentlemanly. One day, Donovan came to Roosevelt (so it is said) and told him that it was easy enough to get spies into Axis-occupied Europe, but it was proving almost impossible to get them back to the United States for consultation and what all. Could the OSS please have a supply of blank passports so that they could be used to document the spies?

Roosevelt is reported to have said that getting the passports should be no problem, whereupon he called in Mother Shipley and put the question to her. She, however, didn't want to hear any of the justifications, how this was so important to the war effort. They say she responded more or less this way, "I have just one question, Mr. President, will these passports be used in accordance with the passport laws and regulations of the United States?"

The President had to admit they would not. Mrs. Shipley replied, "Then, Mr. President, I will not give you the passports and you will not get them as long as I am Director of the Passport Office." Legend has it that Roosevelt went directly to the company that supplied blank passports to Mrs. Shipley's office and had them run off some extras.

"That's a perfectly good passport," I told my visitor. "We wouldn't think of making a false one."

He wrinkled his nose at me, and handed that passport back. "I am with the Embassy of Poland," he said. "I am military attaché; I wish to defect."

For a moment, I just sat there. He did look like a military man, I decided. And as a defector, I supposed he might be of some use, but I didn't know exactly what to do with him. Taking him home with me seemed impractical. Not counting Nanny's quarters, we had only two bedrooms for our family of four. And the piano practically filled the living room.

It seemed to me that this was another problem for Eddie Soper. "I had better put you in touch with someone."

"Who is it?" he demanded.

"Just someone who deals with defectors. Somebody with the embassy."

My visitor stiffened. "Cannot go to embassy!"

"Maybe I can arrange for you to meet him somewhere."

"No!"

"Well, I don't see how I can help you if you won't see anybody."

My visitor thought that over. "Roten Turm. I meet him at restaurant Roten Turm."

"Fine, I'll set it up."

"You must come with."

"Me?"

"You bring him to me; then I know he is right man."

That sort of made sense. We agreed on a date and time.

I called Eddie and set up a meeting for the end of the day. He wanted to know what it was about, but there didn't seem to be any safe way to tell him, assuming that our phone line was not secure. Eddie assured me he was working on my photographic problem and coming to see him wouldn't speed anything up. I assured him that it was something new. He only half believed me.

During the remainder of the workday, I fiddled with an idea. What was needed was a way essential data could be gotten to the CIA. Some simpleminded code that would be used so rarely that it might be safe for such things. Vegetables and colors, I decided. Maybe a carrot could be a political person, a rutabaga could be an embassy staff member, a tomato a literary figure, and so on. Hungarians might be blue, Rumanians yellow, Poles lavender. Daren't use red for Russians; too obvious. Perhaps white?

So I sneaked away early and caught a taxi to the embassy. This time the way was prepared for me and the CIA's floor seemed to be as uninhabited and quiet as a funeral home after visiting hours. Eddie was standing, waiting at his office door. He hurried me in. "Are you supposed to be a visa officer?" I asked.

"Huh?"

"It seemed like a good question to get out of the way."

"I don't—"

"Never mind." Better not mention Groucho. I explained about my visitor.

"A Pole? What's his name?"

"He didn't wish to tell me."

"How do you know he is who he says he is?"

"I don't. This is your business, not mine. I'm just the messenger boy." Eddie agreed to go with me to the restaurant Roten Turm at the end of the week as planned. I rather looked forward to it. Any excuse to have lunch in a good restaurant— "And by the way, I want to give you a copy of our code book." I pulled out a copy of my vegetable and color list. "I was going to use a first edition of *Alice in Wonderland*, but I was afraid Lehar would get after me for reading at my desk. I doubt he'll have any problem with my grocery list."

Eddie examined my code and dropped the paper on his desk. "This is idiotic."

"Yeah, I wanted something we could both understand."

• • •

Tuesday morning, Lehar, himself, walked the length of the second floor, past the Austrians, and entered my office. This had not happened before. "The ambassador wants to see you."

Gawd.

3

My Ambassador

Gone again. It was beginning to look like I would have to come into the office on weekends to do my regular work. I covered my absence by telling the locals I was going out for my morning martini. Disbelief faded from their faces.

The main embassy building was an elegant structure dating from the days of the Austro-Hungarian Empire, when it served as the imperial diplomatic academy. The ambassador's suite reflected this past glory as much as the offices in the spooks' quarters upstairs did not. I marched in, regretting I had not worn a velvet tailcoat with knee breeches. "The ambassador sent for me," I informed the lady sitting there.

She took off her glasses and looked me over. "You are?"

"Richard Conroy. From the consulate."

"You're late."

"I was just told—"

"Sit down."

I did as ordered. I sat where I could look at her. Hair pulled back. Dark but a touch of gray. Nobody to trifle with. Could have been attractive except for her attitude. Forties, I decided. It seemed that she might be suffering from prolonged exposure to diplomats. Prematurely ages the expression. Wouldn't have hurt her to have smiled— No, it probably would have.

I contrived to examine her desk without looking straight at it. Vase of flowers. Fresh or artificial, I couldn't be sure without pinching one. Double pen holder. Black ink, certainly, for notes for the ambassador. Red ink, probably, for death warrants. Small tray for little sheets of notepaper. No big tray for work. Large, leather-bound appointment book in the center of the desk and covering most of a leather-bound blotter. She pulled out one of her pens; I couldn't see whether it was black or red. Tried to read her expression to tell. Red, I decided; I looked away, don't enjoy scenes of death.

Typewriter to one side caught my attention. Cover on it, but I could see a cord running from it. Electric. Nobody in the diplomatic service (in those days) had an electric typewriter except the Recording Angel, maybe. Doubted she (the ambassador's secretary) used it. Too precious for workaday use. Doubtless saved for *Notes Verbales.*

She returned her pen to its holder and opened a drawer. I stared straight at her, expecting I knew not what. Kleenex. She more dabbed her nose than blew it, and dropped the tissue into a wastebasket without looking. The wastebasket was behind her executive-type desk so I couldn't see it, but I was sure it was an executive-type wastebasket. Solid wood, walnut or cherry. Maybe leather bound.

I had been sitting there for eighteen minutes, more or less, when a large man came striding through the office followed by Eddie Soper taking twice as many steps. Showed Eddie's reluctance, I suspected. Eddie avoided seeing me. I didn't know whether that was abnormal. Perhaps it was characteristic of spies. They don't see us so we can't see them. Eddie and the other man breezed right through without pausing and entered the ambassador's inner chamber. The door closed with a solid "thunk." Solid nineteenth-century construction and probably soundproof. I, who notice everything when I don't have anything else to do, noted that the lady at the desk had not smiled at the newcomers, either. I felt better. But she also had not stopped them and made them sit down. I felt worse.

What would my being called in by the ambassador have to do with Soper? One of two things or both. My Red Army applicant, somehow. Or maybe the Polish gentleman. Perhaps I should think of him as the alleged Pole. Or maybe alleged gentleman. I couldn't decide.

For some time, silence emanated from the ambassador's office. That was good. Or maybe it was bad. Or maybe I was right in thinking the door might be soundproof. Anyway, now that I thought about it, silence probably couldn't emanate any more than dark could shine. Something to ponder sometime when I didn't have anything else to worry about. My stomach felt funny; it doesn't much like to dither.

After a while, Soper and the other man came out. This time I caught Eddie barely looking at me out of the corner of his nearer eye. A voice in the ambassador's office grumbled something. It sounded like "Drucilla," but it could have been "Priscilla." I was almost certain it wasn't "Dracula."

"Go in," said the lady at the desk. It would not have hurt her to say please.

The ambassador had a more than passing resemblance to Lionel Barrymore. He didn't get up; he didn't ask me to sit down. Without looking, he reached behind his chair and pulled something from a bookcase. I could see it was the ubiquitous stud book. That damn book would probably be at the Pearly Gates if I ever got that far. I knew what the ambassador would find in it. Without speaking, he turned the pages. Holding it open with a finger pointing at an entry, he looked at me through thick glasses. "Conroy? Richard A."

"No, sir; I believe he's in Argentina. But I sometimes get his mail."

"Ump." The ambassador moved his finger down an inch and a half. "Richard T.," he said.

"Yes, sir. That's me. I mean I."

"Ump." He read the few lines of my entry. "This is not your first assignment."

"No, sir. It's my third."

"And you don't know any better than to get mixed up with the CIA? Why don't you hire on with them if you like them so goddamn much?"

"Sir?"

"I will not have my officers involved with those people. It discredits the whole embassy. The whole service. The State Department." He looked at me in an all-encompassing way, not just at my eyes, but my whole being. "It offends God," he said.

"Sir?" "God" was still ringing in my ears, but shrilly. Like the way the higher-pitched church organ overtones linger after the vibrations of the base pipes have died away.

"And you set yourself up as some sort of go-between between the CIA and this Polish person!"

"Not by choice, sir. He came to me and said he wanted to defect. I didn't know what to do with him; I just said I would inform the proper authority. It was his idea that I had to point out the CIA person."

"You should have let the embassy handle it."

"He was afraid to go to the embassy. Apparently the KGB, or somebody, watches who comes and goes. And I couldn't very well send Soper over to the Polish embassy to call on him there."

"Well, I suppose you have to go through with it. It is not to happen again, is that clear?"

"Yes, sir." Maybe I could post a sign on my door, NO DEFECTIONS ALLOWED.

On the way back to the consulate, I wondered why it was, if the embassy and the CIA station were at such odds, the spooks felt they had to tell Ambassador Kitteldorfer what we were up to? Do you suppose the embassy bugs the CIA's offices? Lord help us all. Was God really offended?

• • •

On Thursday, Soper phoned to say my visa applicant, Mr. Foltin, was in the clear. He didn't explain further and I didn't ask. The phone was probably tapped.

I stayed in the office for a while after work and wrote up a request to the visa office in Washington for an advisory opinion. This was required for reversing a visa refusal that had been posted in the lookout book. I put the request into an envelope for the classified pouch and marked a carbon copy for Lehar. The carbon, I put in Lehar's reading file. He might get around to looking at it someday, or maybe not. No point in letting him see it before it went to Washington, particularly since he had been responsible for Mr. Foltin's most recent refusal.

That was something I had learned in Zurich. Never let your boss know what you're doing until it is too late for him to stop it. I had this case in Zurich that was really interesting, though an explanation of it stretches the limited confines of this book.

But the gist was, this lady was born in an Armenian community at an oasis in the northern Sudan, near the Egyptian border. There were no birth records kept at the oasis, but Armenian Church elders witnessed the birth. Sat around and watched, I suppose. By the time the lady reached school age, her family had moved on to another oasis farther north, but over the border and into Egypt. The first official government record of the child was therefore the Egyptian school record. Still later, the child grew up and married an Anglo-Egyptian banker and produced a number of Anglo-Egyptian-Sudanese (and half Armenian, too) children.

Then General Nasser came to power and had a set-to with Britain over the Suez Canal, among other things. The banker and his family found it expedient to depart hurriedly, from Egypt. They presented themselves to the American consular officer in Cairo, and asked to immigrate to America.

Now, in those days, we had a yearly immigration quota for each country, and what with one thing and another, the quota for persons born in Egypt was oversubscribed by many years, too many to count. But the Sudan quota was wide open because few persons from the Sudan gave any thought to going to America. Maybe they didn't even know where it was.

Also in those days, a whole family, whatever the origins of individual members, could immigrate in the most favorable quota of an individual family member. Hence, if the mother was born in the Sudan, the whole family could be Sudanese immigrants even though the father and all the children were Egyptians or even Martians. Got that straight?

Anyway, the American consul in Cairo decided the mother was lying when she said she was born in the Sudan, despite numerous affidavits from Armenian church elders. So in despair the family fled to Switzerland, where they were able to obtain only short-term residence visas. Then they came in to see me, to try again to go to America, the promised land, before their allotted time in Switzerland ran out.

And I considered the evidence and I thought: On one side there is the Egyptian school record and on the other side there is the Sudanese church record. I concluded that it was fair to say the lady's place of birth could not, from the evidence, be established beyond doubt.

And why did I decide such a thing? Because there was a rule that if the country of birth could not be established, then the quota was to be determined by the country of last residence. I examined the woman's passport; there was a Swiss residence visa, big as life, albeit not for long. "Congratulations, Madam, you are Swiss, as far as American visa regulations are concerned." And the Swiss quota in those days was only a little bit oversubscribed, with only a few months' waiting time.

However (and this is the sneaky part) she had registered months before at our embassy in Cairo, and they had given her a letter to that effect, though they insisted she was Egyptian. I could use the date of her application in Cairo to establish her priority date on the Swiss quota, making her and her family eligible for immediate immigration.

I prepared an advisory opinion request for the Visa Office in Washington. This was necessary, because my determination was in conflict with the embassy in Cairo. I showed it to my supervisor. "She's an Egyptian," he said, and tore up my paperwork. When I protested, he ordered me to drop the matter.

That did not end it. I already had my travel orders for my transfer to my next post (Belize), an assignment that did not improve my attitude toward my fellow Foreign Service officers who had arranged it, one way or another.

I wrote out another request, placed that day's date on it, and gave it with instructions to my senior local Swiss assistant. "Send it to Washington as soon as I'm out the door on my last day in Zurich."

Several months after I arrived in Belize, I got a letter from my old assistant. He said the Visa Office accepted my argument and my old boss was mad as hell, but he couldn't do anything about it. *C'est la vie.* Now, more than two years later, I was sure that somewhere in America a family of Anglo-Egyptian-Sudanese-Armenian children had forgotten all about General Nasser and lived by Howdy Doody time. Made a body feel good about America.

• • •

On Friday, Eddie and I went to the Restaurant Roten Turm. "Who was that with you in the ambassador's office?" I asked.

"My boss."

"Is he the one who tipped the ambassador on this?"

"Don't ask."

I cased the joint. The Polish defector was nowhere to be seen. "Shall we have lunch, anyway?"

"Yeah, but not here."

So we came back to the little restaurant across the street from the consulate. Herr Martinovic, the proprietor-cook-waiter (and probably dish washer), had been a ship's cook on the German liner *Columbus* at the beginning of World War II. When the ship was scuttled off the coast of Virginia rather than be captured by a British destroyer, Martinovic was picked out of the waters of the Atlantic by an American merchant vessel. One of the sailors gave Martinovic a merchant marine cap. Martinovic safely sat out the war, interned first in Canada and then after we came into the war, in the western United States. He spent the time as camp cook, thus he was well fed and missed the hardship and privation of wartime Europe. For this he was eternally grateful and went to extra effort to serve up his best to the consulate officers who dined in his establishment.

Hasenpfeffer, the occasional pheasant, venison, all these appeared in his establishment when available in the market. The proprietor, wearing an American merchant marine cap on cold days, would greet us at the door. "Gentlemen, have I got something for you today!" He would rub his hands together with excitement as well as to keep them warm in the still-cold *Esszimmer*. And, as soon as we were seated, he would shuffle off to the kitchen without asking for our orders. What he had cooked was what we got. *Hasenpfeffer*, *Reh Rahm-schnitzel*, or whatever. Some might have preferred to have a choice, but speaking personally, I was rarely disappointed with the main dishes. However I never acquired a taste for *Sturm*, the cloudy new wine that he foisted off on us in season. I fancied it settled storm clouds onto my brain.

Eddie and I sat in the back room, and while we waited for the whatever, I asked, "What do you think, Eddie? Do you suppose the Polish embassy caught on? Maybe his office is bugged, like yours."

"What do you mean, like mine?"

"Just kidding. But I wouldn't be surprised."

"Ummm," said Eddie and looked thoughtful. "They may have been trying to finger me."

"Yeah, they do that all the time. Particularly the Italians."

Eddie studied me again but kept quiet. He plainly thought me peculiar. I didn't explain how I'd been tricked this way before.

4

My Hungarians

My recollection is that we had four titled ladies on the staff of the consular section, a not unusual number, considering the quantity of such persons in Vienna. Most of mine had Hungarian connections. That was not unusual either; Vienna had attracted such people since the days of the old Austro-Hungarian Dual Monarchy. One did not quite meet these people on every street corner, but that was because they tended to congregate in a few places, seedy salons and the annual Opera Ball, for instance.

The twentieth century had been hard on the gentry. Two wars had taken their toll. Since the establishment of the First Republic in 1920, titles were no longer to be used. Officially, that is. Of course, socially, and in certain places, such distinctions did survive, though often it was as mild ridicule.

There was one person known about town as the Garlic Baron (*der Knoblauch Baron*), who was, if I am not mistaken, of Hungarian origin. He was said to live entirely on raw garlic, and his near approach to a street corner was announced by something akin to biting into a good garlic sausage, only stronger. Several times, when there was a brisk wind at my back and his approach came as a surprise, I was able to observe him at close range. Though he was an elderly man, his skin had the marvelously pearlescent quality of a freshly peeled clove of garlic. Wrinkle-free.

Despite his ambiguous social distinction, I recall the Garlic Baron as having been usually attired in rather advanced fashionable taste. Not quite a dandy, but neat, in muted colors not unlike the fibrous portions of a garlic bulb with perhaps a bit of green in his tie, of the shade found in a clove just beginning to sprout.

But many of the other once-titled Viennese were not so well turned out. In addition to losing the honor of their titles, many were no longer rich and some were abjectly poor. The old sources of wealth had gone, especially among the Hungarians

The Vienna State Opera

who, because of the Soviet occupation of Hungary, were cut off from their ancient sources of wealth, their lands. But this genteel poverty was not entirely new. In many cases it predated the Second World War.

I knew such a lady, an elderly baroness who was the second generation in her family to have fallen upon hard times. Both she and her sister married just after the First World War, during the difficult, politically fragmented, and uneasy years that marked the First Republic. Their mother lacked the money to provide proper dowries for each of the daughters, but to make do, she divided the family silver service for seventy-two into equal portions of thirty-six, and also cut in two the linen tablecloth that was once long enough to accommodate seventy-two at a single table.

What she did about the indivisible soup ladle, I do not know. Every set of Austrian silver (smaller sets, of course) my wife and I bought in the sixties seemed to come with a single soup ladle, but perhaps the baroness's mother's set had two, so that the gentry at the head of the old table would not have their soup grow cold while waiting for those at the foot of the table to be served.

When I knew the baroness, it was some forty years later and she had worked for the American embassy for many years. Long adapted to reduced circumstances, she did not take the waters in the fashionable places but spent her vacations touring the countryside, riding double on a tiny motor scooter with her husband, who also held a title, but no money, from his own family. They were searching, I suspect, for an Austria that had long ago vanished.

After the Second World War, her only sister (recipient of the other half of the tablecloth and the table setting reduced to thirty-six) had become a *Sensal*, a hired bidding agent at the

Dorotheum, the state-owned pawnshop and auction house. She knew quality when she saw it, even if she could no longer afford it.

In my time in Vienna, the best barometer of the financial health of the gentry was the Opera Ball. Held in the winter, and annually since 1935 with time out for the war and postwar reconstruction of the war-damaged Opera House, the ball had its origin in the Imperial Court Soirées of the 1870s. A few years before that, in 1869, the legendary Emperor Franz Josef had opened the new and magnificent Opera House with a performance of Mozart's *Don Giovanni*. The last production before the house's destruction during the heavy and deadly air raids of March 12, 1945, had been Wagner's *Götterdämmerung*. How Viennese, to choose a German opera with the title *Twilight of the Gods* at such a time.

To the Viennese, the burning of the Opera was traumatic, and despite the daunting postwar hardships of Vienna, highest priority was given to the Opera's reconstruction. It reopened in November 1955 with a production of Beethoven's *Fidelio*. Beethoven was always regarded by the Viennese as one of their own, despite the composer having been born and lived to manhood in Bonn. A photograph taken on the evening of the reopening of the Opera House shows the people of Vienna packed like sardines on the sidewalks but keeping clear of the streets surrounding the building to permit the unimpeded arrival of the elegantly attired opera goers.

So you see how important the Opera Ball is to the Viennese and why the old gentry would, in the years after the opera house reopened, wish to attend the ball even if it meant selling the family silver to get enough money to do so. This, of course, often meant taking a silver samovar or several trays with vermeil roses to the Dorotheum. We Americans lurked like scavenger birds waiting for these unredeemed treasures to be sold at auction.

Employed in the visa section, where I was first assigned, there were two Hungarians of noble birth. Both were baronesses, one young, the other distinctly elderly.

The younger one, the Baroness Marlene Thiesen-Weilers (a made-up name), was the rather exotic bird I have mentioned as sometimes perching on the corner of Gerhard Huber's desk, engaged in what I assumed to be harmless flirtation, the sort of thing ladies of her class had done to stave off boredom for as long as anybody could remember. Marlene was a thin, stylish young woman, with dark curly hair cut short. She had about her an air of cosmopolitan elegance that quite set her apart from the other women in the consulate. Indeed, she had been educated, if memory serves, in France.

I was told that her grandfather had, at one time, held quite a high office, first as an aide to Emperor Franz Josef, then as commander of the Austro-Hungarian fleet in the last days of the First World War. He served as regent of Hungary during the interwar period and into the Second World War until he defied Hitler in 1944 by seeking an armistice with the Allies. American forces freed him from his imprisonment in Bavaria. Granddaughter Marlene was married to a prosperous Austrian manufacturer of soap and doubtless could have lived as a lady of leisure, had she not chosen to work for the consulate.

The visa section's other aristocrat, Xenia Hadas, the elderly baroness, presided over our quota control office. Her title, generally considered to be Hungarian, could well have been Slovenian or perhaps Slovakian. Titles appeared from time to time where least expected. Writer Rebecca West tells, in her 1941 memoir, *Black Lamb and Grey Falcon*, of how a whole village in

Croatia was ennobled by an emperor who had come through the village, tired and hungry, out of sorts, and feeling neglected by his retainers. The village united in receiving their sovereign with hospitality and honor, and the emperor returned the kindness.

But our Baroness Xenia was real gentry, and greatly needed. In the nineteenth and twentieth centuries, boundaries and peoples had moved all over the place in the area once dominated by the Austro-Hungarian Empire. This created unusual problems for the administration of our immigration laws.

In those days, the United States assigned an annual immigration quota to each country, based more or less upon the proportion of Americans at the beginning of the century who traced their origins to each country. The idea behind this was to preserve, in years to come, the peculiar mix that made up America. As you might suppose, the British had the largest share, followed by the Germans, then the Irish, and so on. Those countries that had sent the fewest immigrants to America were limited to an immigration of one hundred or so. Austria in those days had a quota of several thousand. (Don't hold me to an exact number; this is not a history book, you know.)

Anyway, applicants were assigned to national quotas according to the nation that governed the place of birth at the time not of birth but of visa issuance. But Austrian borders had meandered all over the place, and place-names had often changed. Hence, an applicant might have been born in what was then Austria-Hungary, but the place-name of the town as shown on the birth record might no longer exist. The town now (in the 1960s) might be in Czechoslovakia, Yugoslavia, Poland, the Italian Tirol, or in a separate Hungary. The town names changed from time to time to reflect the current language or other local practice.

Hence, the Baroness Xenia presided over the huge map that covered one wall of the quota control office. The map showed national boundaries that existed at various times, and the names of towns and districts as they have changed over the years. Only an elderly multilingual citizen of the old empire, with a memory like an elephant, could handle the job.

Another noble Hungarian, our countess, was not in the visa section but had a desk in the lobby on the ground floor. She acted as receptionist for both the visa section and the passport/citizenship section on the first floor, where I would eventually finish my tour of duty. While the *Gräfin* (Countess) Sophie Schaddenstein was of a Hungarian family, she was actually born in the country that was the Slovakian portion of what was Czechoslovakia during my time in Vienna.

Countess Sophie was exactly my idea of a Hungarian—she charmed you, but it was all business with her, and she carefully gauged your reactions. If she saw you resisting her charms, she immediately switched her tactic. Instantly she could be a coquette or sincere and gently bred, or whatever was required to accomplish her purpose.

Nowadays, these traits, taken together, would be called manipulative. In those days we just called it Hungarian. "That Countess Sophie, she's a real Hungarian," we would say. And what did it matter that she was born in Czechoslovakia? And what did it matter that she was to become her husband's mother?

That's right, his mother. She was married to an official of the Royal Hungarian Government-in-exile. Her husband carried himself like a count, but, alas, he was born a commoner. Austrians on my staff, who did enjoy good gossip, told me that Countess Sophie had begun proceedings to adopt him so that he, too, could have a title. People from that part of the world are so funny about titles that the tale did not surprise me. But in fairness, I have to admit that I do not have personal knowledge that it was true, and I never had the courage to ask her, straight out. Looking back upon it, I wish I had done so if only to have had the pleasure of hearing her inventive reply. Doubtless something like, "Ooh Herr Konsul"—she had promoted me from vice consul long before Washington got around to it—"it is not I who adopt my husband, it is the office, the title of countess that does so. So we are equal, the count and I, in the blessings of the *Adelstand.* We stand together."

Later on when you are better prepared I will tell you more about the Hungarian baroness who worked in the Passport and Citizenship Section. For now, it is enough to say that it was she who explained the Hungarians to me. "Hungarians in the old days, Mr. Conroy, Hungarians of our sort, were truly a *Herrenrasse.* They were not like those Hungarians"—her pronunciation of the word took on a different intonation, unmistakably derisive, emphasizing the second syllable—"we see today." I had not heard the word *Herrenrasse* (master race) applied to Hungarians before. It was a new and interesting concept.

5

The Golden Years

*W*hile the functions of the embassy's consular section were divided into two parts, visas on the second floor and citizen services on the first, it was impossible at times for these two fiefdoms not to become entangled, as I will shortly explain.

Citizen services, generally referred to as the Passport and Citizenship Section, was pretty much a catchall for the problems of Americans traveling abroad, just as the visa section, where I first worked, was the gatekeeper for foreigners wishing to go to the United States.

The Passport and Citizenship Section was presided over by an American consul, Wieslaw Budzinsky. Buddy, as everybody called Budzinsky for obvious reasons, was an old hand at consular affairs. He and another American of central European origin were famous when I had been in Zurich in the late fifties, as the two who, with unerring sense, brought order to the post—World War II chaos of American refugee and migration affairs. Of mature years then, Buddy was now well into the usual retirement age, and serving with a term appointment as a Foreign Service reserve officer.

Despite his U.S. citizenship and his official position, Buddy was uncompromisingly European. Indeed, the last time I saw him, after he had retired and I had, at long last, been promoted to consul and had taken over his job, Buddy was walking past my office window, dressed in a dark suit of European cut, wearing a homburg adjusted to a distinctly continental angle (straight as a die), swinging his furled umbrella, and carrying a rabbit (dead, apparently) by the ears. A European gentleman bringing home something good for dinner.

Buddy and his Polish wife lived in one of the apartments on the upper floors of the consulate building. My wife and I were there once, for tea. I don't remember much about the apartment except that the furniture looked antique and European but of no particular style, and the curtains were some sort of gauzy stuff that let in a lot of light without allowing the view of the Vienna skyline to intrude.

But what I recall most clearly was the room full of people all speaking Polish. My wife and I sat there speaking English to each other. From time to time my wife, who is unabashedly, even incorrigibly, social, would ask a question or say something to one of the Polish speakers. They would reply in English that was more or less fluent, and then resume speaking Polish to the others. After we had drunk our tea, we remembered a previous engagement and departed. The others hardly noticed. Perhaps they said good riddance as we went out the door, but it would have been in Polish so the effect was certainly lost on us.

I was never any good at languages. Any, not just Polish. So I hated it whenever Buddy took leave from his job and I had to cover for him. It was easy enough to sign a passport or two, or maybe do a notarial, but what it usually involved was helping out Americans who had to deal with official bodies in Austria.

That usually meant interpreting for them and advising them to "calm down, this is their [the Austrians'] country." That much I could say in English, for what little good it did.

Where possible on such occasions, I took along Teo. That was Dr. Teodor Schlitter, the consulate attorney. Elsewhere in this memoir I will tell you more (lots more, actually) about Teo, his war experiences (he attacked the Soviet Union on a bicycle— Teo being on the bicycle, not the U.S.S.R), his hobby (drinking), and how he established a symbiotic relationship with the American opera singer.

But for now, it is enough for you to know that Teo was an attorney who had never been a lawyer in the usual sense but had since the end of the Second World War worked for the American embassy and kept vice consuls like me from getting into too much trouble. Most of the time.

I recall that once when Buddy was away and Teo was unfortunately indisposed, an American was called into traffic court. He had made a right turn (perfectly legal) and hit a bicyclist (illegal, though possibly unavoidable) who was proceeding straight on but next to the curb. The American was adamant that he had no need to get his own lawyer, and insisted on having someone from the embassy straighten out these crazy Austrians.

Well, what the judge said was all legalese and I probably wouldn't have understood it word for word even if it had been in English. But the meaning was clear. If a motorist in Vienna turns right, he better be damn sure he is smack dab against the curb, because otherwise there might be a bicyclist coming through. The cost of this lesson was five hundred schillings, as I recall. The dollar was strong in those days so it was not as much then as it would be now, and not even as much as a lawyer's services would have cost. Anyway, I did not cover myself with glory in that engagement and the American probably complained to his congressman when he got home, which may explain why I didn't get promoted that year.

• • •

The case I want to tell you about now was one in which the way of two lovers, strewn with orange blossoms, proved to be a primrose path. Despite true love (albeit expressed in pantomime) the course did not run smoothly and indeed it ran quickly from bad to worse and then to utterly dreadful.

It went something like this:

I had been on leave, I don't remember where, but somewhere out of town. We had finally got a good nursemaid (*Haustochter*), Erna, for the children and were beginning to see something of Austria. On this particular Monday morning, I dragged into the office, not particularly happy to be back, and expecting the worst to be waiting for me. The most urgent of my work was to have been seen to by another vice consul who inhabited an office next to that of Consul Lehar. I will refer to the vice consul as Mr. X because I never learned to think kindly of him during the brief period our tours of duty overlapped in the visa section. I could not now make up a pseudonym for him that would not betray my feelings. So, Mr. X he is. It is also likely he was unable to read and write, so X may very well be what his signature looked like. I never looked to see.

Midmorning, one of my Hungarian baronesses stuck her head in my door. The black hair on Marlene's head had what used to be called a poodle-cut. "You have to go to a wedding," she said. She rolled her eyes with some meaning I did not at the time understand.

"Oh."

"You have to go see Miss Brand."

Fraulein Helga Brand worked down in Buddy's office. So that's what Marlene was talking about. Buddy must be away. Just witnessing a wedding; not too bad. "I'll stop in this afternoon."

"Better go now. They're getting married after lunch."

Fraulein Brand had the certificate made up. "Be sure to bring it back as soon as the wedding is over. They need it upstairs."

"Upstairs?"

"Yes. In INS. For the petition. So you can issue the visa immediately. Don't you know about it?"

"I've been away." I wasn't ready to admit to Miss Brand that nobody tells me anything. For the reader's edification, INS, the U.S. Immigration and Naturalization Service, maintained a regional office in Vienna, on the third floor of our building, where Americans could, among other things, file petitions for the immediate immigration of their newly acquired foreign spouses.

The happy couple was waiting for me at the *Standesamt*. A depressing place. Not quite Brecht's hastily furnished stable, but nowhere near a church, I thought, recalling the lines from *Die Dreigroschenoper* when Polly Peachum marries Mackie Messer.

In the *Dreigroschenoper* there had been no piece of paper from the registry office and no flowers on the altar, and who could say where the bride got her wedding dress. Nor was there the traditional myrtle in her hair.

What was important, Brecht had then and I now supposed, was whether *"Die Liebe dauert oder dauert nicht . . ."* and the present surroundings would have little to do with whether this couple's love would last.

There would, of course, be a *Schriftstück* issued by the registrar, and I was going to provide a consular certificate of marriage. And as for the flowers on the altar, the bride-to-be clasped a small bouquet against her best velvet dress. Red, looking rather out of place at a wedding. But, as it turned out, maybe not. I looked in her hair for the myrtle, but couldn't be sure because of her hat. Whether the love was going to endure or not was also not immediately apparent.

"You the American consul?" asked a balding gentleman. Northeast Texas, my ear told me.

"Umm," I replied, not actually wishing to put too fine a point on it or to lie. "Richard Conroy. Pleased to meet you. Mr. Vance, is it?" I allowed Tennessee to show in my own accent. In my experience, a whole lot of Texans passed through Tennessee on the way west. Cousin Davy, who didn't have enough sense to get out of that Alamo, was one.

"Just call me Willy. Willy Vance from Tulsa." A wide smile stretched across the bottom of his face. His eyes played a separate game, sizing me up. Must have gone west from Chicago, I decided. Been away too long. Can't any longer distinguish Texas from Oklahoma.

Mr. Vance crushed my right hand. I suppose that's why we are born with two.

"This here's Anna, soon to be Mizzes Vance just as soon as you translate this Austrian for us."

"Interpret," I said sort of absently. A horrible thought had come over me. "You don't speak German?"

"No, sir. American is all I need."

"And Miss Anna doesn't speak English?"

"Hell, neither of us speaks English. She'll learn American soon enough when I get her to Tulsa."

I asked the *Standesbeamter* whether he spoke English. Most Viennese officials do but he did not. I sighed, and off we went. Anna understood the registrar well enough and I repeated the oaths to Willy, mostly from memory of my own wedding four-teen years earlier. I noticed after it was all over that Anna, now Mrs. Willy Vance, handed the bouquet back to the Standes-beamter, who stuck it in a vase without water in it. Artificial, I decided.

I drove the newlyweds back to the consulate. They sat in the back of my red convertible holding on to each other like love-birds. Or like lovebirds would if they had arms. The image in my mirror did nothing to disguise the fact that it wouldn't be long before the bride said good-bye to her forties, if it hadn't happened already, and Willy would be saying hello to his sixties. I wondered if either had been married before and whether any-body had happened to ask them whether any previous marriages had been dissolved. No point in me asking it now; if my passen-gers were bigamists, I didn't want to know.

At the consulate, I stopped by Fraulein Brand's desk to get the consular seal impressed over my signature on the marriage certificate. Then I sent the Vances up to the third floor to see Tony Bertucci to file their petition with INS. I had no doubt Tony would approve it on the spot and they could come back to see me in the morning for Anna's visa.

Back in my office things had piled up, routine things that jus-tify your salary, but now thirty-five years later, are so unmemo-rable that I couldn't tell you what I did that afternoon. Until a bit after four o'clock, that is.

Frau Jaeger came into my office. I can see her even now. Dark hair, and, except for the color, looking like Blondie's in the comics. There, any similarity ended. Christa Jaeger was the sen-ior visa clerk on the immigrant side. She had been with the con-sulate for a long time, almost eighteen years, since the first years of the Four Power military occupation of Vienna. She was already a young woman when the war began. By now, there was not much she didn't know.

No, that is not quite right. She apparently didn't yet know that I was almost as bright as vice consuls who had gone before except maybe the one who had held my job several years earlier and as I previously mentioned had managed to get made ambassador to that place no warm-blooded Southerner like me would want to go. She let no opportunity go by without telling me how wonderful he had been. I'm sure she was right. We all were wonderful. Except for Mr. X, the vice consul without a name, as I mentioned earlier.

Anyway, Christa knocked on my open door and came partway in. She stopped. When I saw she looked troubled and obviously didn't quite know how to begin, I shuddered. A problem for Christa would be worse than a problem for me.

"Mr. Conroy, there is something you should—I don't know whether Mr. [X] told you—"

"He didn't tell me anything. He never does."

"Yes. I was afraid so." Christa sighed. "It is about the marriage you witnessed this afternoon. There is something wrong."

"Wrong? The marriage looked ordinary enough to me. The bride and the groom don't speak the same language, but that's not so unusual. They obviously have something in common." I stressed "something" just enough to make my meaning clear. Christa smirked. "Don't tell me there is a problem with a prior marriage."

"No, not that. It is her police certificate. She is a prostitute."

"It's on her police report? She's been convicted?"

"Oh, no, she's never been convicted of anything. She's perfectly legal. However, she has her little card from the *Geschlechts und Mädchen Kontrol Amt.*"

"Oh." It sank in. "Oh! Has [X] seen it? I mean, had he seen it, uh—before?"

"Naturally. He checked all the documents."

"Maybe he overlooked it." Not likely.

"We discussed it. He knows we have to refuse the visa."

"You mean, I have to refuse it. And you let me go witness the marriage without telling Mr. Vance?"

"Mr. [X] says that is procedure. We can't tell the applicant about any adverse information until the visa interview. If then."

"You think that's right?"

"No, it's not right, but I suppose that's what the regulations say. We locals are not permitted to see your Appendix A," Christa added with a bit of sarcasm. That appendix of the Foreign Service Manual was confidential and mostly covered political security matters. I couldn't offhand remember whether it said anything about derogatory police information.

"We'll just have to get Mr. Vance to apply for a section G waiver for his wife," I said. That should have been simple enough but it meant the bride would not be flying out with the groom the next day. A background check on the good character of the American spouse would have to be done and that would take weeks.

"Yes, but—"

"Yes, but what?"

"The consular officer has to recommend the waiver—"

"This isn't Mr. [X]'s case anymore. I'll have a recommendation written before closing time. I'm sure I can get INS to waive her ineligibility . . ."

"It's not only that. Mr. Vance—if he doesn't know about Anna, then he might not want to request the waiver."

"Oh, Lord! I hadn't thought of that."

Well, Willy Vance didn't get out of Vienna until the weekend. We had a series of meetings with them, together and separately, and to avoid making this the whole subject of the book, I will try to summarize:

First we spoke to Anna and told her we had information that she was a licensed prostitute. She seemed a little surprised that we were making a big thing of it. Perfectly legal, she said. Yes, we replied, but prostitutes were ineligible for American visas. We suggested it would be best if she explained things to Willy. She said she didn't know how she could do so until she learned English.

Then, because it seemed the only thing to do, we offered to break the news to Willy. Anna was delighted to hand the problem over to us.

Willy was not a bit upset. He explained that their first meeting had come about through a solicitation for sex, and he knew from the beginning that she was a prostitute. The only surprise to him was that her profession was licensed by the police, and he was disappointed that this proved to be a problem with her getting a visa.

I helped Willy prepare his petition to INS for the waiver of Anna's ineligibility, and I wrote a strong supporting statement saying that Willy just wanted to make an honest woman of her and that this was obviously a case of love at first something or other. Willy flew back to Oklahoma and Anna settled down to wait. She had not surrendered her prostitution card, so there was bound to be no problem with her financial support.

Though you never know. I was reminded of another bit of Brecht, this time from his *Seven Deadly Sins*. In this, Anna (not the new Mrs. Vance, but the Anna in Brecht's rather strange song) has split into two sisters, a beautiful one named Anna and a practical one named Anna. The two sisters are journeying from city to city in America to make their fortune. The beautiful one earns money because she *"zeigt ihren weissen Hintern, Mehr wert wie eine kleine Fabrik."* This means, roughly, that she shows her white behind, of more value than a small factory. And the sisters send the money back to their family in Louisiana, where their parents and two brothers are to build a small house on the banks of the Mississippi. However, in the song, the beautiful and productive Anna keeps falling in love with her johns and this gives the practical Anna fits.

This had obviously happened with our Anna when Willy came along, and, I supposed, might happen again while he was back in Oklahoma. I couldn't even begin to imagine how we could ever explain that to Willy.

After several weeks during which Anna stopped by the consulate so often that there was no telling what ideas it gave to the neighbors, Tony, the regional INS officer, appeared at my office door. "I got a cable from Washington," he said.

"On Mr. Vance? Good. Having a streetwalker hang around the office all the time makes a bad impression."

"Not so good. They turned the waiver down."

"Turned her down! Don't they believe in redemption? Besides, she's almost fifty."

"Not her, him."

"Don't tell me he's bringing her back to the States for immoral purposes. Her prospects wouldn't justify her airfare."

"They say he's a child molester. Several convictions."

"Oh, Lord!" The petitioner in such a case had to be of good moral character. And child molester——! "Do you suppose Washington would buy the redemption of both of them?"

"We can but try."

"Yeah, or maybe Willy could learn to like living in Vienna."

"If they would give him a residence visa," Tony observed.

So I wrote to Willy and after some days he was in Vienna again, this time distraught. Christa and I, this time assisted by our Hungarian baroness, Marlene, who was armored with the sort of sophistication that can only be acquired by living (at various times) in Budapest, Vienna, and Paris, sat down with Anna and Willy to map our strategy. First off, we had to know what was in the hearts of the newlyweds, then I would have to decide how to plead for a reconsideration by INS. What we came up with was this:

Anna was plainly getting too old to hustle on the streets of Vienna or anywhere else. Her "Hintern" was no longer as klein and weiss as it must once have been. Willy owned up to having molested children and dabbled in pedophilia in the past, but he, too, was getting too old for that sort of thing. Willy was the only man who had ever treated Anna with kindness and respect. Anna had responded, showing that in real life as well as in musical comedy a whore can have a heart of gold.

Theirs was indeed true love, arriving late in life but therefore all the more sweet. I seem to remember that I compared it with the rich, sweet wine from the *Spätlese* grape. Moreover, it was not possible for their union now to be blessed with children who might be ill influenced by the couple. And finally, this was the last, best hope these two lovebirds were likely to have for salvation. And we all believe in salvation, don't we?

Even INS has a heart, and with their reconsidered blessing, we finally were able to issue Anna's visa. There wasn't a dry eye in the visa section except for two belonging to a disapproving Mr. X, and for those of Mr. Lehar, the section chief, who was beginning to suspect that I preferred issuing visas to refusing them.

In the years since Anna immigrated to America, I have wondered about the marriage. Did it last? Was it happy? Did Willy and Anna give up their wanton ways? I read that half of all marriages end in divorce. But somehow I think that my couple grew old together. I don't know why; it's just a feeling I have.

6

Carmen

*U*nlike our weeks and weeks of Anna, we had barely twenty-four hours of Carmen. Oh, maybe thirty-six if you count tidying up afterward, but only one full day of Carmen herself. When I first saw Carmen she didn't have a cent. Just a pocketbook with a few odds and ends, cigarettes, a book of matches, a comb, a few things like that. And a lipstick in carmine red. After we began to put a few things together, that proved to be significant.

Carmen was pretty, of course. Young, probably in her early twenties, but with an air about her that suggested that maybe she had been around. And so she had, but we didn't know that until later.

That morning Carmen was sort of sprawled on the bench out in the foyer, waiting. Countess Sophie was observing her over her glasses as she sorted the morning mail. The frown on Sophie's forehead suggested that she was as yet unable to put Carmen into some familiar category in which she might be dismissed from further consideration, or, far less likely, welcomed with a smile.

Carmen ignored Countess Sophie. That should have been a clue, right there. I stood there staring, while pretending to say good morning to the countess and talk about some trifle, I forget what. I moved so I could look at Carmen over my glasses, too, but that was a mistake. I can't see anything without my glasses.

A few moments later Wieslaw Budzinsky—Buddy—came in from the street. He grunted at me, ignored Countess Sophie, possibly didn't see Carmen at all, and proceeded into his office. Carmen sat up straight and raised her eyebrows at Countess Sophie. The countess nodded and Carmen sort of slithered to her feet and followed Buddy. With no hope of further diversions, I said something or other to the countess and climbed the steps to the visa section, where I started the day no more late than usual.

But downstairs, immediately below my office, a drama was beginning. Carmen had a story to tell, one so remarkable in its peculiarity and simplicity that everybody believed it. Even I reserved judgment when the first sketchy details swirled around among the Austrian employees. I had seen Carmen and admired her more obvious presentments. These suggested she had little to hide.

Well, now Carmen was in Buddy's office and she seemed to speak only English, albeit with a bit of an accent nobody could identify. It was not so much her phonetics as just a strange way of inflecting her speech.

I was of course not in the room at the time, but I pieced Carmen's story together from Buddy, from the Austrians who never missed anything, and particularly, from my boss Frank Lehar, whose exposure to Carmen was to prove no little embarrassment.

This is the story Carmen told:

Carmen was a member of a large family of German-Americans (this explained her slight accent) who now lived in Cincinnati, Ohio. Her family had always been in the meatpacking business, both in the old country and now, since before the war, in America. And they had grown quite prosperous through hard work and keeping the family together in the business.

Now that the oldest generation was ready to retire, the family felt that they could relax a bit and take a well-earned vacation. And that they would do so, the way they had always conducted their business, together. The old people, the children, the grandchildren and various wives and husbands.

The first part of their vacation would be a visit to the old home in Germany, some small town nobody had ever heard of, one near the Dutch border. Then they would take a grand tour by automobile to the places the old people knew from before the war. And finally the members of the family planned to separate into small groups that would go their own way, touring Europe here and there, before returning to America and the beefsteak, ham, sausage, and hot-dog business.

Since the family was large and as a party would eventually fragment, it was decided that they would come to Europe with five new Buicks. It would be a sight seldom seen in Europe in those days, five expensive American cars, all alike and, initially, all traveling together.

The trip to Germany and elsewhere went as planned and was wonderful, with old friends in the old country greatly admiring the prosperity of the family in America. And the cars. Remember that in those days automobiles were taxed throughout much of Europe according to engine displacement, and small, cheap cars ruled the highways. The few big, powerful cars meant big, powerful money.

After visiting Germany, bit by bit the family worked its way through other countries and came finally to Austria. In Vienna they had a wonderful time seeing everything. They even rode the famous Ferris wheel at the Prater, the one so familiar from a half dozen movies and the one that big as it was, I still could not see from my window. Then they turned south to Neunkirchen, after which the cars would go their separate ways, this way and that, until they converged again in a month's time to load the family and their Buicks on a ship and sail for home. First class, of course.

Near Neunkirchen, the family stopped at a country inn to have a last lunch together. I could just imagine the scene. Toasts were surely drunk and the patriarch must have begun to speak in that peculiar style of German *Tischrede* with its significant pauses and oblique references understood only by the family. At times teasing and other times lugubrious. Pauses to refill glasses and for more toasts. Little exchanges between the old man and several of the younger ones, not fully explained to the others.

Probably the old woman did not speak, except perhaps to make a few pithy comments to show she had her own opinions. Finally it would have been incumbent upon a few from the next generation to say a few words. The others would have attended, to see who might be a contender for the old man's place. The children would become bored and squirm, and perhaps also those of their elders who were related to the family only through marriage. But whatever age, they would surely have remained quiet and respectful.

Carmen told us how it was after the lunch at the inn. The weather was warm and there was behind the inn, which had once been a mill, a beautiful creek with water clear as crystal and a bottom covered with rounded pebbles in many colors. While the others in the family were smoking, saying their good-byes, and maybe having a final *Schnaps*, Carmen decided that she had to go wading in the creek. Though none of the others wished to join her, she was an adventurous sort and went in alone.

The water was cold and after a short time she came out of the stream and sat on the bank letting the warm sun dry her feet and legs and the parts of her dress that had gotten wet. She smoked a cigarette. It was very quiet and peaceful.

After a while, Carmen became concerned that she had neither seen nor heard anything from her family, so she put on her shoes and picked up her pocketbook, the only things she had with her except for her dress and what little she wore beneath that, about which no gentleman would speculate.

Carmen found that the five Buicks had gone, as had all of her family. At first she could not believe that she was not asleep, perhaps, and that she was only imagining, dreaming things. She made inquiries in the inn, ever more frantically, and at length she came to realize that she was indeed abandoned, left behind with only a small amount of money, a few odds and ends in her pocketbook, shoes (penny loafers) without socks, a dress, and whatever, if anything, lay underneath. (You see? I am not a gentleman.) And sunglasses and a ribbon for her hair. That was all.

But Carmen also had her thumb and she was a pretty girl so motorists stopped their cars and *Lastwagens* to pick her up and in this way she made her way to Vienna and to the consulate. The last of her money she had spent on her dinner last night, on a bed in a youth hostel that was unsurprised by her lack of luggage, and on a small *Schinkenbrotchen* and coffee for her breakfast. Oh yes, a few coins for the tram.

Of course Buddy called in Fraulein Brand—Helga—who actually did most of the work of the office when it came to distressed Americans, particularly female ones. Buddy preferred to sit back and make decisions when and if necessary, but to leave the details to Helga's good sense and sympathetic mien. Helga had large brown eyes and when she turned them full on you, it was impossible to tell whether they were welling with sympathy or imagining her next vacation on the Dalmatian coast.

Helga tried all the obvious things. Wouldn't she be missed? Carmen said she had wondered about that, and that she had stayed at the inn for hours, waiting for a car to return, but she had concluded that the people in each car assumed she had decided to go in a different car. There had been ever so much switching about in the final hours they were together.

Where would the various groups from the family be in the days to come, Helga asked. Carmen didn't know, she didn't have the itineraries and hadn't paid any attention to them. Since she was having such a good time, she hadn't cared in which direction she went.

Where would the family get together again? Well, it would be at the boat to return to America, but Carmen was not sure from which port it would sail or exactly when. It would be about a month, she thought.

Relatives in America? None. They were all on the trip. How about the business? Closed down for extended vacation while the family was away. Probably a night watchman, but he would know nothing.

"You do have a passport?" "Oh, yes. It is with my suitcase in the trunk of one of the cars." "Won't they notice the bag?" "Probably not, they are all alike."

The day wound on. Buddy took some money from the tiny office welfare fund and told Helga to take Carmen to lunch. Time passed.

It was late afternoon when Helga faced Buddy and told him

he had to do something. "You can't leave an American girl homeless and starving on the street."

"We fed her lunch."

"That is not a permanent solution."

So it was that Buddy climbed the stairs. That was not something he often did. He did not enjoy the exercise and ordinarily, he saw little point in socializing with those of us in the Visa Section. But it was time for drastic action. Buddy wheezed to our floor and went straight into Lehar's office. The Austrians gravitated to that end of our office suite and a silence came over them. I couldn't hear a thing from my end of the building.

After a bit, the light on Lehar's phone line lit up and stayed on for a while. Then he accompanied Buddy downstairs and shortly returned with Carmen. I pretended to go back to work, setting an example for the strangely quiet Austrians. It wasn't long before Lehar yelled to me that it was time to go home.

I don't like carpooling. It seems to me that the clock has little to do with the requirements of the workplace. Maybe it makes sense when you are on shift work and one body is simply replaced by another, around the clock. But a visa office isn't that way or shouldn't be. But nevertheless I was riding with Lehar in those days.

At the time, I had only one car, a Corvair convertible. Red, conspicuous. And since my wife was discovering the pleasures of antique shopping in Vienna, I left the car with her and rode to work with the boss. Someone else was in our car pool in those days, I don't remember who, I just remember I always sat in the backseat and after I was dropped off at my Chimanistrasse apartment, Lehar and whoever the other one was continued up to Hartaeckerstrasse, the other U.S. embassy housing farther up the hill.

Carmen ∷ *81*

Carmen was sitting in the backseat of the four-door Taunus when I got in. She had lit a cigarette and blew smoke at me through pursed lips. During the ride home, nobody said much of anything except Lehar, who mentioned Carmen would be staying in his town house while her case was being resolved. I did not detect any lust in Lehar's voice. I marveled at his composure.

The next morning I got a call from Lehar during breakfast. He said he would be by to pick me up in a couple of minutes. This was well ahead of the usual time. I asked what was wrong but he cut me off without explaining. I abandoned my second buttered *Semmel* and *Marillen Konserve* and hurried out to the street.

Just in time. The Lehars' green Taunus came purposefully down the hill, with Frank holding grimly onto the steering wheel. The car was crowded—the other car-pool rider was in front and Carmen was in the back, but so was Mrs. Lehar. I climbed in and Lehar had the car moving before I had the door fully closed. The passengers sat in stony silence while Lehar drove on silently, his expression unreadable. "What's up?" I asked. Nobody answered. Mrs. Lehar looked as though her jaw had been wired in an uncomfortable position. I smiled across her at Carmen. Carmen lit a cigarette.

Lehar abandoned his car in a no parking zone at the entrance to the consulate. As we all climbed the stairs, Lehar said to me, "We'll be up with Gerlach. I'll talk to you later." At the second floor, I went into the visa section and Lehar and his wife hurried Carmen up the stairs to the office of Dr. Gerlach, the U.S. Public Health Service's contract Austrian physician.

That was the last I saw of Carmen, her behind fetchingly climbing the stairs accompanied by the determined but less supple Lehars.

The story, as I later pieced it together, was that Carmen had come down to breakfast and while waiting for things to be ready, had been seen by Mrs. Lehar to be slipping a piece of paper under the living-room carpet. Mrs. Lehar told this to her husband, who retrieved the paper and saw that upon it was written, "I do not wish to live. I have taken poison and soon I will die."

A search of her pocketbook did not reveal any container that might have held the poison, and Carmen, when questioned, refused to say anything but had asked for more coffee.

Dr. Gerlach gave Carmen an emetic and found nothing in her but eggs, sausage, and coffee. And orange juice. He called the police, who escorted her to the *Klinik Hof* for observation, as was required for suicide attempts, real or imagined.

Some days later, the police identified Carmen as a Dutch girl who had done similar things before. This was, apparently, the first time she pretended to be an American.

All this upset Lehar. I think he felt that had Buddy not been Polish, and had he, Frank Lehar, not been born in Germany, they would have known immediately that Carmen was not a genuine American girl. Mrs. Lehar now told him that she was sure from the beginning that there was something funny about Carmen.

I tried to assure him that the trouble was not with national origins, but his sex. No man was going to pay much attention to Carmen's speech; it was her body language that said it all. But privately, I fault Buddy. As a refugee officer in Europe after the war, he must have seen Carmens by the yard.

7

Duty One—Tricky Russians

I recognized him at once. Not that there was a Keuffel und Esser in a leather case on his belt, but he had the look of an engineer about him. If you were raised around them, you can tell. The cutesy ones have things like little slide rule tiepins or maybe it's a tiny T-square or something like that. You know, like Sunday golfers with golf-club tiepins. But with real engineers it is in the set of the eyes, I think. Ready to do battle with things. Not with people unless they get in the way but with steel, concrete, electricity, and what all.

"I'm an engineer," he said as he sat down.

"Yes, I know."

Suddenly he was suspicious. "You know? How do you know."

"You just said so. Besides, you look like one."

He thought about that for a moment, and barely perceptibly, he changed, like unstressing a piece of prestressed concrete. "You are right, I think. They too saw it."

Now I tensed. There was something here that did not meet the eye. "Do you want a visa?" He wasn't clutching any forms. I wondered how he had gotten past Gerhard.

"No."

"You know that's what I do here. I issue visas." I considered what I had just said. Better qualify it, I decided. "Sometimes I refuse them. If I have to, of course."

"That is why I am here."

"You were refused a visa?"

"It is the Russians."

Oh, God! The Russians seemed to be responsible for everything, though it was not immediately clear how that iron law applied to the Austrian engineer sitting in front of me. "The Russians refused you a visa? I can't do anything about that. Some people might even consider it a blessing."

"That is the point. The Russians try to make it so I have to work for them."

"Umm. You are an Austrian citizen?" He nodded. "Then you should go to the Innenministerium. I'm sure they will be interested."

"No, they do not care. It is only you who will care."

"Me? I mean, I?" One has to set a good example for foreigners who make some effort to speak English. "You had better explain."

"Soon I receive my *Diplom.* I am aeronautical engineer, first in my class. So I must go to America. You know, to practice my profession. There is not much to do for aeronautical engineers in Austria."

That much made sense. As far as I knew, Austria at the time lacked an aircraft industry.

"So when I am offered a position, it will be in America."

"There are other countries—"

"I will only go to America."

"And why are the Soviets a problem? You aren't a Communist, are you?"

"Of course not! I am not such a fool. But the Russians know I will one day have important job and they wish to force me to give them secrets."

"Blackmail? Do you have anything to hide?"

"Of course not! But they may make it appear so."

"How can they do that?" I looked at my watch and then glanced out the door. There seemed to be no one waiting to see me. "Start at the beginning."

And so he did. "When I begin to make my *Doktor*—you know what I mean?"

"When you began to work on your dissertation—"

"That is it. Then I have not much money. It is the usual thing that students are very poor, I suppose. Anyway, one day this Russian, he approach me and ask would I like to earn some money. So I say, yes, even if I know he is from Russia."

"He told you?"

"No, at least not that time. But he speaks *Deutsch* like the Russians do. We in Austria know the Russians very well so there is no way he can fool me. He said he is engineer and he needs help in translating technical papers. He shows me the papers. Mostly they are written in French or English and the man says he can read these languages a little bit but not enough for technical use.

"So I see these papers anyone can get. Also they are easy and will not take too much time, and I agree to do it for him. He pays very well but not so much I think something is wrong. After that we do this some more and I wonder why is it these papers are important for him. This information must also be available to him in Russian. But I need the money and when he wants more such papers translated, I do it for him.

"We talk some and soon he sees I know he is Russian and he says yes he is with the Soviet embassy but he is not a diplomat, just ordinary engineer in Soviet trade mission, but he is not good with languages and they send him back to Moscow if they find he cannot do his job.

"Then comes the meeting in Germany. This is an aeronautical engineering meeting and people from many countries come to it. For me it is very important because there I meet people in your aerospace industry. I tell this Russian about the meeting but he says he knows it already, and it is important for him but his chief does not understand this and will not let him take time to go. Would I, he asks, collect for him a set of copies of the technical papers, and write summaries of them. If I do that, he will be happy to pay for my travel. Anything that looks to him interesting, later he will arrange with me for full translation.

"This is good for me because I don't know how I am to pay for it myself. The travel, I mean."

"Didn't you see how this might be dangerous for you?"

"No, I only see the money. All the papers I translated and everything I get in Germany, they are not secret and would be available to anybody."

"And now something has changed?"

"Yes, is possible I receive soon a job offer from an American company. The work would be on military contract and if I take the job, I must have what you call a security clearance. This is no problem because I never talk to anybody about the work I do for the Russian. But I think, how would it be if I get the security clearance and the job and someday a Russian comes to me in

America and shows me pictures with the Russian and maybe copies of the canceled checks for the money he paid me."

"You took your money by check?"

"Yes, it was always on an Austrian bank and there was nothing illegal about what I do. Except now it not look so good."

"Are you still doing anything for the Russian?"

"No, not anything. But I have not told him so, yet."

"Before you do, it would be wise if you were to talk to someone at the embassy—"

"I tell you. That is enough. You will issue my visa."

"You said yourself that the problem will come in the United States when you face losing your security clearance, not when you get your visa. If I give it to you."

"If it is a problem I tell them to ask you."

"That's not the way it works. They won't ask me. And even if they do, I may be in Perth, Australia, or someplace. It may be ten years from now and, even if I remember you, all I can say is you said something about it. There goes your clearance. Security problems are always resolved by turning you down."

"You think so?"

"I think so. I used to work for the nuclear weapons program."

"Oh."

I could see my visitor adjusting his thinking. Maybe I wasn't just a bureaucrat. Maybe I was something much worse. Maybe I was CIA or something. I smiled in what I thought was a reassuring way. He blinked uncertainly. "We need to get your statement on the official record while what you say can still be investigated. And confirmed," I added.

• • •

"Eddie," I said, "you need to talk to this fellow. He's just a doctoral candidate now, but if he isn't blowing smoke he may be in a sensitive national security job someday." Eddie and I were sitting at a quiet table and I was eating one of those chocolate Viennese pastries that taste like the chocolate icebox cake that my mother used to make in the thirties. The recipe, if you don't already know what I mean, was in the old *Boston Cooking School Cook Book* so maybe you can find a copy and see for yourself. I was working on regaining the twenty-five pounds I had lost in Belize. A pound a month, despite two years of eating everything that was edible and some things that weren't.

I made it a rule never to talk over the phone to Eddie about anything of substance. Back when I was assigned to Zurich, a couple of men came into the consulate general and told our Swiss receptionist that they were from the phone company and had to check our PBX equipment. (That was what small exchanges in places like offices used to be called.)

The receptionist, who was Swiss and no dummy, said to the men, "Fine, but I have to call the phone company to confirm it." She suggested they go out for coffee, or whatever (probably a beer) and come back in an hour. Naturally, the phone company knew nothing about it and the men never came back. Probably, they found another way to bug our offices. Wasted effort, because in Switzerland we never had much in the way of secrets to talk about. Maybe our spooks did, but that was their problem.

Anyway, there we were in the coffeehouse with Eddie consuming an *Einspaenner* and me having tea and the pastry. Both of the drinks were served up in those funny Viennese glasses like a demitasse, with a big gob of whipped cream sitting on Eddie's coffee. Personally, I never got used to drinking hot tea out of a glass, because it seems to conduct heat more than does china and it burns my lip.

"I suppose so," answered Eddie, "but you work us to death with all your requests for investigations."

"Just making sure your job doesn't get abolished."

"Ummp," said Eddie. He knew very well that nobody was going to cut a CIA position in Vienna just because they had nothing to do.

"But don't try to turn him. He's not in a position to do you any good now. Just show him how nice and reasonable you American security people are. Just convince him he's got to report it after he's in the States and the Soviets make their move. Then he'll have to deal with DISCO. Poor fellow."

"Yeah, poor fellow."

Hands down, I'd rather deal with the CIA than with the Defense Industry Security Clearance Office, but that's another story. I left the matter in Eddie's hands and never saw my Austrian aeronautical engineer again. Likely, I had moved from the embassy's visa section to the passport section before he got his visa or perhaps the job offer never came through. Maybe the Soviets made him an offer he couldn't refuse.

That's one of the things you have to get used to in the diplomatic and consular services. Often, you see only a slice of history and then you are gone. Like reading a chapter or two of a book on a bus and leaving the book behind when you get to your stop.

• • •

"You've got the duty," said Lehar. Already? I thought. There must have been almost fifty officers at the embassy who pulled night and weekend duty for a week at a time. I should come up once a year, or now and then, twice.

The drill was you went over to the ambassador's office on Monday and his secretary, the one with the red and black pens, gave you a folder that showed everything important that was likely to come up, such as arriving congressional junketeers, and listed the names of other embassy personnel who should be able to help out in case of an emergency, and supposing they were silly enough to stay near the telephone. Truth to tell, most emergencies were consular, and in fact had to do with distressed citizens, but other things could happen.

Once when I had the duty the Gulf of Tonkin crisis broke and I had to race across Vienna in the wee hours of night to get to the embassy code room. But most of the time it was some poor sod in jail and screaming his head off. From a career point of view, I would take a dozen war crises any day over some obnoxious American looking for an excuse to complain to his congressman.

But in this particular duty cycle, there was something interesting expected for the weekend. A U.S. Army technical sergeant had apparently defected to the Soviets and, a few weeks having passed, they were now throwing him back to us. Our legation in Budapest had given the sergeant the duty officer's phone number in Vienna (mine) and told him to call as soon as he crossed into the West.

Sergeant—Tomkins, I'll call him—had not been debriefed by our people in Moscow because he had been in the care of Intourist in some small provincial city, and when he came out through Hungary he wasn't prepared to linger in Budapest just to be raked over the coals by our people there.

Intourist, as most people know, was in those days the Soviet state travel agency and people from the west traveling into the Soviet Union back then had to buy package tours run by Intourist. When Tomkins called, I arranged to meet him in a little café next to the Rathaus.

If looks mean anything, Tomkins did not seem the type for a defector. Small town stuck out all over him. Close-cropped hair, innocent eyes. He was assigned to one of our air bases in what was then West Germany, as a radar technician. Might have had a couple of years of college, but probably not (we didn't get into that).

This is pretty much his story: He had some leave coming, so he signed up for a quick trip to the Soviet Union without mentioning it to anybody back home in South Dakota or wherever it was. When he got to Moscow, he saw Red Square and Lenin's tomb. Then he got this idea; he would send his folks a postcard of the Kremlin, surprise, surprise. On the card, he wrote something like, "I have defected to Russia and I'm now in Moscow. Wish you were here." Then he dropped the card in a mailbox and went on his way to the next stop on his tour. He didn't think any more about it. For a while.

Then this one Intourist guide, a pretty one, took him in hand and said she would show him some of the sights that weren't on the regular tour. Somehow, they missed catching up with the rest of the tour group, which was moving on to Smolensk or someplace like that. No problem. His guide held herself and Intourist responsible and they would catch up with the group. In the meantime, he had nothing to worry about, Intourist would take care of every expense.

Well, a remarkable series of foul-ups followed. They kept arriving at city after city, just after the regular tour group had moved on. But people were nice to him and a lot of high-up people who could speak English met with him and were terribly interested in his views on this and that and what he would like to do with his life.

But after a while, these important people seemed to lose

interest in him and he began to think it was because he was only just a tech sergeant. Even his pretty guide, who had seemed to have all the time in the world for him, became inattentive and he found himself spending a lot of time alone in his hotel room. He became homesick, even for his unit in Frankfurt am Main, where almost everybody could speak at least some English and he could come and go as he liked.

Finally, they said the only thing to do was for him to go home by way of Budapest and Vienna, and they gave him a train ticket to take him back to West Germany. He couldn't wait to get home.

"Sergeant, didn't you realize it was probably all because of your postcard?"

"I figured that out. They gave me lots of time to think. Not at first, but later."

"And you never thought seriously about staying in the Soviet Union?"

"You got to be kidding."

8

Right from Wrong

The Foreign Service is loaded with people who think being a visa officer is dogs' work. (Sorry, dogs, I know you get a bum rap.) And it probably is, if you do your job the way it is intended. Look at the evidence, look at the law, issue or refuse the visa, next case, please.

Well, those poor sods miss all the fun. The sport lies in trying to make the system mete out justice. Vienna in those days was particularly rich in such opportunities. Austria had been an enemy country, then came a decade under military occupation and a place of ideological contest, and now, eight years later, its citizens were still in no position to make demands. American visa officers made mindless refusals and there were no appeals.

In addition to the case of the Red Army sergeant I described in chapter one, four more cases come to mind:

The Case of the Two Baskets of Apples

On a crisp fall day, during the immediate postwar days when Vienna was starving and the per capita food intake was down to

The Stallburg building, dating from 1565, and the spire of the Michaeler Kirche

six hundred calories (yes, six hundred calories, I looked it up), an unsustainably low level, a hungry and enterprising seventeen-year-old boy decided that, for the sake of his family, he would ride out of the city on his bicycle and proceed across the Danube River to a place where he believed there would be orchards. Indeed there were, and the trees were laden with ripening apples. Seeing no one around, he picked enough apples to fill the two baskets that he had brought with him. Two of them, so he could balance one basket on each side of the handlebars. As he left the area, he was apprehended by a policeman and eventually brought before a magistrate's court, where he was convicted of two crimes, one for each basket of apples.

Later, the young man became a commercial airline pilot, and when he applied for a visa so he could fly into the United States, he was refused a visa for having committed two crimes, only one of which could be forgiven under U.S. visa law. The visa officer who made the refusal did not choose to look behind the fact of the convictions, and would not tell the Austrian the particulars upon which his decision was made. The official assumption was that the refused applicant would surely be aware of his own sins, whether he would admit them or not.

Thereafter, each time the pilot had to fly into the United States he had to apply in advance for a temporary waiver— [under section 212(d)3 of the law]—on the grounds of his visa ineligibility. A nuisance, time-consuming, and a handicap to the Austrian's career because he could not accept such flight assignments without several weeks' notice.

I, of course, told him exactly why he had been turned down. With this information, he could get a transcript of the court papers and it was obvious that under U.S. law, having two baskets of contraband in order to balance the bicycle would not have made it two offenses.

And so, after Washington agreed with me, the impediment was lifted and the Austrian was able to fly happily westward ho.

The Case of the Austrian Communist

I was always suspicious of Austrians labeled as Communists. In the first place, there weren't so very many, and even the Soviets gave up trying to bring Austria into the East Bloc, finally agreeing to a neutral Austria. It is true that when Barry Goldwater, who was a very fine man, though wrongheaded about a number of things, was running for the presidency, he named Austria as being one of the Iron Curtain countries. For this ill-considered remark he was never to my knowledge forgiven by the Austrians.

The politics of Austria, particularly between the wars, was very complex and I cannot presume to be an expert on the subject. The peace treaty following the end of the First World War separated Austria from Hungary and left it as a country doubting its own viability and having a fragmented sense of its nationhood. In the main, there were three political forces. Many ethnic Germans felt they would be better off allied to Germany. Away from Vienna, there were many Catholic conservatives who wished to use the church as a unifying force. And particularly around Vienna, there was a rising socialist (not Communist) middle class that included many Jews. There were probably 220,000 Jews in Vienna before the Second World War.

To a certain extent, Vienna went its own way, separate from the rest of Austria, and the Viennese socialists introduced many social reforms that still make their mark on Austria today. While there certainly were some Viennese Communists, they did not compete well with successful socialism.

It is my opinion, bolstered with virtually no facts, that during the four-power occupation of Vienna following the Second

World War, the Soviets wanted Vienna to go hungry and were determined not to assist in the flow of foodstuffs from Hungary. My bogus Red Army sergeant had been quite correct in saying that from the earliest days of the former Austro-Hungarian Empire, Hungary had been what he called the "bread box" of Austria. At the end of the war, starving Austria had almost wiped out its livestock, and out in the provinces, farmers were not anxious to share what was left with an even hungrier Vienna.

All of this is a long, roundabout way of getting to two cases, one involving the attitudes of some of the older Austrians toward the natural liberal ideas of the young, and the other, a matter of simple hunger.

The Case of the Communist Entrepreneur

A Viennese businessman was refused a U.S. visa years earlier because we had evidence he was a member of the Communist Party. When he came to see me again, I of course told him that he was said to be a Communist.

I had looked into our files, those lovely old files that preserved the histories of our past misdeeds. The sole evidence of his political affiliation was an old CIC report from the occupation days, at a time when the man had been a university student hardly out of his teens. Like so many of the counterintelligence reports, this gave no evidence as to the reliability of the source. And the Austrian applicant could be of no help here; he was plainly flabbergasted at the news. He was a small businessman of some sort, but I now forget some of the details.

Once again I prevailed on the rather strained friendship with our local CIA people and after a time they were able to get a copy of the original CIC report. The source of the derogatory information had come from an old lady, a monarchist, who said that she was sure the people the young man hung around with were a bunch of Communists. The young man, our visa applicant, was of course her grandson.

We made an effort to find something, anything, that would corroborate the old lady's allegation, but there was nothing. Washington agreed with us to throw the refusal out. It has been my experience that the people in the visa office in Washington could be a lot more reasonable than are many consular officers, provided they get decent information from the field.

The Case of Grand Larceny

During the war, almost a million Austrians were taken into the German armed forces. The regular army, the *Wehrmacht*, got most of them, but some Austrians did serve in the politically oriented *Waffen SS*.

In April of 1945, the Soviet armies were approaching Vienna from the east and their artillery was shelling the city. The defending German armies retreated to the Kahlenberg, the small mountain in the famous Vienna Woods (*Wienerwald*) overlooking Vienna. In happier times, the Wienerwald was a favorite place for the Viennese to go walking and they might stop at a *Gasthaus* in the woods or maybe in the adjacent *Grinzing* district to sit outside in the gardens and drink the local wine. It is not a wine to my taste, but I have heard there is such a thing as good Grinzinger wine if you only know where to look. It was no time to go looking just then, during the battle for Vienna. Those readers who want a firsthand account of Vienna in those days might read *The Berlin Diaries of Marie Vassiltchikov.* The daughter of an expatriate Russian prince, Miss Vassiltchikov spent much of the war in Berlin consorting with Germans of her class, but during the last few months of the war, she was working in a Luftwaffe hospital in Vienna.

Our visa applicant was one of those Austrians serving in the *Wehrmacht*, in one of the units that had moved up to the Kahlenberg. He could look down upon his city and, except for the obscuring smoke from burning buildings, he could with a strong glass have seen the house where lived his young wife and newborn son.

Soon, the Red Army would enter the city and there would be street fighting, but Vienna would surely fall. In time the Germans would turn their artillery on the Soviets in the captured city. It was not a pleasant time to be anywhere in Vienna.

Our young soldier asked his unit commander for emergency leave to go into the city and take his wife and child to a place of safety, after which he would return to his unit and fight with them to the death, if that be necessary. His request was refused. In the latter days of the war, desertions among the Austrians were rife. Perhaps foreseeing this eventuality, the Germans had never established separate Austrian units within their armies but had assigned Austrians to fight alongside the watchful Germans.

Both desperate and enterprising, our young soldier stole a blank leave form, filled it in, and left to save his family. Within hours he had returned to his unit, but his absence had been discovered. Despite the chaos of those final days of the war, he was court-martialed and convicted of grand larceny, a felony rendering him forever ineligible for a U.S. visa.

He was fortunate, I suppose, not to have been summarily shot. I could never have corrected that eighteen years later when I arrived in Vienna.

Well, it seemed to me that what he had stolen was simply a piece of paper with no intrinsic value under the circumstances that prevailed at the time, particularly after he spoiled it by filling in his own name. So, under the District of Columbia Code, the standard by which we measure such things, he was guilty of the most insignificant of pilferage, and certainly not a felony. Had I been a low-down SOB I suppose I could have claimed that the value was enhanced by the value of the lives of his wife and child. But whatever else I am, I am not an SOB.

Washington agreed with me, at least about the reversal of the visa decision. I don't know about the SOB part, I didn't press them on that.

The Jewish Community

I found the final one of these illustrative cases to be the most instructive. In my time in Vienna, the Jewish population was only a small fraction of what it had been before the war. As I have mentioned in the preceding pages, twenty-five years earlier there had been not quite a quarter of a million Jews in Austria, and most of them in Vienna. The holocaust claimed a third of them. The lucky ones got out in the late thirties. Of those who eventually came to America, many made a great contribution to their country of refuge.

Franz Bader and his artist wife came to Washington and established the first art gallery that concentrated on contemporary art. Franz gave many artists, especially painters of the Washington colorist school, their start, and was important to many printmakers as well. That I never achieved very much as a painter and sculptor was not for want of Franz's support and encouragement.

Gertrude and Otto Natzler, a renowned team of potter and glazer, became world famous from their adopted home in Los Angeles. Otto's niece Senta Raizen has long been associated with the National Academy of Sciences and science education.

Lisl Cade, of New York, is one of the greatest of authors' publicists, handling some of the best known writers in the country.

Peter Masters, of Washington, spent the war as a British commando and settled in Washington to rise to the top of his profession in graphic design, not to mention writing one of the best of personal memoirs of the war.

These were just ones of my not particularly wide acquaintance, an infinitesimal sampling. Each tells a story of amazing fortune that allowed them to find refuge in America. It is not pleasant to think about those not so lucky.

As it happened, some Jews went west and others went east, wherever they could go, searching for a way to survive the Nazi times. As I said, a third of Vienna's Jews did not find the way.

Following the war and during the allied occupation of the former Axis countries, including Austria, America watched in horror at the seemingly inexorable advance of Communism as it spread out from the Soviet Union. To combat this spread, this infection, our intelligence people attempted to identify organizations thought to be Communist dominated and thus agents of Soviet expansionism.

Among the organizations thus stigmatized were the Jewish community organizations and their newspapers in Vienna. And therefrom hangs our tale.

One of my visa applicants was a Viennese, a man who had fled to the West, to Britain as I remember, and returned after the war to try to reclaim his family business. Like so many other visa refusals from those years, this one was one I thought demanded a second look.

No one had ever claimed that the man was a Communist, but it was known, and he freely admitted, that when he returned to Vienna from Britain, he had joined some of the Jewish community organizations that we had decided were Communist dominated.

Such a broad assumption seemed to me to be quite unfair, since there were many reasons for joining Jewish organizations that had nothing to do with politics. Foremost was this man's goal of recovering his family's confiscated assets. It ran counter to what I thought about my country, to treat the surviving Jews of Vienna with such disregard for the truth.

Once, when I was in my late teens, I had a job with a crew traveling around from city to city installing communications equipment. My fellow workers came from all over the South, which, as a region, did not have many Jews. When we got to Miami, where there were some, I remember saying something like, "that's typical of a Jew," and the guy I was working with said, "I'm a Jew." I had no idea that he was, and there was no way to take back what I had said. I decided to try and think first before picking up the sort of thing everybody says. I haven't always succeeded, but I try, and so I did in Vienna.

I raised my questions with Dr. Teodor Schlitter, the consulate attorney. The time has come when I should tell you about Teo, but to avoid interrupting my account of the Jews of Vienna, I will hold Teo for the end of this chapter.

Teo was not Jewish, but he knew more about Vienna than anyone else of my acquaintance. I outlined my misgivings for Teo. He listened to me without interruption, then said, "There is a man you should talk to."

That was when Teo took me to see Simon Wiesenthal. He was not so well known, then, as he would later become when he became famous for tracking down hidden Nazis. It is my recollection that he was much involved in the early sixties in trying to operate a clearinghouse for information about the fate of European Jewry. But many people will know far more about his activities than I can recall after all these years.

I remember his office, if you can call it that, was in the First District of Vienna, on the Graben or perhaps one of the streets nearby. I have never seen a workplace like it. Floor to ceiling, it was packed with files, and the ceilings were quite high. There seemed little workspace in between.

A picture of Wiesenthal doesn't form in my memory; I only remember what he said. I recall that he tried to impress upon me what it was like for the Jews during and after the war. Yes, he said, the Jews who stayed in Vienna, frequently *"U-Boot,"* by which he meant hidden like a submarine, were in close cooperation with the Communists. There weren't many Communists, he said, "but they were our friends. The Communists were against the Nazis"—after Hitler invaded the Soviet Union in June of 1941, of course—"and they were the only effective, organized resistance in Vienna." And after the war, those who had been imprisoned and had survived, Jews or Communists, organized themselves into *Kassetteverbände* but the rationale for the groups was their common experience, not politics.

Regarding the Communist domination of the Jewish organizations of Vienna, Wiesenthal said that Jews had fled Vienna both to the west and to the east. Those who went to countries under Soviet control were returned to Vienna during the Four Power occupation. He believed there was an effort on the part of the Soviets to get those Jews who went east to return en masse to take control of the abandoned Jewish community.

However, Jews who went west trickled back only later, many waiting for some sign that the Soviets would not stay in Austria. According to Wiesenthal, it took Jews from the West years to take back their organizations. Within these organizations, there were many battles fought to remake them as representative of the Jewish community rather than Soviet ideology. It seemed outrageous to Wiesenthal that we Americans would impose sanctions against Jews who came back to Vienna to oust the Communists.

It seemed outrageous to me, too, and, I'm happy to say, also to the State Department in Washington. We modified the rule so that membership solely in the Jewish organizations would not disqualify an applicant for a visa.

Now about Dr. Teodor Schlitter, the consulate attorney. You need to know about him because he is important, and this is as good a place as any to tell you.

Teo was a roly-poly fellow with round glasses on a round, pink, cherub-like face. I suppose he was an alcoholic or maybe he just drank a lot, but drunk or sober, he made more sense than most of the other people in the embassy. I relied upon him, a lot.

His background was rather amusing, viewed from a distance. He had just received his doctorate of laws as the war started and was one of the 800,000 Austrians who, in the years following the Anschluss, were inducted into the regular German army, the Wehrmacht. Sometime in August, 1942, Teo was issued a bicycle, a backpack, a rifle, and a box of ammunition, and told to pedal toward Stalingrad, a distance of about fourteen hundred miles. It was a hard trip, taking backroads to avoid the heavy military traffic. And by the time Teo got well into the Soviet Union it was harvest time and wheat was spread out on the roadways to dry, making travel by bicycle even more difficult going.

Despite everything, Teo did arrive at Stalingrad, just in time to be shot through the hand. The hardest part of the Russian winter had not yet set in when Teo arrived, and the German army was still an intact fighting force. Months later, the Germans would be fighting for their lives, often surrounded, and in a few cases (it has been said) would be reduced to cannibalism just to stay alive. Most of the survivors would be captured. But in those early days, Teo was able to get on a train evacuating the wounded for proper medical treatment. Afterward he was sent to Italy to recuperate. He was still there at the end of the war, and made his way back to Austria, into the American sector near Linz, where he was interned.

One day Americans came through the camp asking for persons who could speak English and would be willing to work for the occupation authorities. Teo held up his now-recovered hand. Eventually, Teo came to work for the American embassy, as did so many who wanted a modicum of protection from the Soviets, who, it seemed for a decade, might never go home.

Now Teo was settled in a room right next to Buddy's office downstairs in the Passport and Citizenship Section. It was convenient to the pub that was around the corner, in the basement of our building. So all was, finally, all right with the world.

I could only suppose that the years between the Austrian unification with Nazi Germany in 1938 and the State Treaty in 1955, when the Soviets were finally induced to go home, were very painful for Teo, as they seemed to be for most Austrians. All, for the most part, were silent about it, but Teo also dulled his pain with drink. Only once did he allow a meager bit of humor about the past to show, when he one day exceeded his quota of schnapps and told me about his visit to Stalingrad.

He told me about the high irony, and only incidentally about the pain or the hardship. Ironic that he should struggle for months to get to the hell of the battle of Stalingrad and survive it by receiving a trivial wound to his hand. Ironic that he should get out of an internment camp because he happened to speak English. Ironic that it would eventually land him at the American embassy where food and drink could be had. It was entirely that sort of humor, developed by the Viennese to deal with centuries of Hapsburg rule, that had adapted and was working well in the postwar world.

9

The Czech Agent

Franz Hoch was a Czech agent, or so it was said. There was no doubt at all that he was a bit of a slippery operator. Years earlier, just before the war, he had left Vienna and immigrated to the United States, where he had obtained American citizenship. But he had greatly missed his dear Vienna and after the end of the occupation of Austria, in 1955, he returned and picked up where he had left off. And, by all accounts, he added a bit of espionage, making frequent trips between Vienna and Prague. No hard evidence of espionage, but the worst was assumed.

Spying might never have caused him any real trouble, but enjoying the comforts of Vienna did. A provision in our Immigration and Nationality Act said that a naturalized citizen who stayed abroad for five years, or even for just three years in the country of his former nationality (Austria, in Hoch's case), would have to be expatriated. That meant he would lose his U.S. citizenship. Hoch was careless, lingered long in Vienna, and the day came when he was an American no more. But not stateless, for he was still an Austrian; it was not so easy to lose Austrian citizenship.

Hoch had tried to re-immigrate to the United States and been turned down because, as I said, we were pretty well sure he had become a Communist agent since his departure from our shores. From time to time, thereafter, he would apply for a business visa so that he could make a short visit. With the same result. Though various types of visa ineligibility could be waived for short-term visits, there was no such relief for spies.

But Hoch liked some things American, anyway. In those days I had a Corvair Monza Spyder convertible, supercharged and bright red with black leather upholstery. Despite the bad name later given to the Corvair (by someone who, in my opinion, knew damn little about automobiles), the car was considered very desirable in Europe. Mine was, in fact, stolen three times in three years, but always recovered because it was so conspicuous.

Anyway, when my wife wasn't using the car, I used to park it next to the Rathaus, close to the consul general's Lancia Flamina, where I could see it from my office window to assure myself that it was still there and not off joyriding in the company of some teenager. And on some nice days when I had left the top down, I would look out of my window and see Franz Hoch sitting in my car, imagining I know not what.

Perhaps he could see (in his mind's eye) the blue Mediterranean from the Amalfi Drive or maybe even from the *Corniche des Cretes.* More likely, I suppose he imagined himself whizzing along on the Jersey Turnpike, American passport in his pocket. I didn't begrudge him his pleasure but I did give up discussing state secrets while taking my turn at the wheel. However, after a time I didn't drive the Corvair much anymore. I had acquired a little Fiat that I usually drove to work. I could discuss all the secrets I wanted in that; nobody would bother to bug a Fiat.

Here is as good a place as any to mention the Japanese-

American student and her little Fiat 600. She had gone for a year of study in Prague. She had imported the Fiat to get around because she had been crippled by polio. An automatic transmission was not available for the little Fiat, so some Czech mechanic had devised a means of operating by hand the manual clutch, which the young woman had been unable to manage with her crippled leg. It was very cleverly done and worked perfectly.

The woman was not allowed to sell the Fiat in Czechoslovakia. When she left she had to bring it with her to Vienna. Then, unless she paid high Austrian import duties, she would be unable to sell the car in Austria, either, except to someone such as a diplomat who had free-entry privileges. I put her in touch with various diplomatic missions and international agencies (such as the International Atomic Energy Agency) but when the time came for her departure and she still could not find a buyer for the Fiat, I bought it for my wife. Or to be more precise, I bought it for me so my wife could use the Corvair. Ironically, that's what put a stop to Hoch sitting in my car. Nobody wanted to sit and dream in the Fiat.

One day Hoch came into my office, along with another man, a stocky, vigorous type, like a construction worker wearing someone else's business suit. East European, I thought. Hoch is bringing in a character reference who looks less reliable than Hoch. Maybe he just wants to show me what a real spy looks like.

"Mr. Consul, this is my good friend, Tomas Mladovic. He wishes to go to Chicago."

That rather threw me. I replied with something inane, like, "I don't think you can commit him for that, though some might disagree."

Franz, who was used to me, was not put off. Tomas looked

confused, thought about it, then grinned broadly. "I need visa," he announced.

"Perhaps if you fill out a—"

"I will explain," said Hoch, "Tomas was with the Yugoslav trade mission in New York, until recently."

"Last week," said Tomas, helpfully.

"Tomas had decided to live in Austria. He is going to work for *Gebrüder Lackäfer*. They make varnishes, you know. They are very big. Tomas has a formula for a milk-based paint for cribs and other children's furniture. The paint is nutritious for children to eat." (This is a small lie on the part of the author. The real Tomas had a paint formula that seemed just as peculiar but for various reasons ought to be suppressed.) "*Gebrüder Lackäfer* wishes to license the production of this paint in the U.S., and Tomas must go to Chicago to make the arrangements. He needs a visa."

Tomas had a smile permanently in place and seemed happy enough to have Hoch speak for him. That was okay by me; I thought I knew when Hoch was lying. "What kind of a passport does he have?"

"Yugoslav. A diplomatic one."

"Can he go back to Yugoslavia?"

"Oh, no! He certainly cannot!"

"Then it isn't a passport. Maybe it used to be, but not anymore. May I see it?"

It was, indeed, a Yugoslav passport and it actually contained a diplomatic visa, though now expired. The departure stamp indicated more like two weeks ago than "last week." I thumbed through the pages. He had been authorized a visit of thirty days in Austria, but there was no sign of an Austrian residence visa. "If he can't return to Yugoslavia, then he's going to have to have a residence somewhere else."

"Oh, yes," said Tomas.

"Okay, where?" I asked.

Tomas looked to Hoch for the answer. "I'm sure it can be worked out."

"Fine. When he gets a permit to stay somewhere else after he departs from the States, then we can at least consider whether his passport might be considered good, if we stretch a point. I suppose that as long as a passport is issued by a proper authority, and hasn't been revoked, the authorized residence doesn't have to be in the country of issuance. But I'll have to look into it." I knew the moment I said that, it was a mistake.

Hoch's eyes lit up. "I will fix everything."

It was a day or two later when Hoch and Tomas returned. Hoch nodded to Tomas, who stepped up and placed a passport on my desk. Honduran. I opened it. It was all properly made out and issued by the honorary Honduran consul, Franz Hoch. I looked at Hoch and he smiled at me, sort of consul to consul, overlooking the fact that I was still a vice consul.

"You are the honorary Honduran consul?"

"Yes. I mean, *Sí*."

I examined it further. "It says here that this passport is not valid for Mr. Mladovic's travel to Honduras. Isn't that what it says?"

"*Sí*," said Hoch.

"How can you issue a passport that isn't good to return home?"

"But, Mr. Consul, you said—"

"The Yugoslav passport doesn't say Mr. Mladovic can't go home. It's just that we know it wouldn't be a good idea. But this Honduran passport—"

"The government of Honduras has limited my authority. I

am not authorized to send people to Honduras. In all other respects, the passport is perfectly good."

I sighed. Perhaps Hoch had bought a stack of blank passports, or perhaps he really was the honorary consul with limited powers. I had no way of finding out that would not entail no end of trouble. "Maybe you can get the Austrians to put a residence visa in it." The Austrians would have to decide whether it was a bogus passport or not.

"Yes, we can do that."

A week went by and no Hoch or Tomas.

Too good to last. Eventually Hoch and Tomas returned, and this time Tomas put down an Austrian passport. Made out to the new Austrian citizen Tomas Mladovic.

I didn't actually pull the passport apart, but I did examine the stitching carefully, and the photo and every stamp the passport contained. Perfect. In every way. No pages in it that looked suspiciously old or of a different shade. A degree of amusement spread across Hoch's face. He knew he had me this time. "See, Mr. Vice Consul? Now Tomas can travel anywhere."

Indeed he could. But Hoch's demoting me to vice consul did not go unnoticed.

There is an epilogue to the Hoch affair. A year or so later, when I had been promoted to consul (finally) and had moved downstairs to take Buddy's job upon his retirement, a young lady who was completely unknown to us (at the time) changed everything. She was Rosemary Schneider and was not one to put up with any foolishness. Miss Schneider had immigrated from Germany to the United States and she, like Hoch, had returned to the country of her former nationality (Germany) for more than three years. She, like Hoch, became expatriated.

However, Miss Schneider refused to accept the consequences

of that provision of the Immigration and Nationality Act. The act, she said with the help of her lawyers, was unconstitutional because it established two classes of United States citizenship (native born and naturalized) subject to unequal protection of law. She won her case, of course.

I saw a story about it in the Paris edition of the *New York Herald Tribune*. Apparently Hoch did too, because I heard from him even before the department got itself together to send us a telegram about the reversal. "I think I'm still an American, just like you. I want to apply for a passport."

"Happy to have your application, but better wait until the State Department gives us our instructions. May be an effective date or something like that. Wouldn't want to mess up your case by doing the wrong thing."

So I called my CIA friend, Eddie Soper, and we arranged lunch. I was beginning to take against Eddie. We had had so many lunches in the past year that I had regained almost half of the weight I had lost in Belize, and Eddie looked as though he hadn't gained a pound. Unfair, I thought.

"You remember the guy who used to sit in my car?"

"You mean the Czech agent, don't you? Nothing illegal about sitting in your car."

"Only you say he's a Czech agent; but I know he used to sit in my car. Still does when I can get my wife to let me drive it to work."

"Yeah?" Eddie was not prepared to make an issue of it.

"When I was upstairs, I couldn't give him a visa."

"I should hope not."

"Well, now I'm going to have to give him something better. I've got to give back his American passport." I explained about the Schneider decision. "I put him off for a few days, but you might want to see how solid your information is about him being a Czech agent. If he really is one, maybe we better alert Washington before he gets his passport."

Well, it took a few days, but not long. Eddie reported back to me that Hoch was in the clear. He never was a Czech agent.

Normally, we never ask the CIA how they know something. Saves them having to lie. Of course if the derogatory information comes from old military counterintelligence (CIC) files, the CIA doesn't care. But if it is something they've discovered themselves, they wouldn't even tell their lawyer or their priest. In this case, I was curious enough about Hoch to pry a bit.

"Why were we, in the first place, so sure he was an agent?"

"I don't know that I ought to tell you."

"If he's totally in the clear, what's the harm?"

"Yeah, well"——Eddie looked around the restaurant and mumbled in my ear——"your friend Hoch was all the time making trips to Prague, and there were a lot of suspicious currency transfers."

"That doesn't sound to me like you can be all that sure he's not still up to something."

"Oh, he is. He is. It's just that it's not espionage. I got the real skinny from my best source."

"Who's that?" I asked, albeit knowing he would never tell me and perhaps I didn't even want to know.

Eddie frowned at me, but whispered, "My son."

"Your son?" I almost yelled at him.

Eddie looked as though this would be our last lunch together. "Yeah, my son. He goes to the American School. Hoch's son goes to the American School, too. They're buddies. You want to know why Hoch goes to Czechoslovakia? He buys and sells antique cars."

I was more or less speechless, but it made perfect sense. I had been in Prague once and was struck by the number of old cars, particularly from the classic period. Prague had been a prosperous city during the early part of the automobile era and had not suffered the bombing that had destroyed so many of the other European cities. Coupled with that, the 1948 Communist takeover had put a virtual stop to the importation of new cars, and there were enough skilled Czech mechanics to keep the old cars running and in good repair.

And there was my little Fiat. Now that I thought about it, I had imported a car from Czechoslovakia myself, albeit indirectly. Couldn't very well argue with Eddie about this, now could I?

10

On the Run

$\mathcal{T}$he case of Hoch, my Czech spy who wasn't (or probably wasn't), reminds me that while Hoch was traveling so freely to Czechoslovakia to buy old cars, there were people in that country who wanted nothing more than to get out.

One such person was a flame photometer technician who floated out, crossing a river into Austria on an inflated air mattress in the dark of night and in the middle of January. He came into my office and dropped a large hunk of metal in the middle of my desk. "What is that?" I asked.

"Platinum," he said. "I save it. It is all I can take with me."

As he explained it, his job involved heating specimens for spectral analysis, suspending them on platinum wire. By letting the wire get too hot, he was able to melt some of it, slowly accumulating his dowry for the free world. I convinced Eddie that he might be useful, so he was flown out of Austria to one of our air bases in West Germany.

• • •

We weren't so lucky with a nuclear physicist from Hungary. She presented herself in my office and I recognized the type. "Aha!"

St. Ruprecht Church, believed to be the oldest in Vienna

I said to myself, "a nuclear scientist." During my days at Oak Ridge in the fifties, I had seen lots of such people. I recall one who looked for all the world like that famous WWII cartoon of the Wehrmacht soldiers doing the goose-step. One particularly simpleminded soldier, with buck teeth and his hair sticking out every which way from under his helmet, has both legs straight out in front of him. The soldier behind says, "Psst, Hans, alternately." Well, that cartoon character was a dead ringer for an Oak Ridge scientist who was working on a weird isotopic separation process and was so spaced out the management had to send a car for him in the morning to be sure he got to work. Once he got the process up and running, he got his teeth fixed, his hair cut, and looked just like anybody else. Better than any of us instrument mechanics, as a matter of fact.

Just that sort of person, this Hungarian lady. So I called up Eddie. "Take it from me, Eddie, she is what she claims to be." Eddie couldn't see why I had any particular knowledge about such things but he telephoned our science attaché in Bonn who said send her along. Unfortunately, by then it was late in the day, and Eddie had to put her up for the night in a hostel for distressed women.

The hostel was right next to our embassy and that was probably Eddie's mistake. When he went by for her the next morning, he was told that large men in overcoats had come during the night and taken her away. Perhaps they took her back to Budapest, where she got some sort of project up and running, got her teeth capped, had a perm, and now she looks like any other fashionable lady having tea at the restaurant Hungaria.

• • •

One weekend, when I had the duty, a young American showed up. She had just been released by the Czechs. An unhappy lady and her story was a rather sad one.

She, like the Nisei from whom I would later buy the little Fiat, was crippled with polio. Younger readers may not realize how common that was in the days before the polio vaccine was developed. There was a time when polio rivaled alcoholism and psychological problems as one of the principal health hazards of the Foreign Service.

The American woman had been visiting West Berlin, for reasons I have now forgotten, where she met this charming young man, an East German refugee. He told her all about the East German girl who was the great love of his life. He had left her behind when he escaped to the West and she was to try to follow him later when he had found work and a place to live, and when she saw an opportunity to escape safely. Though he wanted to keep moving farther west and maybe even to America (of course), where he could be sure of being out of the reach of the *Stasi*, he had remained in West Berlin hoping that his girl could eventually get out to join him. Several years had gone by and it was becoming more difficult, not less, to get over or around the Berlin Wall.

The American woman was at heart a romantic, and when she saw his unhappiness and longing, she resolved that she would set things to rights; she would smuggle the young East German woman out and reunite the lovers. No one, she believed, would expect such a bold act by a crippled American woman who had no East German connections.

And so she passed through one of the checkpoints, driving her ancient 1949 Chevrolet. The car was then only fourteen years old, and because its owner was perhaps not a practical woman, the vehicle was not in the best of mechanical health. Or possibly the lady being crippled, but determined and able to carry on, she expected no less of her ailing Chevrolet.

She found the East German girl without difficulty, but the girl, who had been trying for months to find a safe way to the West, told her that it was madness to try to drive back into West

Berlin. Any passengers in her car would have their identities checked and she would surely be discovered.

No problem, said our American, she would hide the East German girl in the trunk of her Chevrolet.

No, not even that, said the East German. Every driver was required to open the trunk. But finally they agreed that there was another way to get out of East Germany that just might work. They would drive into Czechoslovakia, which they could do without difficulty, and then proceed from there into Austria. The Czechs might not be so vigilant at the Austrian border, and even if they were caught, the East German thought she would only be sent back home and nothing worse. So, off they went, chugging south, trailing blue smoke.

Some distance before the pair reached the Austria-Czechoslovakia border-crossing point, the East German girl was stuffed into the small trunk of the Chevy. Now, it was most unfortunate that fumes from the exhaust leaked into the trunk of the car. That it did not also become tragic was only because the engine also burned oil and before the East German girl could expire from the carbon monoxide she became violently ill from the oil smoke at the border station.

If they had been able to whisk through the border station, their escape might have succeeded, but the Czechs typically took forever to decide that you weren't trying to take out *Kroner* illegally. This, as I remember, required checking your passport for the number of days you were in the country and comparing that to the amount of foreign currency you had exchanged for Czech currency, as noted in your passport. Tedious and petty, but it gave time for the girl in the trunk to become so ill it was audible to all.

The American woman was locked up and questioned, and the German girl taken away never to be seen again by the American. Eventually, the Czechs decided that our crippled American was only what she appeared to be, someone rather foolish but more or less harmless. She was let go.

• • •

I visited Prague only once. My Corvair insisted upon true high-octane gasoline, which was not available then in Czechoslovakia, insofar as I was able to determine. Regular Czech gas was 72 octane which would probably pour as long as you kept it warm. Their high-test was 84, which still was unwelcome in a super-charged engine. I worked out an itinerary that involved gassing up at the Austrian border, driving to Prague, then leaving via Pilsen for West Germany. It was late fall of 1963 and I do not remember it as a particularly pleasant visit. My wife and I passed through some rather dreary small towns, where loud-speakers seemed to be mounted everywhere, and someone was making announcements in what I took to be Czech.

Out on the narrow roads, unimproved since before the war, we faced death from madmen driving large trailer trucks with sec-ond trailers attached behind. There was no way these behemoths could come to a tactical halt, if you were passing them and got caught by oncoming traffic. I downshifted and let the super-charger whine; my wife, hair already turning gray, went directly to white. It was misting and dark when we arrived in Prague, and after a few wrong turns, we managed to find our hotel.

I was tired, hungry, thankful to be alive, and eager to get to the men's room. There, I encountered a lady attendant who spoke pass-able English and assured me that she was really a countess whose title had been stripped away and she had been set to doing menial work. Leaving the men's room, I found my untitled wife and we checked in. The bellman did not appear interested in Kroner for his tip but wondered whether we might have some spare cigarettes.

When we descended later to the dining room it was only to find that, since this was a Thursday, no meat was being served. According to the menu, on the other, nonmeatless days, meat entrées were calculated by the gram. In those pre–pocket calculator days I always carried a small slide rule for such emergencies.

The next day, Friday, I visited our embassy. I had never been in one of our East European embassies before and was unprepared for the sight of the conference room made entirely of Plexiglas and suspended inside a larger room in the embassy so that all sides and top and bottom of the conference room were visible. If this is a difficult concept, imagine a glass-topped jar supported on glass legs inside a box. I wondered if this wasn't a bit extreme, maybe even paranoid. However, several years later I met a security technician who had debugged some of other embassies in Iron Curtain countries and had found that even stone buildings were tunneled through with listening devices. When I got back to our hotel room, I poked around and took apart the telephone but couldn't find anything. Not very flattering, I must say. (Long afterward, my friend Virginia explained that the bugs were often hidden in ceiling light fixtures, too high up to reach. That makes me feel better.)

My wife wasn't neglected, however. During our stay, someone slit the lining of her big fuzzy coat to see what she might have hidden inside.

On Friday we saw the Laterna Magica, that peculiar and peculiarly Czech creation combining live actors with film projected on fixed screens, moving screens, and see-through screens. An art form that makes full use of that essential building block of art, ambiguity.

There seemed to be little in the stores to buy, and after a dispiriting tour of the shops, we found our way to U Fleku, a brewery-on-the-premises beer hall. The first mug of their beer made the trip to Prague worthwhile. And students—the place was packed with them. They recognized us immediately as Americans, and insisted on talking to us about Prague not really being what you see, that one day it would change. They, the students, would see to that. Five years later, they did, briefly, with the short-lived Prague Spring, until their minds were changed by 200,000 Soviet-led troops.

• • •

Czechs I have known have been, on the whole, admirable. I met my first Czech in Washington before I came abroad for the State Department. My wife and I were so fortunate as to take an apartment in the same building with Brett Pliske and his wife. Brett was, as I remember, an overage major in the U.S. Air Force. He had actually served during the last days of the First World War in the Austro-Hungarian air force, that being before the creation of an independent Czechoslovakia, and after armistice Brett had gone to Canada to become a bush pilot, flying the old rotary engine aircraft.

On such engines, the cylinders revolved around a fixed crankshaft, creating a strong gyroscopic effect that made it almost impossible to turn the aircraft against this force, limiting the pilot to left-hand turns or right-hand turns, depending upon the direction of rotation of the engine. These engines also were not well sealed and tended to catch fire. According to Brett, those pilots who survived the experience developed a technique of diving to blow out the flames.

Brett met his future wife, a Texan, when he took her up in a light plane, long after the era of the rotary engine. The lady was quite tall and had, at an early age, lost a leg to bone cancer. She wore a prosthesis, which during their flight managed to get entangled with the controls of the airplane, putting it into a long descent that seemed certain to lead to an unfortunate and disharmonious encounter with the ground. Brett explained that the only way for him to save them was to unstrap the lady's artificial leg. This successful act led to an intimacy that, in turn, led to marriage, a long and happy one.

During the Second World War, Brett served mostly as a ferry pilot, flying four-engined B-24s. After the August 1944 liberation of Paris, U.S. forces in England decided that they had earned the right to drink some champagne. The British were not at all sympathetic, though just what the problem was, Brett never explained to me. He did, however, describe what the Americans did about it. They arranged with U.S. forces in Paris to lay hold of a goodly supply of champagne and sent Brett over in a B-24 to fetch it.

At Orly airdrome (I believe that's where Brett said) there was quite a lot of the champagne, a planeful, in fact. It was loaded into the B-24 and Brett taxied out to the end of the runway to await the signal for takeoff. Instead, a message came from the control tower to wait for two high-ranking passengers.

There was some little argument between Brett and the tower about how the plane was full of cargo and there were no seats for passengers, with the tower countering that Brett would just have to make room. Before that was settled, a jeep arrived with two British generals, who said they simply had to get to London and they didn't care whether there was a seat or not.

Reluctantly, Brett, who after all was only a major, allowed the generals to climb up on top of the champagne cases next to the ceiling of the plane, where they lay as Brett revved up and took off for London. Brett flew the plane at treetop altitude because it was not pressurized and he was afraid that at normal cruising altitude the champagne bottles would pop their corks. Unfortunately, as they approached the Channel the weather turned bad and Brett had to take the plane up to a safer cruising altitude. The air was bumpy, so in addition to having decreased atmospheric pressure, the bottles were thoroughly shaken.

Well, they lost a few. A few hundred, that is. And when they arrived at Croydon the British generals were unconscious from the mixture of alcohol and CO_2 fumes. But Brett still had maybe 90 percent of a planeload of champagne, so he had the generals delivered to their BOQs with a few cases of champagne. He heard nothing further about it.

Sometime later, during the occupation days, Brett's wife, Mary, became president of an American military wives organization in Europe and as such was presented to the Queen of England. When she made the expected curtsy to the Queen, her troublesome leg prosthesis locked on her and she had to be carried away from the throne. She threw the device away and never used it again, depending on the simplicity and reliability of crutches.

Brett later retired and became a teacher in a California boys' school.

• • •

Another Czech, one I knew in Vienna, was Dr. Trcka, the Austrian representative for the American Fund for Czech Refugees. He, too, was an old-timer. Trcka had joined the Czechoslovakian diplomatic service when the country was created at the end of the First World War. He was exactly as you would expect: tall, thin, well scrubbed, elegantly dressed, and courtly. He had been friends with all the interwar leaders of his country, Beneš and both Masaryks, Tomáš and Jan.

If I remember Trcka's story correctly, he was serving as

Czechoslovakian ambassador to Venezuela just at the end of the Second World War. A new Soviet ambassador arrived in Caracas but did not know Spanish and was in the beginning quite isolated. But Trcka, who like many of his countrymen knew many languages, took pity on the Soviet diplomat and introduced him around and where needed, interpreted for him. Then, and perhaps it was in 1947, the Soviet ambassador said to Trcka something like this, "You have been a good friend to me and I want you to know that I appreciate it. I have sent your name to Moscow, and if you ever have trouble in your country, you must insist that they ask Moscow, and you will not have any more difficulties."

Trcka said that he tried to get the Soviet ambassador to tell him what sort of difficulties there might be, but the man would say nothing more. Shortly thereafter, Trcka was transferred to Mexico City. And, as it was beginning to become clear to him what problems there might be in Prague, he arranged to have Mexican citizenship granted to his daughter, whom I believe he loved very much.

Then, after the Soviet takeover of Czechoslovakia in late February 1948, and the setting up of a Communist government there, Czechoslovak diplomats were ordered home. Friends advised Trcka not to return, but he still remained strongly loyal to his country and he went to Prague sometime before the end of 1948. For several years thereafter, Trcka worked in the Foreign Ministry in Prague.

After many times asking to be sent out again as a diplomat, Trcka was finally sent to Geneva as Czechoslovakian representative at an international conference. I believe it was an ITU conference or something of that ilk. At the conference, simultaneous interpreting in a particular language was only provided if there were enough delegates wanting it. Trcka told me that the Spanish-speaking delegates lacked one delegation to qualify for simultaneous interpreting, so Trcka, who could speak almost anything, opted for Spanish under the condition that the other Spanish-speaking delegates would support the provisions sought by Czechoslovakia.

Thus it was that when Trcka sent in his report to Prague, his government was astonished that the Czechoslovak delegation had wide support and was able to get just about everything they asked for. Then Trcka's report said good-bye, he wasn't coming home. To prevent his possible defection, Trcka had not been allowed to bring his family to Geneva. However, he arranged to have a signal passed to his daughter, who ran the gauntlet of guards to get into the Mexican embassy. The Mexican ambassador later took Trcka's daughter out of the country in his embassy car. I believe his wife remained in Prague, by choice.

The last I heard (more than thirty years ago), Trcka's daughter was serving as a Mexican diplomat in Switzerland. Doubtless she was able to speak just about any language.

• • •

We have known other Czechs, and a Slovak or two, since our return to Washington, and I have generally found them amazing, particularly a former dancer cum art impresario who probably deserves a book unto herself. But this book has to have a cutoff somewhere, and it had better be with Vienna.

One last Czech, therefore, and then we call it quits. In Vienna, we knew a Jewish woman whose family had been very wealthy in Prague before the war. Her house, where she learned to ride her bicycle on the balconies overlooking the streets of Prague and where there were several room-size vaults devoted solely to storing the family silver, was later to become the Chinese embassy.

This lady married an American artist living in Vienna in comfort but by no means opulence. It was from her husband that I learned (in the days when I fancied myself as a painter) that almost anything can be used to apply paint to canvas. Neither of us was allowed by our wives to dip naked models in blue paint and roll them on our canvases, but from this expatriate American painter I did learn that the end of a board works pretty well as a brush.

One day my wife asked the painter's wife whether she missed her grand house in Prague. The woman replied, "Well, it was nice, I suppose, but what I really miss is our little twelfth-century castle in the country."

11

Espionage and the World Federalist

Frau Eva Prosl, one of my Hungarians but not one of the royal ones, thus disproving a conclusion one might otherwise easily draw, presented herself before my desk and assumed a pose of mystery. A pose typically Hungarian, I had come to realize. It was usually that, or barely controlled laughter. Only rarely, fury. But always something. I had become quite attached to Eva in a general way when she tried (unsuccessfully) to teach me enough Hungarian to give the oath required of all visa applicants. I had more or less mastered it in German and had it down pat in English, but the Hungarian version seemed to begin with what I would expect of a Sicilian fish peddler saying excuse me. I would break up and could get no further. The mood of serious bureaucracy would be lost.

Nevertheless, Eva seemed to believe that my linguistic failings were no more than what could be expected of an American. But today she had something choice. I could tell.

"Herr Konsul, Frau Dr. Gellert is here to see you. She says it is very urgent. But first I must tell you about her husband. There is something you have about him in—in there." She sort of pointed to my safe, not being able to bring herself to say the word.

I studied her closely and she dressed herself in an expression of utter innocence. Yes, I forgot that. Innocence was her other mask.

However, I knew what Eva was talking about. The first time I had looked in the safe, months before, on the day when the Red Army sergeant had come in, I had seen the Gellert file. As fat and full of facts as the sergeant's file had been thin and full of flimflam.

"Tell Mrs. Gellert I will be with her in a few minutes. I just want to review the file."

"Do I say that to her? About the file, I mean?"

"What do you usually say to applicants? You can tell her to keep her shirt on, if you like."

"Ja, Herr Vizikonsul," she said, demoting me back to my proper rank.

It had been a number of years since anything new had been added to the file. Several times, my predecessors had summarized the misdeeds of the woman's husband, Dr. Gellert, so it wasn't too difficult to get a general picture of the man. He was on the blacklist of former Nazis. He had been an electrical engineer in 1938 at the time the Germans marched into Austria and took over. In addition to appropriating the country (which many Austrians at the time welcomed) the Germans took over a number of Austria's basic industries, including the one that employed Dr. Gellert. A prudent, though not farsighted man, Dr. Gellert had joined the Nazi party.

When the war went badly and the Russians arrived in April of 1945, Dr. Gellert found himself in that portion of greater Vienna that was under Soviet occupation. Our prudent though still not prescient Dr. Gellert threw away his Nazi Party book and got a red one, a Communist Party membership book. This was a time when the Soviets were doing whatever they could to increase membership in the Austrian Communist Party, though with rather limited success, except for Dr. Gellert, of course.

When the Soviets gave up and traded political domination of Austria for substantial reparations, especially oil, Dr. Gellert began to realize that nothing in Austria could be counted on as being forever. So he immigrated, first to Canada and then to Australia. (I may have these countries in the wrong order; it has been thirty-five years since I last saw the file.) In those long-ago days, we tried to keep track of former Nazis and Communists, but the use of computers had barely begun in the mid-sixties. The result was that Dr. Gellert's past caught up with him only after he had immigrated to these countries, and he was summarily thrown out for having misrepresented his past. At some point (I no longer remember when) he tried for immigration to the United States but was turned down, courtesy of the file folder I had in my hand.

So the Gellerts moved on to Indonesia, and we quit being concerned with him. New additions to the file ceased.

Mrs. Gellert looked to be a rather ordinary woman, perhaps in her early fifties. Not particularly stylish; nothing suggesting she bought her clothes in Djakarta. She looked tired; I invited her to sit down.

"You have to do something, Herr Konsul. You must make your CIA stop bothering my husband. Not anymore will he have anything to do with politics. It makes only trouble."

"You should speak to the American embassy in Djakarta——"

"No! No more Djakarta. We are now in Egypt."

I uncapped my pen. There would be new additions for the file, after all. Mrs. Gellert told me how it was that her husband had worked for Sukarno on various projects as the country became progressively more anti-Western and descended into chaos. (As we know now, this would eventually lead to the military takeover by General Suharto, but not for another three years after I first spoke to Mrs. Gellert.) Getting out just in time, as they thought, the Gellerts moved to Egypt, where Dr. Gellert went to work for Nasser's port authority.

"And now the CIA try to make him a spy for America. My husband never have anything to do with politics anymore. You make them stop."

I assured Mrs. Gellert she would have no more trouble. I had no authority to do that, but I knew that once Eddie saw Gellert's file he would not wish to be involved with him in any way. Besides, I was so relieved she didn't want a visa, I would have told her almost anything.

Eddie didn't disappoint me. He said he would send a report back to Washington and that would be that. And I saw no more of Mrs. Gellert—for a month or two. But more about that, later.

• • •

I had the duty again. It seemed that I, and maybe a couple of other fellows, were the only ones pulling duty. My misfortune that particular week was that a former assistant U.S. attorney general chose it to come to Vienna. In his retirement, he was devoting his energies to advancing the cause of United World Federalism. I should say at the outset that the World Federalist movement is one about which I have long had certain misgivings. No crazier, of course, than the case of the young man I encountered some years before in Switzerland. That one had abandoned his U.S. passport and had a print shop make up one identifying him as a citizen of the world, a nationality not well received by the immigration authorities who presumed to speak for this country or that.

I shall name this United World Federalism advocate Pascal Anderson. Tall, as so many great men seem to be, overbearing as so many tall men are, and blind, which could happen to anybody. He was traveling around Europe, devoting his declining years (he was seventy-six) to his great cause.

Anderson found it convenient to employ two young Americans to help him with his travels and to act as his secretaries. I will call them Tweedle Dum and Tweedle Dee and try to limit my comments about the two young men to comparing them to Cohen and Schein, assistants to Senator McCarthy: They did not look particularly like Cohen and Schein, but they did manage to share their personalities in most important respects.

I had not met any of this trio before the night in question, but at about three A.M. I got a call from the First District police station saying that Tweedles Dum and Dee were in the drunk tank and demanding to see the American consul. I crawled out of my perfectly comfortable bed and went down to the police station.

The police told me that they had been apprehended as follows: At around midnight, they had been dancing around in the middle of an intersection in the Vienna First District (the old town inside the Ring) and had declined to get out of the street when told to do so by a policeman. Suspecting they were foreigners (after all, they were acting crazy), the police demanded to see their passports. The boys declined, saying they did not understand German.

The exasperated policeman called for reinforcements to help him move the boys out of the street. They went into what we used to call the spaghetti-leg mode, one that had been used for some years by American students wishing to provoke the police. The technique, as I understand it, involves completely relaxing all limbs so the subject cannot be made to walk.

This was a miscalculation on the boys' part. The police had a perfectly good way, developed through long experience, of handling people who were hopelessly drunk. I have seen this procedure employed several times and can therefore describe it.

Vienna paddy wagons in those days were VW vans with a wide door opening on one side. Two policemen would take a drunk, each by an arm and a leg, and after a few good swings would throw the subject into the van headfirst. If subjects were sufficiently drunk, they were sometimes not seriously injured.

Well, Tweedles Dum and Dee were dirty and looked a bit knocked about, but no more than could be expected, given the circumstances. In the morning, after the proper offices had opened up and the boys could be released, Teo and I came back and sprung them from jail. We took them to see the consulate physician, Dr. Gerlach, who examined them and pronounced them not seriously damaged, though he admired the perfect shoe print on one of the boys where a policeman had tried to encourage him to get out of the street.

The boys were released and told they could go get cleaned up, but they would have to appear at a hearing later. In the afternoon, Mr. Anderson appeared on the scene. Finding we had not yet gone to war with the Austrian government over this, he was preparing to indict the embassy, and particularly me for complicity in the Austrian police brutality against his two boys.

I suggested they get private legal counsel, since there was legal redress that could be sought under Austrian law. This was not enough. Mr. Anderson thought it might be better if the embassy summarily fired me, and when the ambassador and the consul general (my fellow Baylor man) declined to do so, Mr. Anderson put his suggestions to the Secretary of State and the Assistant Secretary for Special Consular Services. Just in case they failed to do their duty, he made his suggestion to my senator, Estes Kefauver, a ploy that possibly failed because the Senator was a friend, as was also his father to my father. It had no effect, of course, that Anderson had been a Republican appointee and my senator was a Democrat.

Most important, Consul General Trudgeon was solidly on my side and did not hang me out to dry as a sacrifice to appease all the worthies who had been stirred up by Mr. Anderson. Something good had come of my years at Baylor, after all.

Well, all that ever came of the Tweedles Dum and Dee matter was a pile of correspondence between the embassy and the Department of State. No more than a couple of inches thick. Eventually, Anderson and Tweedles Dum and Dee moved on to find other poor bureaucrats to battle.

Perhaps it was all this high-level publicity that soon got me promoted to consul.

• • •

I should have known Mrs. Gellert was not gone for good. This time she pushed right past Eva and my other Austrian protectors and demanded to know why I had not called off the CIA. Yes, they were still bothering her husband, and no, he was not going to have anything to do with them.

Naturally, I reported all this to Eddie, who said that there had been no response to his earlier request. Maybe nobody knew what was going on in Cairo, since all the CIA station records were in the process of being entered into a central data bank. He would, he said, try again to do something about it, but it was not clear what.

• • •

At about this time, I learned that Consul General Trudgeon would soon be leaving and would be replaced by Luke Townsend. The name was familiar, but I had to think about where I had heard it. Then it came to me: the Mad Bomber. At last I would find out the truth.

I had met the Mad Bomber in Zurich four years earlier. I will give him the name Geikle, and now that I think about it, he was originally from Bohemia and perhaps might have fit into the foregoing chapter, though he was not one of the people from Czechoslovakia whom I admired.

Geikle had wanted, in the worst way, for me to give him a U.S. immigration visa. After the war, there must have been a lot like him knocking around Western Europe—no fixed address, no visible means of support, and a willingness to tell the consular officer almost anything if only the *Herr Konsul* would tell him what was wanted.

Some of these stateless floaters could be rather polished, or at least oily, the sort that might be thought a lounge lizard in some other setting. Geikle, however, was distinctly scruffy. A roundish little man who might blend in better with a shift change at a glue works rather than with the lunch crowd on Threadneedle Street. He carried a cheap, bulging black briefcase, the sort with two straps closing it, and containing God knows what, maybe all his worldly possessions. Maybe even a bomb. He was soon known around the Zurich consulate as the Mad Bomber.

I say that the Mad Bomber was without visible means. That

really requires some clarification. He claimed to be a dentist. The thickness of his little round comic anarchist spectacles kept me from wanting to offer up my teeth to test him. Swiss police files (you betcha, we checked, and since he wasn't Swiss they were more helpful than usual) had him under deportation orders if only another country could be found that would take him. He had used up all the countries surrounding Switzerland and therefore could not simply be booted across the border. And airlines were sticky about accepting undocumented passengers of dubious repute and no fixed residence, who might end up flying with them forever like a modern-day man without a country.

The files also reported that he was apprehended in Switzerland with a large quantity of passports (nine as I remember) all bearing his likeness (poor choice) and an assortment of names, only one being the one in his current use. The Germans wanted him for gold smuggling and the Czechs were mad at him for illegal border crossing. I no longer remember what France, Italy, and Austria had against him, but it was something of the same sort.

To support his case, the Mad Bomber dumped endless questionable documents on my desk. Some typewritten pages were interlined with something that looked a bit like shorthand. "What is that?" I asked. "Just my notes, not for you to worry about," he more or less explained. Then I asked how come all the passports. "For my work." His eyes unblinking, he looked mysterious. Like Peter Lorre in one of his early German films.

Then the Mad Bomber asked to go into another room, away from the two Swiss employees who, with banks of files, shared my office. (Don't you believe it if anybody says a new vice consul rates a private office. Besides, my predecessor had seen to it that one of my Swiss office mates was a double for Marilyn Monroe. Or maybe she was Mary Pickford. I can't really recall.

When we left Zurich my wife swung my gold watch in front of my eyes and repeated, "You will forget . . .")

However unsettling it was to be closed up in a room alone with the Mad Bomber, I was soon absorbed in his story. He was one of us, he explained. He was one of our agents. His mission was to cross the border into Czechoslovakia and bring out information on Czech uranium-ore mining and reserves. As for the passports, he said, "I just do what you Americans teach me to do." What Americans? The Mad Bomber bent close. Finally I knew something for sure about him. He was fond of garlic salami. "There is a man in *München*," he breathed. "Yeah?" I wasn't surprised. I had visited Munich; you could find just about anybody there.

"This man, he is at the *Generalkonsulat*. He is a very big man. He can tell you about me." Well, that didn't surprise me either. Munich in those days was full of people in the market for information. CIA, military intelligence, the other side, free agents, it could be anybody. But a consular officer? I looked skeptical.

"It was not my wish to go back over so many time. I sure they catch me. Czechs or the *Deutsch*. But this man swear to me if I go back across and I be—in some kind trouble, you know? I get visa to America. *Sofort.*"

"Does this man have a name?"

"Ja. Townsend. That his real name, Luke Townsend. I make sure of that. I investigate."

Well, before I left Zurich, I sent a message to Munich asking about Geikle, couched in the most circumspect of language, as you can imagine. It took a while to get an answer, which, as I recall, was something to the effect that, "Yeah, we know him, he's a nut, run him off." Not too satisfactory, considering all the questions left unresolved. But about that time the Mad Bomber quit coming into the office. Out of sight, out of—you know.

I supposed he had made up a new passport and had gone off to bother some other vice consul or maybe the Swiss had him locked in solitary. He could even have gone into the practice of dentistry, but I doubted it. And anyway, I was being sent off to Belize, "Devil's Sandbar," a maximum security prison for sinful vice consuls, somewhere in the jungles of Central America.

Well, now this Luke Townsend would be coming to Vienna and everything would be explained. I looked in the Foreign Service List. Townsend had been in the West Indies for four years. He must have been already gone from Munich when I queried them about Geikle.

I settled down to wait. It wouldn't be long.

• • •

Mrs. Gellert again, now more frightened than mad. Something had to be done about the CIA in Cairo. Eddie had not seemed to be very excited about this, the previous times we discussed the Gellert case. But now I told him that something had to be done or it might become rather public. He agreed, and said the CIA sometimes had trouble with other U.S. agencies doing intelligence gathering on their turf, and sometimes they did not make any special effort to keep their informants from thinking they were dealing with the CIA. More classified cable traffic back to Washington.

• • •

Trudgeon climbed the steps to the visa section one afternoon just before quitting time. He called us all together. Luke Townsend and his family had come over in the American Export Lines ship from the United States, had off-loaded their car in Italy, and driving up to Austria had been in an auto accident.

One of his three sons was dead and Townsend and his wife were injured and in a hospital. I forget whether it was in Klagenfurt or some other town in the area.

Trudgeon delayed his departure, and we all went down to the hospital to see the Townsends. It was clear Luke Townsend would not be able to take over the consulate for a while. I thought I would wait for a better time before bringing up the subject of the Mad Bomber.

Weeks went by and Eddie finally reported back on the Gellert case. No U.S. agency was involved. So that was that. Whoever was bothering Mrs. Gellert, it wasn't us.

Not long after that, Consul Lehar was transferred, and when Townsend was able to come to work, he took Lehar's place. Trudgeon would stay on a little longer to manage the consulate general.

• • •

Mrs. Gellert, back again, not so much frightened as desperate. I told her the United States was not involved. She didn't believe me.

What else could I do but go back to Eddie? "I know, Eddie, but even if it isn't us, shouldn't the agency be concerned if someone is pretending to be a CIA agent?" Eddie agreed. It might be a good idea if someone in Cairo looked into it.

Weeks later the Townsends were released from the hospital and were able to come to Vienna. Sometime later Luke Townsend began visiting the consulate for an hour or two. He was a restless man, unable to keep still, always pacing around. I wondered whether the accident had something to do with that. Perhaps it was just his nature.

One day I asked Townsend about the Mad Bomber. "Him? Yeah I remember him, he was crazy as a bedbug." Did he ever do intelligence work for us? Townsend looked at me as though I was out of my mind.

Another time we were talking and the subject of Townsend's previous post, the Dominican Republic, came up. I mentioned that in Belize I had given an immigrant visa to Trujillo's first wife and she had sent me a bottle of the best rum I had ever tasted. "Yeah, they could be generous," Townsend said. "After the uprising against Trujillo started, I got a call from some of the Trujillo family. They wanted visas to the States. While I was talking to them on the phone I looked out my window and his troops were burning my car. I said, 'You got your nerve asking me for a visa while you people are burning my car.' After an hour or two, they delivered me a brand-new one."

• • •

It took a while but Eddie got back to me. They had finally located the man bothering the Gellerts. He was an Israeli agent pretending to be an Armenian working for the CIA. Our people suggested to the Israelis that they find another cover. It must have worked, because I never heard from Mrs. Gellert again.

12

Black-and-White Wing Tips

*N*ow, for a while, after Lehar had gone but before Trudgeon felt he could put the full weight of running the consulate general upon the recovering Townsend, I had the pleasure of working for both men, directly for Townsend, but still closely with Trudgeon.

In the short time that I worked under Townsend, I learned a lot about what a consul could and could not do. I won't go into details, because this is not, after all, a manual on consular operations, though it must at times seem like it to the reader.

But before Trudgeon leaves the scene, I want to tell you a couple of things about him that I remember. In my next life I'm going to keep careful notes so I won't forget things, but if the reader will not demand perfect historical accuracy, I will do the best I can.

The first thing is trivial. Trudgeon was a golfer. Every chance he got, he played golf with, or perhaps I should say against, an American physician, Dr. Gross, who represented the American

Medical Association in Vienna, where many American students came for medical school. When I arrived in Vienna, the Austrian staff could not wait to tell me that the competition between Consul General Trudgeon and Dr. Gross was fierce, and that upon at least one occasion Trudgeon had broken up his golf clubs after losing to Gross, an action usually reserved to the comics.

The second thing is domestic. Trudgeon was married, and I will call his wife Ida. The truth is I don't even remember her first name; having been properly brought up, I always addressed her as Mrs. Trudgeon. But for this tale, since this was all long ago and I am now old enough to call almost any woman except the First Lady by her first name, and since the name Ida is shorter than writing Trudgeon, easier to spell, and takes less typing, I will call her that.

Anyway, Ida was a Sephardic Jew, which meant that her family originated on the Iberian Peninsula. In 1492, the same year that Ferdinand and Isabella dispatched Columbus on his New World voyage of discovery, they also drove the Jews out of Spain. Many of these found refuge in Turkey. In the almost five hundred years that led up to our time in Vienna, the descendants of at least some of these lived as foreigners in Turkey. That is, they were born, lived, and died in Turkey, but they did so as documented citizens of Spain, a country that many of them had never seen.

Ida's parents lived in Istanbul, a city that absolutely everybody knows was founded as Byzantium around 660 B.C., renamed Constantinople when Emperor Constantine made it the capital of the Eastern Roman Empire in A.D. 330, sacked by the Crusaders in 1204, and taken by the Turks in 1453. The Turks changed the name to Istanbul in 1930, several years after Ida was born. Thus Ida was barely born in Constantinople, or would have been had her mother not decided that Vienna was more suitable for her lying-in. So Ida was really born in Vienna, but from the strict point of view of nationality was no more Austrian than she was Turkish, or Roman or Byzantine. She was a Spaniard. Is all that clear? I thought so.

Ida had a passion. At least one, and a gentleman would not inquire into any others. This passion I'm writing about was antique shopping, a character failing she shared with my wife. The two of them, Ida and my wife, neglected their husbands to shop for various things, but most notably for ornate gilded picture frames, sometimes containing mirrors, but more often empty. On one occasion, there was a picture inside and on another, bedbugs.

We have the picture even today. It is of a sort of Pre-Raphaelite naked lady just stepping into her bath. The bath is very grand, of Roman or perhaps Byzantine proportions. The lady is very naked. Something akin to a charcoal brazier glows in the background, keeping at least her hindquarters warm. She needs it; she has been poised on descent into her bath for more than a century.

However, it was another frame that Ida abetted my wife in buying that almost destroyed our marriage. The frame had a nice mirror inside, covered with a wooden back. We mounted the framed mirror in the bedroom where my wife could check to see if her slip was showing and things like that. We went to bed. We read awhile as we usually did and do. We turned out the lights.

In the dark of night little creatures migrated from the mirror to our bed. They smelled blood, warm blood. They were hungry; there had been little blood in the antique shop. I spent the

Sarah's $10 purchase, artist unknown

final hours of that awful night standing on the bed, with all the lights on, slapping at bedbugs. They were full of my blood and made red splotches on the sheets when I squashed them.

In the years that followed, I found that wee bloodsucking

creatures consider me as gourmet fare. It was not bedbugs but fleas, when raccoons moved into our attic a number of years later when we came back to Washington. The fleas would abandon their furry hosts, hop down through the walls, exit where the quarter round failed to meet our bedroom floor tightly, and would then hop into my shoes and lie in wait for me to join them in the morning. I noted, too, that I could simply walk across a rug in a house with pets, and my socks would become heavy with fleas. I could have hired out as a pied piper. It would be another twenty years, and more, before I would find that I have a genetic disposition to take up too much iron in my blood, and it becomes heady fare for bloodsuckers.

One could forgive Ida almost anything, even the bedbugs. Not only was she charming in an odd, amusing sort of way, like the second lead in a thirties movie comedy, but it was she who introduced my wife to the used furnishings shop called the Volksladen. It was there that my wife found our most prized Viennese acquisitions: the *Damenzimmer*, a set of furniture for a lady's sitting room; and the Luna. Though unmarked, the art noveau settee, two armchairs, and two side chairs had obviously been designed by Georges de Feure for Samuel Bing's Paris shop in the nineties. Two accompanying pieces, a desk and a vitrine, were made to match in Vienna by Gebrueder Ludwig.

But the great find was the Luna, a wonderful, small grand piano that we bought for forty dollars. It was in perfect condition and of a truly odd design. The strings were straight, that is, on a single plane without the overstringing that cross-lays bass and treble strings in modern instruments. This had two effects, it decreased the overtones that add fullness of sound at the expense of clarity of individual tones. And having all the strings on a single plane made possible a mute, in the form of a leather-edged blade that could be lowered onto the strings by depressing the middle foot-pedal. This, of course, required the elimination of the sostenuto pedal that otherwise permits already raised dampers to remain lifted while the player goes about his staccato business with other keys. That is a trivial price to pay for having a piano capable of muted tones that transform some of Mozart's sonatas into something approximating what the composer may have had in mind, or should have, if he didn't.

The Luna was distinctive for its Viennese action, capable of light touch, rapid return, and thwarting any temptation the player might have to shake down the plaster, crack the windows, and deafen the wife and children. And the cat, if you happen to have one.

But enough of that. I have to remember not to go on and on about pianos, however much my readers (if any remain) need to hear it.

• • •

There was a story that Trudgeon used to tell about the war that raged in what is now Israel, when the British Palestine mandate expired and the Arab Legion and Egyptian forces engaged the new State of Israel in combat the day after Israeli independence was proclaimed. At the time, Trudgeon was assigned to our consulate in Jerusalem, and he told how the consulate compound lay between the opposing Arab and Israeli forces. Shells continually whined overhead, now and then falling into the compound itself.

The American consul general Thomas Wasson became a peace negotiator shuttling between the two sides. If I remember correctly, the consulate car was soon put out of commission by gunfire, was replaced, then was disabled again. The Department of State said it couldn't keep replacing vehicles, but arranged to borrow one, I think it was a jeep, from the U.S. navy. But the navy jeep had something wrong with the drive mechanism and had to be abandoned. So it came to pass that our consul general was reduced to walking between the Arabs and Israelis to carry on his peace negotiations. Thus exposed, the consul general was killed by a sniper. Trudgeon always blamed Washington's parsimony for the death, but perhaps it was inevitable, a human sacrifice for peace.

When Trudgeon left Vienna at the beginning of 1965, it was to return to Israel, this time to Tel Aviv, so as not to miss the seven-day Arab-Israeli war. Some people have all the luck. I can almost hear Trudgeon telling his staff in Tel Aviv, "This is nothing; you should have been here in forty-eight. I remember those mean suckers in the Stern Gang—"

When I considered Trudgeon in Jerusalem and Townsend with his car burning in Cuidad Trujillo, I realized what a cushy life I had led in the Foreign Service. I won't even try to tell you the story told by our embassy's communications officer about how he was held prisoner in China with Angus Ward, about Mrs. Ward's dozen cats, and how newspaperman Roy Howard finally hired a train to go in and bring out our people. It is a story I am sure is better told by people who were there.

• • •

One day I took up the DCM's long-standing offer for a game of chess. DCM means Deputy Chief of Mission, who ranks second only to the ambassador. DCMs are almost always drawn from the ranks of the professional Foreign Service officers, whereas many (but not all) ambassadors are political appointees, the percentage of such varying from one administration to another, and depending upon the demands political contributors make upon the President, and whether the President's party holds a majority in the Senate, where ambassadorial appointments must be approved.

I had played a certain amount of chess at my previous post, Belize. In recent years I have given it up completely, ever since I found my younger daughter, when she turned thirteen, could beat me. One can't allow them to get ideas.

DCM Bowen set up the chess board and put on a record of Casadesus playing the Rameau *Gavotte and Variations*. He drew the white men and the first move. Few pieces of music can be as lovely as the Rameau, when in the right hands. The music took most of the sting out of losing two out of the first three games with Bowen.

Bowen put the sting back in with a casual remark about now departed consul general Philander Trudgeon. "You know," he said, "Phil wasn't such a bad officer, for a consular type." Bowen caught himself and looked at me and blushed. He had the good sense not to make it worse with an apology, but it threw him off his stride and he made several mistakes from which he could not recover. I profited from this advantage and called it a night with the score two and two. Good rule for anybody: If you can't quit while you are winning, at least try to quit when you are not losing.

Bowen's attitude was fairly typical of the Foreign Service. Many look down on consular types. Indeed, diplomatic and consular officers were quite separate until passage of the Rogers Act in 1924 made it possible for individual officers to serve in either diplomatic or consular assignments. But the prejudices persisted and were certainly still alive forty years later.

About that time, Rose Jones arrived, she was an experienced consul who believed (probably rightly) I sweated too much over whether to issue or refuse visas. More to the point, even though I had been promoted to consul, Jones still outranked me. I progressed, therefore, from fourth man to fifth man in Vienna. Or maybe it was now fifth person. Sooner or later I would probably find myself back on the bottom, like I was in Belize. It was time for me to move on.

Downstairs in the passport and citizenship section Buddy finally retired. "You ever do any passport work?" Townsend asked.

"Some, in Belize." Damn little, actually.

"You want Buddy's job?"

"Will that make me third man in the consulate?"

"I donno, never thought of it that way, but I suppose so."

"I'll take it."

"I don't know why being third man in a fuckin' consulate should make any difference. Third slice of shit pie is still sh—"

"I said, I'd take it. It'll suit me fine."

I gathered up my stuff and moved down to take over. Thus the most interesting part of my work began.

• • •

The move downstairs meant clearing out another desk. And Buddy had left me a full in-box of stuff: circulars, airgrams, Foreign Affairs Manual amendments. Most of it could probably be pitched out, but it all had to be looked at first.

In one corner of Buddy's office, now mine, was a closet. I looked inside. Urns. Three or four containers of the inorganic residue of human beings. American human beings awaiting return to their homeland, awaiting money for the final trip. More discouraging than these few urns was the considerable amount of empty shelf space just waiting for some awful disaster. It set me to thinking.

It made little sense for me to send an American's ashes home to Chicago at the same time an Austrian consul in Washington was sending Austrian ashes home to Vienna. Why shouldn't we just do a little swap. I could take an urn of ashes out to Vienna's

Central Cemetery and the Austrian consul could send his urn to the waiting loved-ones in Chicago. Much cheaper and faster for all. Of course from time to time there would be an international imbalance of bodies in one country or another where tourists simply weren't dying fast enough, but that could be rectified by filling a freighter with the excess bodies from some unhealthy country and sending them to where they were most needed. Cheap transport, much more economical than sending individual bodies here and there by air freight.

Thoughts like these were brought into sharp focus when Teo came into my office and asked, "You remember this American, Mr. Metcalf?"

Naturally I didn't. Upstairs, I had been concerned with Austrians. I looked blank.

"He's a medical student. Or he was. Now he's a cadaver, I believe you call it."

"Well, tell him to wait. I don't believe I'm up to seeing anybody for a little while."

"I don't think Mr. Metcalf will care. But his landlady is very excited. She doesn't like having a dead body in her house."

"Dead? Did you say dead?" I was beginning to pay attention.

"Yes, dead. That's what a cadaver is."

"I know what a cadaver is! Why doesn't she call the *Rettungswagen*? Or the police?"

"I suggested that when she telephoned. But she says Mr. Metcalf is an American so he is our problem. I'm afraid we have to go out and attend to things. We'll have to go right away if we are to get there before his room is looted. They'll take everything he's got as soon as they're sure he's dead."

"Why would they do that, and who's 'they'?" asked I.

"This is Vienna and 'they' is everybody."

"Maybe if we wait a while, they'll steal his body, too," I suggested, hopefully.

It was a rooming house and Teo was probably right. There seemed to be a lot of people hanging around, one in almost every doorway. Waiting to loot, or perhaps just finished. There was no way to tell.

Mr. Metcalf was sitting cross-legged on his bed, dressed in his underwear. A glass adrenaline nebulizer was still clutched in his dead hand. I didn't have to study medicine to know Metcalf had died in an acute asthma attack. I felt my own bronchial passages constrict as I remembered how my own mother had died that way when I was ten, and my grandmother, when I was fifteen. I found it necessary to get outside into fresh air.

"You get used to it, Mr. Conroy," said Teo, rather unsympathetically, when he emerged from the apartment some time later. "I have called the coroner's office and the police. There aren't any personal effects worth conserving. The place has already been cleaned out."

"I use one of those nebulizers when I have severe asthma. They are dangerous, but I never knew they were that bad. Metcalf is younger than I am."

"Let's go get a drink," suggested Teo, kindly.

"It's still morning," I protested proforma.

"We can have some more after lunch."

• • •

Within a few days of my move down from the upstairs visa section, word came that an American was being held by the police. Such occurrences are usually restricted to weekends so the well-earned rest of consuls can be spoiled. But this was, I believe, midweek. Most peculiar. Teo and I went to see about it.

Before I go further, I want to assure the reader that despite the shabby way my wife and I were treated by Buddy's friends, it is not my intention to disparage Poles or Polish-Americans in any way. I'm sure that many of my best friends would be Polish if only my acquaintanceship were wider. As it is, I can only recall a Polish lady who, on her seventieth birthday, won the polka contest on the U.S.S. *Independence*, who displaced the wife of a gentleman a dozen years her junior, and taught me how to cook properly with capers. Oh, yes, she transited Nazi Germany, alone, during the war, with her diamonds hidden in her bra. That sort of woman. Also sorry I never had the privilege of knowing Wanda Landowska, but our paths never crossed.

But to get back to this next tale, it concerns a Polish-American gentleman we shall call Arthur Wozniak. A grown son of immigrant parents in Wisconsin, if my memory is correct. Mr. Wozniak had become a schoolteacher in Illinois, and as he left his ethnic Polish neighborhood behind he was taken with a countervailing desire to get back to his Polish roots.

It was unfortunate, I thought when this affair was all over, that Buddy had retired and had thus been unavailable to extend proper understanding to his fellow New World Pole. But Buddy was now gone, leaving only me, an assistant (a new vice consul you will meet later on), and Buddy's wonderful staff of Austrians and Austro-Hungarians. Most wonderful of all, of course, was the irreplaceable but often inebriated Teo.

The police supervisor read the charges to Teo and me. Arthur Wozniak, a schoolteacher, age forty-one, from Waukegan, Illinois, had been disorderly and had refused to pay his debts.

"In what way was he disorderly?" asked Teo a bit laconically.

"He was yelling in a hotel."

"In which hotel?" The supervisor named one, out close to

the *Ring* and near *Kärntnerstrasse.* Teo perked up. "Is that not a *Stundenhotel?*"

"Yes, I believe it is."

"Then it is perhaps not the same as if he had yelled in the Hotel Sacher."

I must have looked blank. Stundenhotel? An 'hour' hotel? Vienna has such a thing? Really, I could imagine having a transient hotel at the airport, but downtown?

"It is a place for prostitutes to take their customers. Rooms are rented by the hour," Teo explained.

"This makes no difference," said the supervisor. "There is nothing illegal about it. And the guests are all the more concerned if they are disturbed," he mentioned as an afterthought.

"*Na, ja,*" said Teo and frowned, "maybe we should speak to Mr. Wozniak. Perhaps there are things he does not understand."

Mr. Wozniak was led into the supervisor's office. A thinnish man of average height, and wire-rim glasses. Good head of hair, I thought, conscious of my own vanishing crop. The ladies in the visa section had been quite outspoken in their disapproval of my usual haircut, which was about a quarter of an inch long. Or less.

The most unusual thing about Mr. Wozniak was that in spite of being dressed in a suit, shirt, and tie (all rumpled), he was in his stockinged feet. In one hand he carried a pair of the most remarkable shoes I had seen (up until that time, of course), a pair of new black-and-white wing tips, full of elaborate, nonfunctional perforations. Except for the shoes, he seemed most unlikely to be a consorter with prostitutes. "Whore-hopper" came to me, a term from the East Tennessee mountains I had not heard in years. No, Mr. Wozniak certainly didn't look like one of those.

"They said you were yelling and making a disturbance in a hotel."

"I was just trying to get that lady out of my room."

"You are staying at a *Stundenhotel?*"

"No, not what you would call staying there."

"I should think not," commented the policeman.

"It was just so I could rest my feet."

"Your feet?" "Your feet?" "Your feet?" we all three asked.

"Yes. My new shoes pinch. They are too narrow, I think." Mr. Wozniak held them up for us to see. They didn't look particularly narrow to me, but then, I wore (in those days) a double A.

"Why didn't you go to your hotel to rest your feet?" I asked.

"But it was much too far. My feet hurt too much."

"We do have taxis, they could have taken you there." The advantage of Teo's legal training. Get right to the point.

"But I couldn't tell them where to take me. I don't know where my hotel is."

Teo tipped his head and pounded it the way a swimmer does to clear his ears. "You don't know where your hotel is," he said, to make sure he understood.

"I walked from my hotel this morning—no, it is yesterday, now. The day before that when I came to Vienna, I asked the taxi to take me to a good hotel that did not cost too much. I had my dinner and I went to bed. The room is not too bad. Nothing fancy, but it is clean—"

"We do not need to know all that—" interjected the policeman.

"But that is important. The next morning, I had breakfast, what they call an English—"

"You can skip that. What did you do after breakfast?" There was a sigh in Teo's voice. I could tell he had begun to think all this was going to intrude into lunch hour, which meant missing *ein viertel Wein.* Perhaps two.

"Oh. Well, I asked the man at the desk where downtown was and I started walking. It is very far. Vienna is a lot bigger city than I thought. But I do not mind because there is so much to see. So much that I forget to look at the name of the hotel."

"The key," said Teo. "I don't suppose you have your key in your pocket."

"No, you are supposed to turn it in at the desk."

"So naturally you did so." This time Teo's sigh was quite audible. "But you think you can find your way back to the hotel."

"If I walk."

"If you walk. But your feet hurt."

"Exactly! You understand!"

"No, we don't understand. If your shoes didn't hurt when you came downtown, why is it they hurt now?" Teo being lawyerly, again.

"They are not the same shoes. I bought new ones."

"Oh." "Oh." "Oh," we all said. "Maybe you had better explain," I suggested.

"Yes, maybe I should. My family, that is my parents and my sister, she is older, they come from a small town in Poland. It is 1928. I am born in the United States, I'm proud to say. None of us ever went back home. Though it is not home anymore, of course.

"It took my parents awhile to learn English so they would be able to make enough money to make a proper visit. Then the Depression came along and then the war. Right after the war was not a good time to visit Poland and now my parents are old and should not travel.

"But I saved enough money and my parents asked me to go

back to Poland while some of the old people still remember our family, and I can show them how well we have done in America. As I walked into the city I looked at my shoes. They are comfortable but they are old and scuffed, and nothing you can do to them will hide the fact that they are not a rich man's shoes."

"With some good polish, maybe nobody would notice." I followed Teo's glance down at his own shoes. I had seen better; I went to a boy's military school and the one thing that has stuck with me was polished shoes.

"Oh, they would notice all right. In our village, in the old days, everybody used to be a shoemaker, that was the town occupation. Not anymore since the Communists came, but the old people will remember. So when I saw these beautiful shoes in a store I had to buy them and I didn't care what they cost."

"What about your old shoes?"

"I left them in the store. When I get to Poland, if they see the old ones, they will know I buy these just to impress them."

"Okay, I think we're with you this far. Your only pair of shoes hurt. But what's with you and the prostitute?" To tell the truth, I was beginning to worry about my lunch, too.

"I didn't know what she was. I knew I couldn't make it back to my hotel without taking off my shoes and resting my feet. So I asked people if there was some place around there I could go. Most of the people didn't speak English or they were in a hurry. But then there was this young lady and even though she didn't know English very well, she knew right away what I wanted."

"I bet," I said, letting my professional composure slip.

"It was this little hotel. At the desk, she told me what to pay. I pulled out my Austrian money and she picked out how much it was. Then she took me upstairs to the room. It wasn't big but it was enough. I took off my shoes."

The police supervisor read from the file in German and Theo interpreted: "He said you started yelling and pushing the lady out of the room. And you struggled with her. What was that all about?"

"She started to take off her clothes. And I realized she thought I wanted—you know—so I gave her a little money and told her I didn't want any of that, I just wanted to rest. Then she screamed at me and said something, which I think was it was not enough money. She didn't seem to care that we weren't doing anything, she wanted a lot of money, anyway. Well, I wasn't going to have that!"

"You yelled at her?"

"Of course I yelled. She bit me!" Mr. Wozniak took off his jacket and tie, and began unbuttoning his shirt. We watched as he pulled it off, favoring his right arm. On his upper arm were two arcs of tooth marks, very regular. The prostitute had had fine teeth. And he was lucky he had kept on his jacket, otherwise there would probably have been a hunk of his arm missing, like in a *Tom and Jerry* cartoon.

Teo arranged for me to take Mr. Wozniak into the waiting room while he talked to the police. After a bit they came out and the policeman instructed a constable to return the items taken from Mr. Wozniak's pockets. Teo extracted two hundred-schilling notes from Wozniak's billfold, handed the money to the police in exchange for a receipt. Wozniak started to complain, but Teo silenced him with a look.

After we were outside the police station, Teo explained. "You are getting off lightly, Mr. Wozniak. The woman was a licensed prostitute and perfectly entitled to charge you if you go into the hotel with her. You don't have to do anything; some men only hire a prostitute to look or even to talk. But I explained to the police that you do not speak the language and did not know she was a prostitute. They will give her your two hundred schillings, or at least some of it, and she will prefer to take it and not take you to court, which would just take up her time, which she can put to better use elsewhere. Such as in another room of the *Stundenhotel.*"

It took us several hours of driving Mr. Wozniak back and forth while he looked for his hotel. By the time we found it, I needed a drink as much as Teo did.

13

Eliza, the Foot Slicer, the Lion, and the Genius

We had (and have) two daughters, whom I shall call Eliza and Ann. Ann, we can dispense with in short order. She was not quite three when we came to Vienna. Now she is a writer, considerably older than that, and has informed her mother and myself that she has taken out a copyright on her childhood. So much for that.

But Eliza is the interesting (by which I mean unusual) one anyway. At five and a half, she had not spoken a word. She was not deaf. Anywhere in the house she could hear a can opener cut into a can of ravioli, just as a cat knows when a can of salmon is being opened. She could also read the labels on cans. When she would hear on the radio a piece of music we also had on record, she would pick out the record.

She also refused to look into a mirror. Even in the backseat of the car she always demanded her seat directly behind the driver so she would not see her reflection in the driver's mirror. Initially, we thought it might be because she was a vampire and knew she would have no reflection. But upon occasion we found from the proper angle we could see her reflected, so it couldn't be that.

We tried Eliza in the local English school but they did not know what to do with her. She wouldn't speak and she wouldn't often respond to spoken commands. Those days were long ago and we did not well understand autism.

We bought her a Golden Book dictionary, with pictures by the words, so she could enlarge her reading vocabulary from its basic spaghetti, ravioli, vegetable soup, and such. Eliza understood the book at once. She waited with it in the shadows and when guests came to call, she attacked. Disturbing but fascinating. Eliza would open the dictionary, plop it down in the lap of the visitor, grab one of the poor soul's fingers, and force it to point at a picture. Small, weak fingers in Eliza's viselike grip were bent, bruised, and fingernails sometimes broken. Resistance was impossible. Then Eliza would take her other hand and grab the visitor by the throat.

Most of the time, when the visitors overcame initial shock, they would catch on that Eliza intended for them to say the word pictured. Only when they did this, did Eliza release them, dropping their pointing hand like a used Kleenex and casually abandoning their not quite crushed larynx. Thus did Eliza begin her difficult journey to speech. Picture, written word, and the feel of the sounding vocal organ. Unusual, perhaps, but effective.

Still, Eliza did not immediately abandon pantomime, and indeed still drew cartoons from time to time. Multifloored buildings, for instance, having elevators with windows showing heads of passengers descending on the floor above and their feet arriving in the upper reaches of the floor below.

One day, when Eliza was very small, the pediatrician came to call. Some minor illness, I forget what. The doctor had encountered Eliza before and knew her as one of his most difficult patients. This time, however, after the examination, Eliza took him gently by the hand and led him down the stairs. Amazement became delight. He had won over another patient, one thought to be intractable. Eliza took him to the door, opened it, and pushed him out. Hard.

If Eliza felt ill-used, she would not cry, but would draw a cartoon of herself, crying. If she felt I was responsible, there would be a picture of me, doing whatever it was—making her go to bed, or come inside from her play.

Sometimes, Eliza's silence worked to some advantage. I am given to fits of playing the piano for hours on end. Imagine how it would have been if Eliza had been making a racket. And one day, Eliza wandered away from what was called our *Siedlung*. That was the American embassy's housing development. These were tiny, two-story modern row houses, perhaps better called garden apartments, because they enclosed a grassy commons on three sides. Here was where the children played. In front of our unit (on the commons side) there was a playhouse made from solid mahogany. It had been the lift-van for our household goods when they were brought from Belize. I had so designed it that, with windows and a door cut in, it became a small house.

The embassy's Marine Guard detachment had installed a new dance floor in the house for their unmarried personnel, and some of the old flooring was salvaged for the playhouse. So, it was a mahogany house with a polished dance floor. Hard to beat, if you were three feet tall.

But I was telling you about Eliza. The commons full of children and the little house made it hard to keep track of a particular child. We never knew Eliza was missing until the Austrian police brought her back. They had assumed that she must be from the American *Siedlung* because she didn't understand German. A reasonable, if humbling, presumption.

I no longer remember how we learned about Frau Stolzberger. She was a tall, redheaded Welsh woman, married to an Austrian. They had an apartment in the First District, upstairs over the Bosna Restaurant, a place for magnificent food in those days, provided you were able to eat your dinner and get out of there before the Gypsies arrived. I'll get on to the subject of Gypsies in a moment.

Frau Stolzberger—how can I describe her? Most valuable teacher? What you would get if you mixed up Michael Redgrave's daughters with a dash of Royal Fergie? Traveler from another planet? Whatever Frau Stolzberger was, she took over Eliza's education. She taught Eliza to act out the English language. For jump, they would jump, for laugh they would laugh. She began to break through the shell of isolation that had so long encased Eliza. Frau Stolzberger also worked with Eliza's natural aptitude for mathematics. In a short time Eliza was doing long division, and by the time we were ready to leave Vienna, she could do calendar calculating. That means, you could ask her, what day of the week July 4, 1922, fell on and she would say, "Tuesday." As I write this, she is not close at hand but in West Virginia, where she works for the Treasury. But Tuesday is correct. My computer can do calendar calculating with no sweat.

It is, I believe, due to three people, Frau Stolzberger, to a similarly gifted American teacher after we returned to Washington, and to Eliza's own determination, that she is a self-supporting adult today.

...

The safe in the Passport and Citizenship Section had its own interesting things. Money, among other things. Not much, but some. Various small sums went into a fund for distressed Americans. The sources were irregular. For instance, an American might die in Vienna and his relatives might say, Don't send his clothes back, just get rid of them and give the money to charity. The embassy wives (mostly wives, not husbands in those days with a very few exceptions) had a thrift shop and raised a little money. Sometimes it came in unexpected ways.

Mrs. Sekevasy, for instance. Mrs. Sekevasy was a wonderful woman from Brooklyn. She had lived most of her adult life in Brooklyn, but she had grown up in Budapest. She was also of a certain age when one may realize that the old ways and the old things were best. Particularly the clothes, she thought.

Mrs. Sekevasy was an ample lady and she could not find any dresses made in America that were comfortable and did not look as though she had borrowed them from someone else. She knew exactly what she wanted and she was convinced that in Budapest they could still make such dresses. Though it might be that in a Communist country perhaps there was not such good material as in the old days.

One of the functions of the citizenship consul, that is, myself, was to counsel Americans going into Eastern Europe, especially those of Hungarian birth. In 1956, the aborted revolution in Hungary had been put down, ruthlessly, by the Soviets before the fervor for freedom could sweep over the whole of the Soviet satellite empire. But during the few weeks that the border between Hungary and Austria was more or less open, perhaps as many as 200,000 Hungarians left their homeland for the West.

Shortly after that brief uprising, I arrived in Zurich, Switzerland, as a visa officer and found myself examining applications by some of these refugees for residence in the United States. One such family was memorable, a physician, his wife, and two young children. Toward the end of 1956, when it became clear the revolution was going to fail and the border was closing again, the doctor obtained a hay wagon, drugged the children to keep them quiet, hid them and his wife in the hay, dressed himself as a farmer, and pointed his mules west, toward Austria. Once in Austria, for a number of reasons, he just kept going west, finally coming to rest in Switzerland, until they could make arrangements to go to the New World.

Those who had fled Hungary, illegally (from the point of view of the restored Communist government), were subject to arrest should they return. And then, as time passed, the government began to see the advantages (hard currency) of tourism, and they gave assurances to Western countries that for anyone to whom they issued a visa, any outstanding charges would be suspended for the duration of the visit.

Nervously, at first, Hungarians began making visits. And my job was to talk to these people, and to other Americans who planned visits to the East, to try to anticipate troubles. Most were routine interviews; a few were not. One that was not was the American visiting Czechoslovakia who had been handed a camera by a stranger at home. The stranger asked him to take the camera as a present for his relatives in Prague. The stranger said that the camera contained undeveloped film, pictures he had taken of family members in America, and that the relatives in Prague would develop these and then send back similar negatives for pictures of family members still in Czechoslovakia. I convinced the young man that unless he particularly wished to make a study of Czech jails, it would be wise to let my friend Eddie examine the camera.

Not so with Mrs. Sekevasy. All she wanted were good old-fashioned dresses, black, commodious, but suited to her figure, and showing the fine work that she was convinced could still be done in Budapest. And she had sent ahead to her hotel many bolts of fine black fabric, enough for dresses to last for the rest of her life. I wished her well.

It was weeks later when I saw Mrs. Sekevasy again. She hobbled into my office on crutches, barely able to move, it seemed. "Sit down," I said, "tell me what's the matter."

"Mr. Consul, I don't know Budapest anymore. Everything has changed. And in the night, they come and slice off the bottoms of my feet." She raised one of her feet with great effort and rested it on my desk. The foot was all bound like those of a mummy. She offered to unwrap it, but I declined. Her word was good enough for me.

Well, it seemed that each night in Budapest as she slept, Communists or somebody would come into her room with something like a baloney slicer, and they would take a slice off of the bottom of her feet. To save herself, she had to return to Vienna while she could still travel.

I expressed my horror and amazement. She asked what she could do to keep herself safe. I thought about that one for a bit. "Well, I certainly would not go back to Budapest. That might be fatal."

She said she realized that, of course. But she said she knew of nowhere in Vienna that the sort of dress she wanted could be produced.

True, I countered, but wasn't her own well-being more important? She agreed it was.

"If you go back to Brooklyn, I'm sure you will be safe. I will make sure that nobody from Budapest comes after you with a baloney slicer. We simply won't give him a visa."

"But there is all my fabric—"

"Take it home with you."

"No, the shipping is too expensive when I don't get any dresses out of it."

"You could give it to charity." I explained about the thrift shop, and thus it was that the ladies got many bolts of fine black dress fabric, and in time, the welfare account got a few schillings.

Epilogue: I never saw Mrs. Sekevasy again, but next Christmas she sent a large box to the consulate. With some apprehension I opened it. A box of chocolates. Ten pounds of it. There was a note from Mrs. Sekevasy: Her feet had fully recovered, nobody had followed her from Budapest, and she found a dress that would do in Macy's basement.

• • •

There was also the very peculiar account of the dancing lion. "Mr. Timmer to see you, Mr. Conroy." Helga Brand, senior passport clerk disappeared from my office doorway, to be replaced immediately by the Cowardly Lion. It is a fact. Lacking a shoulder ruff, claws, and a tufted tail, of course, but his ears did look fuzzy. He was wearing a suit, but everything else was right.

"Uh, come in. Sit down." I caught myself before I said lie down.

"Just visiting, Mr. Timmer?"

"No, I live here. I'm studying ballet."

I almost hiccuped. "You are?"

"Where is Mr. Budzinsky?"

"He retired. End of the month."

A great sadness spread across the face of the lion, not quite bringing forth tears. "But I want my money."

"What money? Maybe you better explain."

A real tear coursed its way down one of the lion's cheeks. "Mr. Budzinsky gave me money every month. I have to have it!" Menace tinged the lion's voice, not quite a roar.

"Just a moment, I'll be right back." I slipped sort of sideways out of my desk chair and bolted for the door.

"Miss Brand, Miss Brand! What is that all about? He's demanding money!"

"You're supposed to give it to him. Didn't Buddy tell you?"

"Mr. Budzinsky never told me anything. He just retired and went away. We had some drinks. You were there."

"Oh, Lord! Well, give him some money so he'll go away, and when he's gone I'll tell you what I know."

"How much?"

"How should I know? Just give him what he asks for."

"I don't have much on me."

"Not from your pocket, from the safe!" She may have thought "dummy" but she didn't say it.

"Oh." I went back in my office. Mr. Timmer had gotten up and was pawing around on my desk. "Sit down, Mr. Timmer, I'll get the money."

I opened the safe, keeping my body between Mr. Timmer and the combination lock. It took some time, but in the second drawer I found a file marked Harwick Timmer. A fat file. I looked at the most recent material. There was an envelope holding Austrian schillings, and several sheets of paper with dates and amounts written on it. And a signature that looked a bit like a paw print was by each entry, the last being about a month ago. I extracted what seemed to be the usual number of schillings and made a new entry. "Sign here, Mr. Timmer." He scribbled something and huffled off.

I counted the rest of the money. In three months we were going to have a problem. I called Miss Brand into my office.

"I don't know where to begin," I began.

"I know. Weird, isn't he? But he is an American. We issued his last passport here."

Typical, I thought. He was an American and that explained everything. To an Austrian. And to me, too, I have to admit. Admit only to myself, naturally. "Is that usual? Are we a welfare office?"

"Of course. For distressed—"

"I don't mean repatriation—or an emergency loan—anything like that. I mean, what about Mr. Timmer's monthly allowance? The file suggests we've been paying him for years."

"He's a special case."

"I can see that—"

"No, I mean he is one of you, he was a Foreign Service officer."

I opened my mouth. And closed it again.

"He was in Russia."

"In Russia? In the Soviet Union? Him?"

"Yes. Before the war. Buddy told me. He fell down the stairs."

Before the war—"That must be when Davies first went to Moscow. That's— that's—" I calculated. Must have been about. '37. "That's twenty-eight years ago."

"That's about right. Mr. Timmer's over fifty. He was never right—you know, in the head—after he fell. Starting after the war his family pays for him to stay in Vienna. To keep him out of the way, I suppose. Fortunately for them, he wants to be a ballet dancer."

"I can just see it."

Fraulein Brand could, too. For a moment she lost her composure. But quickly regained it. She had worked for Americans too long to allow herself to get carried away.

"His family must be pretty old. When they go, what happens then?"

"I believe it's already in a trust."

"Well, I hope they don't forget about him. There isn't much money in the safe."

• • •

I was trying to write a letter and the sound of two women arguing kept penetrating my concentration. My attention gradually shifted and I could pick out Miss Brand and another voice—Miss Prosl? What was my nonroyal Hungarian doing invading our tranquility? I went to the door.

Helga Brand was sitting at her desk, but with her hands on her hips as if barring the door. Eva Prosl was leaning over her desk obviously trying to get her way about something. She saw me first.

"Mr. Conroy! You have to talk to this man! He can tell you things"—she fumbled for just the right expression—"things that might have military importance!" She had dropped her voice to an intense whisper.

"What man?" I asked. Helga rolled her eyes, abandoning any attempt to keep this mad Hungarian out of my office.

Eva was on me at once. She was quite tall, with long arms and a sharp chin. When she pounced it was akin to being caught by a reddish-blond spider of unusual size. "He is from Yugoslavia!" She flattened the first *a* and dragged it out, like Yugo-slave-ea.

Already she was beckoning to a bespectacled young man who was rising from his seat out front and hurrying around the counter. He had a notebook in his hand.

Before he reached us, I said, "I thought Miss Jones was handling these cases now." Rose Jones was the no-nonsense consul who had taken over the visa section.

"Die Frau Konsul would not speak to him. She is all business, that one," she said disloyally. "Ah, Mr. Consul, this is Mr. Rogic, he has something very interesting to show you." Mr. Rogic understood the gist of that much English, but that was about all.

With Eva interpreting and Mr. Rogic pointing at his drawings, he showed me two inventions that were bound to revolutionize warfare. I won't try to reconstruct the dialogue, which was chaotic, but here in summary form are the inventions (remember, Mr. Rogic thought of them first):

The Submarine That Could Submerge to Any Depth. To prevent the hull of the craft from being crushed by the pressure of deep water, the hull would be perforated with a great many holes. From each hole, a tube would be welded that would lead into the vessel for a short way, then make a U-turn and return and be welded to an unperforated spot on the outer hull. The genius of this idea is that the pressure on the outside of the hull would be brought inside and then redirected against the inside of the outer hull, thus equalizing the pressure, in and out. Not quite like pulling yourself up by your own bootstraps, but almost.

The Soundproofed Airplane. This brilliant idea relied upon the ability of identical sound waves directed at one another to cancel each other out at their point of contact. Mr. Rogic's idea was that microphones would pick up the sound of an aircraft engine and from speakers mounted on the wingtips could be directed at each other in order to cancel each other out. While this idea was inspired nuttiness, with dozens of reasons for its impracticality, a few seemingly idiotic applications of the principle had actually worked. I seem to remember that in some factories of the Western Electric Corporation the sound from machines has been similarly redirected to reduce the racket.

And when I was in boarding school, my genius roommate hooked up his record player to twin speakers on either side of the door to our dormitory room so the sound would cancel out, allowing us to play music during study hours. Our music could be heard in the rooms on either side, but not at our door. The faculty monitor was driven crazy, sneaking up and down the hall and bursting through our door trying to catch us with our forbidden enjoyment. A simple switch on the door shut down the system the moment the door was opened.

So I was prepared for Mr. Rogic. Eva interpreted for him my words of amazement, and how this was too important for me to handle. I would send it all to our science attaché in Bonn who would surely be in touch with him. With any kind of luck, the Austrians would send Mr. Rogic back to Yugoslavia before he could cause me any more trouble.

14

The Military Life

It did seem that unlike upstairs in the visa section, the work down here with mostly Americans was uneven. Sometimes there was too much to do and sometimes hardly anything.

I had an assistant, a rotational vice consul. It was a new idea in the Foreign Service, a fledgling officer would be given a first posting abroad and would be expected to work for a while in a number of different sections of the embassy. I had never had that advantage, if it was one. I had just been set down in consular operations and left there. It was fortunate that I was born and bred in a briar patch.

I'm happy to say that George Langley, the rotational officer I was given for a time, was as good at languages as I was not. I have a notion I was hard on him in some ways. For instance, when I did not yet have my little Fiat, I sometimes rode to the office with George in his little VW. As we left work one evening, I was pontificating, as is my habit, on some boring detail and George was so spaced out he drove right through a caution light.

Traffic lights in Vienna were peculiar. First green, then blinking yellow, then steady yellow, and finally red. If you drove

Dedication of the memorial apartment building, the J. F. Kennedy Wohnhaus

through the steady yellow you could be fined on the spot. Cash. Right then. Well this particular time George was fined some paltry amount and I wouldn't let him pay it because I thought it set a bad precedent. Since George could speak German better than I, he had to explain to the policeman just why it was that I, his boss, wouldn't allow him to pay the ticket. Since returning to Washington, I've changed my mind about this. Erring diplomats should not be fined for traffic violations, but should be locked in stocks on the public street, the way we did with Sabbath breakers in Puritan times.

If this seems like I'm straying from my subject, well, I'm sorry. It's just that I wanted to impress upon the reader that on some days when I didn't have much to do, I even had help not doing it. And I wouldn't even bring up this character-damaging matter were it not for the Baroness Margrit Richter von Richtersdorf. I mentioned her when I was introducing my noble Hungarians in chapter four, and she was the impoverished aristocrat who, with her sister, divided their mother's silver service and tablecloth.

It was also she who explained how it was in the old days that there existed in Hungary, side by side with but apart from the peasantry, a noble "Herrenrasse" as she called it. A master race. Not just the rich and the poor, but separate races. So much for social mobility.

Buddy, who had held my job for five years, had the place working with marvelous efficiency, a regular perpetual-motion machine, much of it depending upon Baroness Margrit, who, with her subordinate Austrian staff, did virtually all of the work of the office except where it involved the more troublesome American underclass—those who were destitute and otherwise distressed, or plain out and out insane Americans. All this I learned when I took over Buddy's office.

"Mr. Consul, sign this please." The Baroness Margrit would spread papers on my desk and hand me my pen.

"Shouldn't I look at the case?" I asked the first few times.

"Oh no!" The Baroness Margrit would look shocked and a little insulted. "You have too much to do to worry about this." I had nothing to do at the moment.

Buddy properly appreciated his smooth-running, trouble-free staff, and rewarded it appropriately with checks in all the right boxes on the annual performance evaluations. Everybody, especially Baroness Margrit, performed with the highest distinction. Best in the world. Best in any world. Best in any world that could be imagined. Well, they were good, I could agree to that.

But one day the Baroness Margrit and I were discussing something about the war, I now forget what, and the baroness said something so extraordinary that the exact words live for me today even though more than a third of a century has passed. "Mr. Conroy," she said, "that Mr. Hitler—he was a ruffian, but, you know, he was not entirely incorrect." I can hear her now, rolling those r's in "ruffian" and "incorrect," pointing out to me the saving grace that would spare that Mr. Hitler from eternal damnation.

I was, at the time, speechless. Later, when I had somewhat recovered (I have never fully recovered) I dropped the subject. Months afterward, it came time again to provide ratings for my staff. When I considered the baroness, I found it impossible to put all of the check marks in the boxes that were at the highest end of the scale. "Superior" was simply as high as I was able to bring myself to go. I admit it, my ratings were a bit arbitrary, but I believe they reflected a higher truth. She was very, very good at her job, but she was not perfect.

The Baroness Margrit came into my office in tears. She had never in her entire career received such a terrible efficiency report, she said, and as she was about to retire, I had ruined her career. I urged her to write a letter to the file, and I would see that it came to the attention of Consul General Townsend.

I have thought about that report over the years, and I draw comfort from Ogden Nash, as one so often must. In the Strange Case of the Dead Divorcée, Nash, in his wisdom, explains how this woman has one failed marriage after another, each spouse divorcing her for infidelity, because none is able to bring himself to state the real grounds, which would besmirch her good name. Finally, for the good of all, her last husband does her in with an ice pick that was a priceless heirloom. Her unspeakable sin was that at parties she always refused mint juleps, saying, "No thank you, I'll just drink half of my husband's."

I did not have an ice pick handy when the Baroness Margrit told me that Mr. Hitler, though a ruffian, was not entirely incorrect, but—

• • •

The sort of case that did get sent right in, without the intercession of the almost but not quite perfect locals, was the one involving Astridur Bjarnisdottir. (I hope Icelanders will forgive me if I blunder ignorantly into implausibilities as I try to make up Icelandic names.) The lady, who came into my office, would be called by someone more gauche than I "a real classy dame." A proud lady dressed in exquisite taste, on a mission that would have humbled anyone lesser. She was from Reykjavík, she said, and she had a problem. I explained that visas were issued upstairs. She ignored the implied suggestion.

As she explained it, her difficulty was she had a new daughter, whose father, she said, had been a member of our embassy's Marine guard in Reykjavík, but who was now posted to Vienna. She wished for the Marine to acknowledge paternity of the child.

Did she wish him to marry her, I asked with as much delicacy as I could muster (not much). No, she said, she did not want that. Did she wish to have support for the child, I asked. If so, it seemed to me that she should have a talk with the Marine's unit commander. Oh, no, she said, she just wanted a signed letter wherein the Marine said he was the father.

I observed that if she did not want financial support, it was a long way to come from Reykjavík just for such a letter. No, she countered. It would affect her daughter's whole life. Then she explained that in Iceland, surnames are constructed from the father's first name plus the Icelandic form of "son of" or "daughter of." An example being Ingolfsson, for a boy, or my visitor's name, Bjarnisdottir, for a girl. The problem arose when paternity was not established and the child's name might have to be Astridsdottir, forever perpetuating the uncertainty of paternity.

All of this was news to me, but I called the Marine in and explained the problem to him. And I told him that I, personally, doubted that child support payments could ever be enforced if required by a court outside the United States. I also told him that I did not want to know what he decided to do about giving the letter.

• • •

Miss Brand brought me the sailor. An ordinary sailor, off one of our navy ships parked in Italy, had been taking leave to see a bit of Europe while he had the chance. He had lost his passport, Miss Brand told me, and giggled.

The sailor didn't appear to be disturbed by the loss of his passport, though he was a little uneasy about overstaying his leave. "They turned me back at the Italian border. Said I needed a passport."

I asked him for his identification and he dangled his dog tags at me. "That's all?"

He pulled his billfold out of the pocket of his pea jacket. He had a U.S. driver's license and a navy ID card. "I lost everything else."

"You had a passport?" He nodded. "Where did you last see it?"

"In the head."

Head? Oh. I was not a navy man myself but I had known some. "You mean in the toilet?"

"Yeah, on the train. The Italy Express."

"You took it out in the toilet?"

"No. There's no pockets in navy pants. I had it tucked into the waist band. Before I realized it, it fell in when, uh, you know—"

"When you pulled your pants down."

"Yeah. I saw it go just as I flushed it.

"Go get some pictures. Two inches square, full face, got to show both ears."

"You going to give me a new passport?"

"Yes, your story is just screwy enough to be true."

"Going to be late getting back to my ship—"

"I'll give you a letter, too."

The baroness came in and asked me if I wasn't going to cable Washington to confirm he really lost a passport. I said no, it would just make him later returning to duty. Weeks later the snow melted on the railroad right-of-way in Kaernten and a railway employee found the sailor's passport. The railway sent it to us. Miss Brand brought it into my office, holding it carefully with a piece of tissue. I returned it to Washington with appropriate comments.

It seemed to me the sailor should not be criticized too much. Consider the American student who met a girl he liked and tore the picture out of his passport to give to her. Or the woman who came all the way from Amsterdam to Vienna with her ticket, but with no identification at all except for a thirty-year service pin from the American phone company where she had just retired.

"You accept a service pin—" said the baroness.

"A thirty-year pin. Anybody who stays with the phone company for thirty years deserves some consideration."

"But—"

"What should I do with her? They wouldn't take her at the pound. Besides, her American friend identified her. And I made the passport valid only for immediate return." I should have explained to the baroness that the lady's St. Louis accent couldn't be faked. Something Buddy would not have had an ear for.

• • •

Lest the reader think I was always right and my Austrians always wrong, I better tell you about Oscar Schlegel, the seasonal exile from New York. Oscar was a tiny man, not much over five feet tall and probably 115 pounds including his cigar. He was a Jew who had been lucky enough to have escaped from Vienna in the days just before the war, and had become an American citizen.

During the busy season, Oscar worked in a tobacco shop in a New York hotel. I no longer remember whether this was summer or winter, but whenever it was, his employment ended when the business slackened. His boss was a kindly man, and when he had to lay Oscar off, he added a little bit to his final paycheck so Oscar could take the plane, tourist class, to Vienna and stay with relatives until business picked up again. Oscar was lucky to have relatives in Vienna who had managed to survive the war one way or another. And they were always glad to see Oscar. Once a year. As long as he didn't stay too long.

When the relatives had put up with Oscar long enough, and besides, he was needed again in New York, Oscar would come to the consulate and explain that he was destitute and needed to be repatriated, which meant being sent home at U.S. government expense. In such cases, the ride home was a loan, and the indigent's passport was marked good only for return to the United States. The repatriation loan would have to be repaid before the passport could be used for leaving the country again.

So in the long run, each year Oscar (and his employer) paid for the trip to Austria and Oscar paid for the return, sort of like putting it on a credit card that has to be repaid. Eventually. Back in the early sixties, credit cards were not common, of course. But the reason Oscar paid for his travel in this peculiar way was that it was the only way he could afford it. The United States in those days was sending people home in military planes for dirt cheap, an amount that even Oscar could repay from the little salary he got working in the hotel.

This went on year after year, despite the repatriation system being intended for people who found themselves in emergency circumstances, and not for cut-rate vacation travel. Washington was getting more and more resistant to paying for Oscar's annual travel. But how to stop it before Oscar found himself stranded in Vienna forever?

Miss Brand came up with the solution, which we cleared with Washington, and on Oscar's next trip we put it into place. We got Washington to authorize sending Oscar back to the United States, flying first class on Pan American's flight No. I, the most expensive air travel in those days short of hiring your own jet. Oscar was never able to repay his repatriation loan again. I hope he found off-season employment in New York.

• • •

Remember the bedbugs? Well, we put their lodgings, the mirror with the gold leaf frame, outside but in a sheltered spot where it wouldn't get actually rained or snowed on. I squirted it well with DDT. Back then we used DDT for everything and it came from the United State Department in U.S. Army—issue olive drab aerosol cans. As a consequence, any eagle who tried to lay an egg in the ozone layer was one dead dodo. Still, I had little faith that the bedbugs were really dead and I refused to allow my wife to bring the mirror into the house.

One day Mrs. Townsend, the now recovered wife of the new consul general, stopped by our town house. There, on our doorstep, she saw the mirror and admired it greatly. She said it was bound to get ruined if we didn't bring it in out of the weather. I said, "You like it; you keep it," or words to that effect. My wife hissed in my ear and said, "There goes your career down the tubes," or something of that sort. I whispered back, "Better that than have the damn bedbugs again."

The Townsends never had any trouble with the bedbugs, or if they did they kept it quiet. People are funny about bedbugs, sometimes.

15

Matters Dental, Ocular, and the Big Broadcast

About this time, I suffered an attack of double vision. I don't know whether it has ever happened to you. If not, I can assure you it is very disconcerting. I awoke one morning to find that everything had doubled during the night. Two wives, four children, that sort of thing. I did the best I could shaving around both of my noses. You can get something of the same effect by the children's trick of closing your eyes, crossing the forefinger and middle finger of one hand, and then, fingers crossed, touching the end of your nose. See? Or perhaps I should say, feel? You've got two noses. Eyes open, I stared in the bathroom mirror at my eyes, all four of them. I almost expected to see that they had compounded, like those of an insect, but they looked like people eyes except of course for there being too many of them.

Made it through breakfast by closing all four, and using my fork very carefully. Then I asked my wife to drive me to work. Easily the most frightening ride of my life. Each intersection was made up of six streets not counting the two we were on. Other cars seemed to come at us from all directions at once. I closed my eyes again.

The town of Weissenkirchen, in the Wachau valley

Made it into my office somehow, a bit late, but there on the same day as expected. Sat in my chairs, thanked the Lord the chairs had arms and thus it was not easy to fall out. Designed for sleeping bureaucrats, doubtless. My helpful Austrian staff helped me dial the phone for an ophthalmologist. A sign I had not yet lost my optimism. Otherwise, I might have started with a neurologist or even a psychiatrist, this after all being Vienna. The Herr Professor Doktor could see me day after tomorrow if I survived that long. I would grow a beard, I decided, and maybe take up polygamy. Didn't know what to do about the extra children, however. No way to accommodate four of them in a two-bedroom apartment. Forgot to count the bedrooms. Maybe there are more of them, too.

I did pretty well up until she came in. That belly dancer. Blond and somewhat skinnier than the ones you see in the movies. She was, or maybe they were, American, or so she (they?) said. I tried to get Miss Brand—oops, sorry, the Misses Brand twins—to deal with them, but she—they—said, no way, the belly dancer insisted on seeing the consul. Even then it might have been all right if only she had been willing to sit still and just talk. But she kept moving around, all the time moving around. An occupational problem, I decided in retrospect, when I was able to think clearly again.

The lady obviously really was a dancer; I could tell that from the way the multiple images of her moved. She was going on and on about how she gave up everything to move to Cairo and now that the Egyptians had refused to extend her work permit, she had had to leave Egypt.

"I'm afraid the Egyptians aren't terribly friendly to Americans, just now."

"The Egyptians loved me. It's only the officials."

"They're the ones who issue the residence and work permits. Or don't, as in your case." I closed my eyes.

"Well, what are you going to do about it?" she demanded, almost yelling at me. I opened my eyes. She was still on the move, crisscrossing my office with her skirt and some sort of frilly stuff streaming behind her. Or maybe it was mostly the effect of my optical problems.

And because you think of the darnedest things at such times, I was suddenly back in the Carousel Theater on the edge of the University of Tennessee campus and fifteen years had vanished. My imagination had given my belly dancer a role, that of the actress who arrives on stage in a sarcophagus in *The Man Who Came to Dinner*. Back then I had been doing stage props and somehow the actress was talking on the phone and loping all around the stage. We had not tied the end of the phone line down very well and it was whipping along behind her. The audience enjoyed it more than we did, but somebody told me that, after all, this was supposed to be a comedy.

So it was all right. I smiled at the thought, smiled for the first time that day. The belly dancer brought up short, "I don't see what's so amusing about it. I'm stranded here."

Well, I explained that I was just thinking about the joy her dancing must have brought to the men of Cairo and said I was sure their wives had made them give her the heave-ho. Then I gave her a list of Vienna restaurants that might need a belly dancer. It must have worked out, because I never saw her again.

• • •

In a few days the eye problem cleared up as mysteriously as it had come upon me. And back to normal, I was getting pretty good on the restaurant scene. There were still at least ten pounds left from the twenty-five I had lost in Belize that had to be gained back, and the dollar was as strong as the Austrian schilling was weak. Dining first class was my duty.

Austrian restaurant food used to be a delight, tempered only by the lamentable tendency of many restaurant owners to employ Gypsy violinists at dinnertime. On principle I avoided the few restaurants offering belly dancers.

The most vile of the Gypsy violinists was the one who fiddled solo at a restaurant on *Billroth Strasse* near *Chimanistrasse*. He played, furiously, upon a tiny dancing master's violin that looked to be a quarter of the size of a regular instrument. He grinned like a satyr and would bend over your table, his bow slashing the air, his strings screeching, the volume undiminished by the small size of the fiddle, until you bribed him to go away.

But there were times of the evening when it was possible to bolt down your food and get out the door before the entertainment began their nightly onslaught. Thus it was that I began my Gypsy-free list, my list of restaurants where, at certain times, it was possible to get something to eat in peace and quiet. "Get seated by 5:45, have a drink," my listing for a particular restaurant might say, "kitchen opens at 6:00, so know what you want; be ready to order. Be sure to ask for your bill when you are served. Get out by 7:30 if humanly possible." That sort of thing.

It was natural that I expanded the list to such restaurants in Budapest, a city that has long been plagued by the Gypsy violin, even at lunchtime, if you can imagine. The reason for this extension was, as I mentioned earlier, that part of my job was to brief American citizens planning visits to Eastern Europe, especially to Hungary.

At this far remove, It is hard for me to give you the actual numerical breakdown, but somewhere around 90 percent of the people I briefed seemed to find me presumptuous and that included a fair number of people who wondered whether I was properly an American. Some few actually said they came to Europe just to hear Gypsy violins, but I believe they were pulling my leg.

But a solid ten percent of the people I briefed were delighted with my Gypsy-free list and have held me in high regard since those days. I like to think that I was in some small way responsible for whatever good feelings a few people, the ones who counted, had about the State Department in the sixties.

In the interest of furthering this research I made visits to Budapest where I found unexpected riches: editions of early, middle, and late Baroque keyboard music published before the Second World War, and some before the First World War. These were mostly, but not entirely, German editions from what had become East Germany. In Budapest I was told, but cannot verify, that the East Germans were devoting seventy percent of their music publishing capacity to nice modern stuff almost as good as Gypsy music, and that their warehouses of priceless, irreplaceable keyboard scores were being cleared out at fire sale prices. I bought all I could lay my hands on.

• • •

Another study I conducted at the time for personal rather than altruistic reasons was my great American national peajib study. This came about because in the process of renewing passports for Americans abroad, I became privy to the places and dates of birth, information that cried out to contribute to scholarly examination, the so-called information age having not yet been invented. And it seemed to me that one of the great unstudied fields was to draw a linguistic map of America according to the local names of one of the meanest, most insignificant objects, the peajib. The peajib was lowest common denominator of consumer products. Their origin may, for some, require an explanation. For those of you too young to remember the Great Depression, it was a time when the playing of marbles entirely with little glass spheres (marbles) was a conspicuous display, costly if playing for keeps, and generally to be avoided.

It worked perfectly well to restrict the use of expensive glass marbles to the taw (the shooter) which would not ordinarily be lost in the game. The expendable spheres were small, cheap terra-cotta things called, at least in the Ducktown Basin where I grew up, peajibs. (Don't hold me to the spelling; references to such insignificant objects were oral, not written). Peajibs were dyed various colors, bluish, reddish, yellowish, greenish, and some were left natural, which means terra-cotta colored.

In the course of my research, I found three other names for these objects: migs, miggels, and commies. My transfer back to Washington (for reasons still unclear to me) interrupted this research, leaving it fair game for future graduate study. But you better hurry. Old-timers who played marbles in the thirties are fading fast.

One day, perhaps, I will track down the term gibnut (possibly spelled gipnut) that I have heard the old people of the mountains call the chipmunk. So you see, in my retirement, my mind is still not idle.

• • •

But to get back to this account of Vienna in the sixties, there are several things you should understand. The first is that travel of Americans was virtually unrestricted throughout Western Europe, requiring no visas for sojourns of less than thirty days (sixty days in some countries). American tourists and their dollars were welcome just about everywhere.

Travel into Communist-controlled countries was much more restricted, all requiring visas, though some were willing to issue visas at their borders. The Soviet Union, as we saw in the case of the American sergeant who sent the postcard from Red Square, required tourists to take government-arranged tours, or in the case of Czechoslovakia, there were tight currency controls. I don't remember about Poland, but it seems to me that the schoolteacher with the tight shoes had to wait a few days for his visa, at least long enough to get himself into trouble.

I tell you all this because it helps explain why people with mental troubles collected in Vienna like flies on a kitchen door screen. It is my observation that certain types of mental illnesses cause people to try to keep moving so as to leave their demons behind. They run and run until eventually something, in this case the Iron Curtain, causes them to stop and allows their pursuers to catch up. Some examples:

• • •

The man sat in front of my desk; I could tell by the set of his jaw that he was uncomfortable. It was either his teeth or maybe his jaw was out of joint. Something in his mouth. "What can I do for you, Mr.—"

"Wuh—"

"I'm sorry, I didn't understand your name."

This time he made a real effort, but covered his mouth, trying to keep imps in or out, I couldn't tell which. "Watts," he seemed to say. "Barryk Whatts. Wi-an haach."

"Oh, Barry Whatts. I wrote that down on my yellow pad. "Now—"

"No—" He got up from his chair, took the pen out of my hand, crossed out Barry and wrote "Barrick."

"Oh. Mr. Barrick Whatts. Now, how can I help you?"

"My teeth."

"You need a dentist? I've got a good one. Mornings he's an artist and afternoons he's a dentist. Good at both, actually. Fix you right up."

"Well, maybe. But he'd have to see me in the morning." (Due to his pained mumbling, I give you here only what I understood Mr. Whatts to be saying.)

"Leaving town tomorrow afternoon?" I tried to suppress the hope in my voice. Rule number one for consuls: Get any kind of problem out of your consular district as fast as possible.

"No, it's just it bothers me worst in the mornings."

"Your toothache?"

"Not tooth, teeth. Someone comes into my room in the night and jumbles all my fillings around. Takes most of the day to get them straight again."

Well, I could sort of understand that. There's been mornings when I swear every one of my teeth hurt, though mostly its been when I had too much to drink the night before. "Maybe you could ease off on the sauce."

"You suggesting I drink too much?"

"No, not at all," I assured him, backpedaling. "You know, spicy foods."

Mr. Whatts rewarded me with a sour look. "Nah, it's my fillings."

"Lock your door."

"What good would that do? I pulled the bureau in front of it, but that's no good; they don't come through the door. They come up from under the floor someplace."

"You mean like a trapdoor?" He nodded. "Nail it down."

"Can't find it."

"Then I've got the answer for you." The trick in cases like this is to try to think like the customer. "What you do is go to *Slama's Schwemme*. It's on *Mariahilferstrasse*. You can buy irregular glassware there very cheap, like about ten cents a glass. Get a bunch of glasses, fill them with water, and place them around on the floor when you go to bed. In the morning, you can see where the water's spilled and that tells you where the trapdoor is. Then you just nail it shut."

Mr. Whatts seemed to like the idea, and after asking directions to Slama's he hurried off. I relaxed, with a feeling of accomplishment rare in my business.

Epilogue: I never saw Mr. Whatts again, but about three months later I got a telegram from Bangkok. Mr. Whatts was driving them all crazy with his problem, and he kept insisting that the American consul in Vienna had been of tremendous help to him. Would we please advise them what to do? God's own truth, that's what the telegram asked.

• • •

About the same time that the man with the migrating fillings came by, the man with the built-in radio visited us. I was running late that morning and when I sat down at my desk there were a bunch of things waiting to be signed. That took me a little while because I had taken to ignoring the baroness's advice and was at least glancing at everything I signed.

The man who came in and sat down across from me had that hollow-eyed appearance of someone who chronically does not get enough sleep.

"Sorry to keep you waiting, Mr.—"

"Rideout. I'm Earle Rideout. That's all right. I was listening to the radio."

"The radio?"

"Yeah. I guess you can't hear it. I can always hear it."

"I've heard of people picking up radio stations with their fillings. What station do you get in Vienna?"

"I always get the same station. They don't ever give any station identification. There's just talk and sometimes music. Sometimes it talks directly to me."

"What does it say?" I asked.

"It varies. Sometimes it asks me to misprison a felony. Sometimes it just wants me to kill somebody."

That pushed my alarm button. Once, back when I was stationed in Zurich, I declined to issue a visa to a Dane because he didn't give a good reason for not applying for his visa before he left Denmark. The man then took a train to the mountain resort town of Davos, went into a hardware store, bought himself a hammer, killed a policeman with it, stole a car, and crashed it into three other vehicles. "You can hear the radio now?" I asked, to make sure I'd heard right.

"Clear as a bell. Sometimes, like on a plane, it comes over the PA system, like, 'Fasten your seat belts, please, and will Mr. Rideout please kill the lady on his left.' Other times, like if I'm out on the street, it comes right out of the air."

"And do you do it?"

"What?"

"What the voice says."

"Oh. Sometimes—sometimes I almost think I'm going to have to."

I took Mr. Rideout over to talk to Mr. Townsend. "You might want to tell your story to our consul general. He's a lot more experienced than I."

Townsend talked to Mr. Rideout for the rest of the day.

Maybe three or four hours. Eventually, Townsend came into my office. He paced around—Townsend as I mentioned earlier, was one of those people who simply can't sit still. He said, "I donno" two or three times. "I almost called the *Polizei*, two, three times. But I don't know what this guy is going to do if I pick up the phone. And I don't know what I could tell the Polizei, anyway."

"How did you get rid of him?"

"I told him to go see a doctor. Doctors get paid for stuff like that."

Later, I looked up "misprisonment of felony." My dictionary said it was failure of an innocent person to report a crime. That sort of made sense. What Mr. Rideout seemed to be saying was that he was supposed to commit murder and somehow he was not to be an accessory to his own crime, but maybe he would be guilty of not turning himself in. If you assumed he was two persons, it would all work out. I thought again of Anna in Brecht's *Seven Deadly Sins.* There are two of her, one beautiful and one practical. The two can talk to each other, *"Nicht wahr, Anna? Ja, Anna."*

My wife, who reads my copy after me to correct my mistakes, purposeful or otherwise, says this chapter is ninety percent piffle. (I might agree to eighty percent.)

16

The One-Way Street
and Hats

I have suggested that Teo tippled. Ordinarily, this caused no particular difficulties, though it had bothered consul general Trudgeon a bit. Townsend took it more in stride. And I learned that if Teo was sitting in his chair, his face cleft by a happy smile, his hands folded over his middle, and his eyes open but motionless behind his thick round glasses, then I should just come back a little while later and I would find that his consciousness would most likely have returned, and he would again be his old, invaluable self.

But that was before the one-way street business. It came about despite the often demonstrated fact that when Teo was driving under circumstances of diminished capacity (i.e., drunk) he always took extra care and exercised great caution. Consequently, he never damaged anybody or anything with his auto. And the time spent driving on the sidewalk saved wear and tear on the streets.

Whether it was because he spent all those years speaking English to the likes of us, or for some other reason, Teo began having problems with those little signs that said *Einbahn Strasse*, for what we would call the one-way street. Or maybe the round, red, international shield with the horizontal white bar (DO NOT ENTER) reminded him of the other, his favorite kind of bar (CUSTOMERS WELCOME). Whatever the reason, he would upon occasion drive up such streets the wrong way. But carefully, of course.

At first he received warnings but the police could not help noticing that Teo was in his cups, so to speak. So it was that one evening Teo drove the wrong way up a particular *Einbahn Strasse*, on what was to be his last trip, as a driver, for six months. Or so the magistrate in the traffic court said.

Most of us would find it inconvenient to be grounded for six months, but ordinarily it would not cause employment problems, unless one drives a taxi or a delivery van, of course. But for Teo it was a disaster, because he lived in the 22nd district, in the far reaches of Vienna across the Danube River, from which public transportation to the consulate in the First District was long and difficult and required considerable presence of mind that Teo did not always have handy when he arose in the morning.

So it was that Teo began to arrive at the office late and sometimes not at all, and when he was there, he was morose, his usual sunny disposition altogether lacking.

This is how it was when Miss Clara Davidson arrived. "I am Clara Davidson," she announced. I said I was pleased to meet her, but apparently I wasn't pleased enough. "I'm the singer," she said, so as to give me a second chance.

"Oh," I replied, and looked at her carefully. Should I recognize her? Probably not. Opera and I are not what you would call cozy. I'm sure that was one of the reasons I was transferred to Vienna.

Apparently she took my searching gaze for one of speechless admiration. Satisfied, she moved on to the purpose of her visit. "I want protection."

"Have you been threatened? Maybe we should call the police."

"No, that would be bad publicity. I just want you to make him go away."

"Him? What sort of a him? A fan?" I had read about fans. Singers, movie stars, and such couldn't live with them or without them, it seemed.

"Of course not a fan. I can deal with those. He's a singer. A countertenor. English, of course, and neurotic. All countertenors are neurotic."

"What do you think he might do to you?"

"I shudder to think." She shuddered.

"You're not married to him or anything like that?" It was something I had to ask. I have gotten in the middle of domestic disputes before. Avoid it; that's rule number two for consuls.

"Heavens no! I met him when we were singing in Cannes. Since we were both traveling in Europe it seemed logical that we travel together." Miss Davidson paused a moment and looked at me thoughtfully before proceeding. "To shorten a rather long story, this man did not benefit from close inspection, and I decided when we got to Venice that we should go our separate ways. He seems to have found me somewhat more satisfactory, however." She fluffed her hair a bit while inflating her chest (needlessly), so I could see just how satisfactory she was.

"You left him in Venice?"

"It was my intention. I had an engagement in Zagreb. I hired a car in Trieste and he actually followed me. Right along behind!"

"Did he then follow you to Vienna?"

"I don't know; maybe not right away. I had one more performance and I sent word to the theater I was sick. Then I disguised myself and got the hell out of town."

"Disguised yourself?"

"Of course. It was easy. I do it every night onstage. But I don't know how much good it did. As soon as my understudy's name went up outside the theater, he must have caught on. Of course if he tried to follow me out of Yugoslavia he's probably still lost somewhere. I've never seen such country."

"Maybe it would be wise for you to leave Vienna." That, as I have elsewhere explained, was rule number one for consuls. Get such people out of town. Forthwith.

"Singers can't hide. Wherever I sing, my public will know about it. If you can just protect me for a while, I know he'll lose interest eventually. After all, he's a countertenor."

After work, when I got home, I would have to look up the term in my copy of *Grove*. I seemed to think that such singers nowadays took roles originally written for castratos. What the significance of that might be, I couldn't imagine. But for now, this appeared to be a case for Teo, though I didn't hold out much hope, considering his current condition. I led her to Teo's office next door.

"Miss Davidson, this is Dr. Schlitter. If anyone can help you, he can." We sat down and Miss Davidson went through the whole story again, adding details dredged up either from her memory or her imagination. Probably a little of both. But she caught Teo's attention, I could see that. For the first time in days, he was showing some interest. I thought part of it might have been because the Viennese always find opera singers irresistible, but it seemed there was something more. Teo was looking thoughtful. And awake, too, of course.

Miss Davidson had come to the conclusion of her story and once again threw herself on the mercy of the embassy. Vulnerable, but with unplumbed depths. Seeing her do it twice, like a matinee followed by an evening performance, put me in mind of watching again some final scene from some opera where the Diva lays her soul bare to some king and, more important, to the audience. I resisted clapping, but was sure she would have smiled to me had I done so and perhaps might have made a small curtsey.

Teo thought for several minutes, from time to time surveying Miss Davidson. One could see he found her comely, as indeed she was. In a mature way. Then Teo spoke. "Tell me, Miss Davidson, do you have an international driver's license?"

The lady instantly disappeared from her imaginary stage, and reappeared in some disagreeable place, such as her business manager's seedy office, but she did reply to Teo's question. "Of course I have a driver's license. Everybody has a driver's license."

Teo smiled. Fully himself for the first time since his difficulties with the police began. "I do not see how the embassy can protect—"

Disappointment, woe, and a soupçon of outrage washed over Miss Davidson's face. Onstage, again. I prepared myself for her to express these feelings in song.

"—can protect you," Teo continued, "unless someone, perhaps myself, stays with you twenty-four hours a day."

Miss Davidson was surprised, but adjusted quickly. A new script, but a pleasing one. She considered it a moment as I watched her face. Teo was somebody she could handle; it would not be, as was her first thought, simply trading one problem for another. "We might work something out," she replied.

I left the room. It seemed intrusive to be present when an opera singer was making arrangements with a new lover. But almost immediately, as I was going to find out, Teo was his old self again. Clara Davidson and her piano moved in with Teo and for almost half a year she drove him here and there, and he protected her and sat in sober admiration as she rehearsed her role at the Raimund Theater, or perhaps it was at the Theater an der Wien, wherever she was singing at the time.

Epilogue: Clara Davidson stayed with Teo for about five months, until Teo got his license back, then she moved on to an opera company in West Germany. She abandoned her piano, however, which Teo gave to me. The piano was a monstrous Czechoslovakian instrument called a Schrimpf, ironically measuring more than seven feet. It was very old, having only a partial metal frame and no overstringing, which means, as I previously explained, the base and treble strings did not cross. It probably dated from the 1860s, though possibly a little earlier. We tried to tune it at the old concert pitch of 435, but it began making alarming noises—groans, crackling sounds, and the like—so we settled for tuning it lower, at 430. I often wonder whether Miss Davidson lowered her singing pitch to match the limits of the piano and how that went over when she sang her opera roles. When my family and I left Vienna, we passed the Schrimpf on to Mrs. Stolzberger, our daughter's tutor. The last I heard, the instrument was living in an apartment above a Balkan restaurant where the Gypsies played their violins every evening beginning at eight o'clock. I hope the Schrimpf drowned them out.

• • •

I was sure I knew the roads Miss Davidson had been talking about in Yugoslavia, the ones where her countertenor was certainly lost. My wife and I had once driven in our little Fiat 600 down from Vienna to Zagreb, and across through Ljubljana to Trieste. Now, even after all these years have passed, I have a vivid memory of it. When we entered Yugoslavia south of Graz, we came to an intersection with road signs pointing both ways to Zagreb. We took the left fork, not realizing the sign must have been put up by wreckers hoping to prey upon the vessels of tourists. But we did not see them, these brigands; perhaps they ignored the sparse pickings from tiny Fiats or maybe they were having their afternoon slivovitz when we passed. In any case, the road got narrower, the gradients steeper, and we left paving far behind as the little car struggled through the mountainous country. Then there was snow on the ground, old snow, probably there for days, and without car tracks, not even footprints. I could not look for paw prints as my full attention was devoted to finding some reassuring sign that this path would eventually lead us to Zagreb.

After night had fallen and it was beginning to rain, the road that had climbed steadily for miles began to descend and we came to a tiny river and some sort of a small factory town. An unfriendly-looking place. We kept going as I looked anxiously at the gas gauge. Peculiarly enough, we finally joined a real road with two real lanes, one going and one coming. The one going led into Zagreb.

The food in Zagreb was delicious, some sort of strips of veal prepared in a cream sauce with paprika. Of course anything tastes good when it comes along after you have become convinced you had the last meal of your life ten hours ago.

The other half of our journey, through Ljubljana, across real mountains and finally down into Trieste, was quite different. Whereas the trip down from Austria had been dark and wild, the one going west to the Adriatic was quite beautiful. Not so, Ljubljana, of course, that was another factory town, or so it appeared to be from the parts we saw. But the mountains to the west had bright, deep, fluffy snow, with shiny crystalline high-lights, of the sort that usually exists only in Hollywood movies set during the thirties in rural Connecticut. As we began our descent to the Italian border, a truck we were following stopped to let people get off. I stopped the Fiat. Another car, an almost identical but Yugoslav-made Fiat, slid into us from behind.

We had a little pantomime discussion, the sense of which was that nobody in his right mind would wish to bring the local police into the matter. That made sense to me. Later, back in Vienna, I replaced my rear bumper (all that was damaged). Cost, twelve dollars. I marvel nowadays that such accidents cause two thousand dollars damage and more.

• • •

One of the best things to collect in Vienna of the sixties was crested silver. It was very durable stuff, being made from 800 silver (80 percent) rather than the softer sterling (92.5 percent). And the pieces were huge, soup spoons big enough for a bird-bath, forks for pitching hay and knives you could use for getting the upper hand at Hastings. A slight exaggeration, maybe, but only slight. The knife handles were hollow silver with sharp iron blades set in beeswax. Consequently, knives had to be cleaned immediately after use and even then they stained readily, and washing them in a dishwasher was out of the question.

The crests were something else, again. Often, there was a coronet engraved on the handle and the monogram of the origi-nal owner worked into the engraving, under the coronet. My wife wrote to her mother describing the monograms on silver we had bought, and asking whether she should have the lettering ground off. Her mother said of course not, and sent us a list of relatives with names matching the monograms. Family silver. The coronets were another matter, with the number of points on the crown indicating the rank of the owner, in inverse order. Hence, a Baron had 5 points, a count 4, a duke 3, an archduke 2 (I can only suppose. I never saw such a one on the used silver market. I also presume a king had a single point, though I never saw one of those, either). The silver we bought all originated in the nineteenth century, when there must have been a lot of gentry dining well in Vienna. We just smiled, enigmatically, when anyone inquired about the crests.

I tell you all this to prepare for an odd little encounter I had with a prince. The name and indeed the family will have to be suppressed as they are well known, but this young man came into my office one day and asked me to assist him in executing his renunciation of United States citizenship.

Ordinarily, the Department of State takes such acts very seriously, hoping to avoid having Americans commit such irreversible acts in a fit of pique over something that might quickly pass, such as the day income tax is due. So it is, or was, generally the case that the department insists the person think about it, and will delay accepting the renunciation for as long as possible.

But in this case, the one I am telling about, the American was born a German prince. There was no reason, of course, why he could not have used the title and remained an American citizen, but he told me that for him it was a moral dilemma. And this was the reason:

The prince's mother had sought refuge in the United States during the Second World War. The prince was born in the

United States as a citizen of the United States, but he also derived German citizenship from his mother and his father. (I believe his father may have died before the prince was born.)

It was a centuries-old tradition in the princely house of which he was a member that the heir to the title serves as an officer in the German army. However, such voluntary service was an expatriative act under U.S. law. That is, he would thereby lose his U.S. citizenship.

I suggested to the prince that since joining the German army or renouncing his citizenship would both have the same effect—expatriation—he could just leave it at that, and no formal renunciation would be necessary.

No, that was not his way, said the prince. He felt an obligation to the United States for giving his mother and himself refuge, and he did not wish to lose the resulting citizenship through inadvertence. It was better, he said, to make it clear that he was abandoning U.S. citizenship reluctantly, and was only doing so because a higher family loyalty was involved.

For once, Washington approved this renunciation without argument, which I suppose shows that there were still a few romantics left in the Department of State.

• • •

It is trite, surely, to move from the sublime to the ridiculous, but no other simile really suits. And this was the homburg man. Another sort of crown in its way.

We got word from the Vienna Psychiatric Clinic that they were holding an American Jew of Austrian parentage who had demanded a hat from a downtown Vienna haberdasher. A small thing, it seemed to me, but I drove up to the clinic to see about it.

The man was indeed an American and admitted to being an Orthodox Jew. He said he had long been having dreams of a black hat. He drew me a sketch of it and it appeared to be a homburg, with the brim curled upward. A bit odd, I thought, because the Orthodox Jews I had seen in New York wore black hats but with straight brims, as I remembered them. But I was no expert, having abandoned any sort of religious affiliation at an early age.

The man said that he was convinced that the hat was, in some mysterious way, very important, transcending any ordinary utility of a hat. And he knew, for some reason or maybe for no reason at all, that he would someday find exactly the hat of his dreams, and, when he did, it was absolutely necessary that the hat be given to him. It would not do, to have to buy it. Immediately I was sympathetic. I have had such dreams about pianos.

Since the dream first occurred, the man had been traveling around Europe, where he somehow knew the hat must be, and at last he came to Vienna. He was walking the streets of the old part of the city, the First District, when he saw the Hat. He knew it instantly.

The man went into the store and spoke to the shopkeeper. The shopkeeper was Jewish and the man took that to be a good sign. The man pointed out the hat in the window and asked the shopkeeper to give it to him. The shopkeeper refused. Any shopkeeper in Vienna would have done the same. Such a thing was not done.

The American insisted that the shopkeeper reconsider, but the shopkeeper would not. The man got more than a little excited and the shopkeeper feared for his life. The shopkeeper called the police. When the American still would not leave the shop and continued to demand that he be given the hat, he was taken to the psychiatric clinic.

The clinic doctor said that after the man arrived at the clinic, some sedatives were administered, and the man had improved greatly. I was taken in to see the American. The man was sitting on the bed, shoeless but dressed in a shirt and black trousers. He had no belt or suspenders, and his shoes, on the floor by the bed, had no laces, all of which I took to be reasonable precautions for a madman.

The man seemed perfectly rational and indeed, calm. We talked about the incident in the haberdashery and he agreed that everything happened just as the police and the doctor described, but that he meant no harm. Unfortunately, it was necessary that he be given the hat if his dream was to be fulfilled. He spoke with such calm reasonableness that it was disturbing. When he was talking to me, everything he said made perfect sense. Of course Viennese shopkeepers might easily become disturbed at the thought of giving anything away, but a dream is a dream and it was unusual but hardly irrational for the young man to ask the haberdasher to do such a small thing as giving him the hat.

I found myself nodding in agreement. Then the young man called for a pencil and paper, which he received under the watchful eye of an attendant. He drew an umbrella with a hooked handle. Perfectly ordinary, a line drawing of an umbrella fully opened. Then with a few additional lines, he transformed the umbrella into a face suggesting Groucho Marx. Cute, I thought. Cute but crazy. We parted amicably. I said I would see what could be done to get him safely back to New York.

• • •

Things calmed down for a bit. There were a few minor disturbances. The God of Carinthia was active again. The God was a former Austrian who had become an American citizen but had returned to Austria to set things right. The God, who had some tailoring skills, had made a suit fashioned from a patchwork of brightly colored pieces of cloth that he wore when he stood by the side of the highway near Villach with two fingers extended, blessing motorists as they drove by. Sometimes, however, when he would see a car traveling too fast or otherwise recklessly, he would step into the highway to slow it down. There had been many near misses and numerous complaints.

The police, in turn, complained to the consulate, but since we had no arrest powers, and were disinclined anyway to remove God by force, we could do nothing but assure the police that we would support whatever they felt it necessary to do to assure the safety of the American citizen.

Farther north, in Salzburg, where we had recently closed our consulate, there was the old American of almost ninety who rode around the city on a Puch, an Austrian equivalent of a Vespa. As he went, he tried to pick up children. But the children, seeing that the man was old and obviously gaga, and riding with him on the motor scooter was clearly dangerous, declined to go with him.

Also in Salzburg was the house rented by American students who played jazz piano in the house at 10:30 P.M. Salzburg, being the internationally famous city of music, sent a policeman around to arrest the Americans. Served them right; they should have played Mozart. Another American student fell off a small mountain in the neighborhood and was hopelessly broken.

There was plenty of work for me and the now fully functional Teo, but it was not very satisfactory trying to do everything from Vienna. It seemed to me that our consulate in Salzburg should never have been closed.

17

The Guitar and a Death in Baghdad

My wife came home with a bunch of chandeliers. It wasn't as though we needed them, but they had been crying to be rescued. The Viennese had in those days something called the *Abfallstation,* which was somewhat like the recycle stations we have nowadays. You took things such as old metal, paper, and the like to an Abfallstation and received a small amount of money. This trash was then resold by the station to make new whatevers.

Among the favorite commodities were old copper and brass and sometimes *Kaiserzinn,* a nonrusting alloy often used to make the decorative objects of which the Viennese used to be so fond.

My wife had learned from that canny shopper Ida Trudgeon that many of the things that found their way into the antique shops to be sold at high prices originally were gleaned from Abfallstations. I am not certain of my facts, but I believe Ida must have learned this by following along behind young Herr Kohlhammer. Herr Kohlhammer's mother operated a famous

The Joseph Olbrich building, home of the Sezession art movement

antique shop in Klosterneuberg, just up the river from Vienna.

Sezession, the unique Viennese decorative style that lasted hardly more than the two decades just prior to the First World War, was not as highly prized in Vienna in the sixties as it is today. People were throwing out such things and replacing them with that nifty modern stuff. However, there was a Mr. Stanley in Chicago who visited Vienna a couple of times a year and was buying up all the Sezession he could get his hands on. It was said that in addition to buying from Mrs. Kohlhammer, he hired her son to guide him around Vienna to ferret out things from other sources.

One of the tricks Ida learned was to visit the *Abfallstationen* regularly, so as to arrive after the Viennese had sold their junk and before it had been disposed of either to the Kohlhammers or to the melting pot. Tricky business, requiring a fine sense of timing.

Well, Sarah (my lady wife) brought home a carload of lighting fixtures, among them a fine Sezession brass chandelier with three globes, showing the style's art nouveau antecedents; a similar one of more eclectic style (which lights my study as I write this thirty-four years later); a couple of fixtures clearly made for a bawdy house in the last years of Franz Josef's reign (these I combined to make our stairway chandelier); and a number of other table lamps and hanging fixtures of various turn-of-the-century styles. The Viennese greatly prized the Biedermeier style, so such items were already too expensive for us. Biedermeier lamps were a rarity, anyway, because there was no electric lighting in the early nineteenth century.

The reader will shortly find out why Abfallstationen need to be explained in such detail. But meanwhile, the case of the guitar player demanded my attention.

• • •

It seems that the first thing that comes to mind of mental hospital staff when they receive a foreign patient is to call the consul. I have thought about this a lot. It surely cannot be that they expect the consul to take the patient home. Otherwise our houses would be filled with our countrymen and women. No, I really believe that since most people regard foreigners as being at best a little bit crazy, the mental hospital wishes to confirm their diagnosis by watching our reaction. If we think the patient is crazy, then it isn't just the ordinary, expected degree of irrationality with which all foreigners are burdened.

Take Miss Epperson, for example. She was a young lady, early twenties, who had come to Vienna to learn ballet. You see, she was another one of my dancing Americans, along with the improbable Mr. Timmer (my Cowardly Lion), and the various images of that out-of-work belly dancer.

Miss Epperson had taken a room in Vienna, and her landlady was worried about her, since after some initial promise she had ceased going to classes and spent most of each day sitting in her room, playing her guitar.

Then, as the hospital resident Dr. Haas explained, "She tried to commit suicide. She met a German student and took a train to Munich with him. Then, in a hotel she cut her wrists. That was two weeks ago. Wrist cuts can bleed quite a lot. The frightened young man must still be running."

"I assume the suicide attempt was halfhearted."

"Who can tell? She didn't hurt herself very much, but she may not be very good at it yet. We find that sometimes it takes practice. They may eventually get it right."

"Why didn't they keep her in Munich? There must be a psychiatric hospital there." It seemed unfair that she was sent back into my consular district.

"She is a student here. She was only a tourist in Germany."

"Oh." It seemed like an unnecessary distinction, but I dropped the subject. The resident used his key to unlock the door and stood aside for me to enter the empty room. Empty! Were they trying to trick me? Did they remember about how I was sympathetic to the Jew and the hat? Was this their chance to get me? I would like to say that such things didn't cross my mind, but sometimes we can't help what we think. I turned around to leave and bumped into the resident.

"No, Herr Konsul, this is the right room. Miss Epperson is usually in the closet." He strode across the room and tried to open a small closet. It was locked from the inside. "Miss Epperson, you have to unlock the door. You would not wish us to break it down!"

There was some thumping about and then a small click. The resident tried the door again and it came open. A dark-haired young woman was folded up in the bottom of the closet, under some shelves. She had a mass of almost curly hair, covering her head and elsewhere, exposed by the inadequate hospital gown and her folded-up position. Her hands covered much of her face and her wrists were heavily bandaged, apparently because of the suicide attempt. "Please come out, Miss Epperson, the consul is here to see you."

The head shook and the large, dark-rimmed eyes stared at me. She didn't say anything and made no move to get out. I sat down on the floor with my head on a level with hers. It was easier that way, because I didn't have to look at her lower parts. I supposed that hospital personnel didn't give such displays any thought, but for others, it was very distracting. "Hi," I said as cheerfully as I could.

"Hi," came back a small, tentative voice, followed by a ghost of a smile.

"Do you like it in there?"

"It's okay." She didn't sound like it was very okay.

"I'm the American consul. You asked me to come see you, Miss Epperson."

"Goldie."

The Guitar and a Death in Baghdad ▪ *219*

"Beg pardon?"

"My name is Goldie."

"Oh. I'm pleased to meet you, Goldie. I'm Richard."

Goldie stared at me. She seemed to be trying to make up her mind about something. Then there was a change in her eyes, a look of decision. "Do you have a cigarette?"

"No, I don't smoke."

"All right, I'll come out now." Goldie thrashed about trying to stand up in her confined space. I got up and extended my hand to help her. She got upright but her knees kept trying to buckle. I helped her to the bed and sat down beside her. "They burn me with cigarettes when I come out. I had to be sure about you." Goldie felt my pockets to check on the cigarettes. Once satisfied, she bent forward and would have fallen off the bed if I had not caught her. She reached under the bed and dragged out a guitar case. Still suspended, rag doll–like, from my restraining arm, Goldie snapped open the catch on the case and hauled out a guitar. With a little help, she straightened up and laid the guitar across her lap. She began to tune it.

"Are you a musician, Goldie?"

Goldie gave me another of her little smiles and started to play a tune. She sort of sang along with the guitar, though neither the tune nor the words had much coherence. Several times the resident tried to get her to stop and once attempted to take the guitar out of her hands. She swung the guitar at him and would have hit him if he had not jumped back. She resumed her playing and eventually seemed to come to some sort of conclusion. I applauded enough to be polite.

"Miss Epperson," said the resident, "we will have to take away your guitar if you insist on playing it when we have business to attend to."

"Would you like to go back to the United States?" I asked.

"That would be nice." Goldie collapsed back on the bed. I caught the guitar.

"Where does your family live?"

"I don't have a family." Goldie sat more or less upright again, looking very sad with her eyes welling up with tears.

"Somebody must send you money to live on."

"That's my mother. She won't let me come back. Do you want to know why?"

"I bet she would let you if I told her to. Can you tell me her name and address?"

"She changes her name all the time. I don't know what it is now. Do you think I'm pretty?"

"You're very pretty, Goldie." I turned to the resident. "Does the clinic have her passport?"

"I assume so. We can stop by the office when you are ready to leave."

"I'm ready to go now. Good-bye, Goldie. I'll be back when I've made arrangements for you to go home."

"Don't go," said Goldie, with the edge of panic in her voice.

"I think it's against the rules, Goldie. I'm sorry I can't stay."

Goldie swung herself onto the bed with her face to the wall and curled up into a fetal position, oblivious of us as we left.

Some days later, the department approved our request to repatriate Miss Epperson. I called Dr. Haas at the *Klinik* to arrange for Goldie's release, and shortly before lunch I drove to the clinic to pick her up. The change from a hospital gown to her regular clothes made her look more or less normal, almost as though she belonged outside.

"Did Dr. Haas explain that I would be putting you on a plane to New York?"

"No."

"Did he tell you anything?"

"Good-bye. And he said he was going to turn me upside down."

I thought about that one. "Did he say he was turning you over to the embassy?"

"I guess that's what it was. Do you have any cigarettes?"

"No, not a one."

Goldie smiled at me tentatively and allowed me to lead her to my car. We loaded her suitcases and her guitar into the car and drove off. "Your mother will meet you in New York. You will take off at three and be going with the sun so it should still be daylight when you get there." Goldie sat quietly beside me and didn't respond. Other things being under control, I thought about my stomach. If I didn't eat now, I would miss lunch altogether. I looked at Goldie. She looked calm enough. She was probably hungry, too. "Let's stop for some lunch," I suggested.

Goldie was not prepared for the number of people smoking in the restaurant. We had not even been seated when she panicked and ran out into the street. I followed her. She sat down on the curb, opened her guitar case, and began playing. The Viennese stood around and gaped. "*Amerikanerin Hippie*," I explained.

By the time I got her to stop and put up the guitar, there was no longer time to have lunch. I loaded her into my car and drove off for Schwechat Airport. On the way, I thought about all those people smoking on the plane. When I handed her over to Pan Am, I suggested, "If you have enough toilets, you might let her ride in one to New York. She likes being in a room she can lock." I didn't stay around to see whether they took my advice.

Had something to eat at the airport. Also had a beer. Or maybe it was two.

...

The lady, a bit more than thirty. She looked hollow-eyed and tired, but I saw that she was normally very pretty. She collapsed in a chair and for a moment just looked at me. She seemed to be trying to decide where to begin. When she was ready, she took a deep breath and began speaking with a quiet, almost confidential voice.

"Mister Consul. I have killed my husband. I have to have your help." She spoke English very well, with a discernible southern accent, but underneath there was something else. "Mr. Consul"—Unlikely a native American would begin that way. She might be a native Austrian. If I dwelt on such a detail, it was because I didn't want to think about what else she had said. I stared at her.

"I said, I have killed my husband," she repeated.

Silently, I sighed. The orderly and pleasurable digestion of my very good lunch was about to be disrupted. I forced myself to concentrate. "I imagine you need an attorney. I'm not in a position to give you advice regarding Austrian law. Have you been to the police, Miss, uh—"

"Ilse Schmidt. My married name is Mahmoud. My husband is—was—an Iraqui. I killed him in Baghdad."

"And now you are in Vienna," I said because I couldn't think of anything else to say.

"That's the capital of Iraq."

"I—I have heard of it."

"But I am an American. And Austrian. And I may also be an Iraqui, but I'm not sure. I had better explain from the beginning."

I got to my feet. "Before you begin, I think I had better ask the consulate's attorney to join us." I went to the door and yelled for Teo. Thank God Miss Davidson had got Teo straightened out. It was midafternoon and I noted that Teo had acquired his usual smooth pink glow, but he seemed smiling and alert. I made the introductions and filled Teo in on the essential facts as I knew them. "It seems that Mrs. Mahmoud has killed her husband in Baghdad and come here to tell us about it."

"Oh," said Teo and sat down. He favored her with a careful smile.

"I immigrated to the United States in 1954, just before the State Treaty was signed," she began. "My mother is a professor at the *Neue Universität* in Innsbruck. We weren't sure what would happen to Austria, and she decided to send me to America. I completed my studies at the University of Indiana and got a job in Texas. I'm a petroleum geologist.

"After I was five years in America, I got my citizenship. That's why I am an American. See?" She pulled a green passport out of her purse and waved it at me.

"Then I met Fouad. I was on vacation in Panama City. That's in Florida."

"Yes, I know the city," I said. I once had a memorable meal there, too.

"Well, Fouad was training in Florida to be a military pilot. We, uh, we got married."

"I didn't know Iraq trained pilots in the United States," Teo said.

"We train pilots from almost everywhere. I think it has to do with promoting military equipment sales. Did your husband get U.S. residence?"

"No, he had to go back home. That's what he said, anyway. When his training was finished we returned to Baghdad. As soon as we arrived, he got me a small apartment. That's when it all started." She paused and fumbled in her purse and brought out a cigarette. I opened the window a crack while she lit it. I adjusted the window until the smoke drifted toward the door. It was cold outside. She shivered. I supposed she had gotten used to warm weather.

"He was gone most of the time," she resumed, "and I asked him why. He said he had to spend some time with his family because he had been away so long. I said I would like to meet his family, but he said no, not yet. They were very traditional, he said, and he had to work up to it. I took that to mean he had not told them he had married me, an American.

"It went on like this for weeks. I thought I was going to go crazy, shut up all the time. You don't know what it's like." Both Teo and I nodded sympathetically. "When I kept after him about it, he would take me out to a restaurant or someplace like that. The restaurants we went to weren't very nice. I thought it was because he didn't have much money. A few times we met another pilot who had been in training with him in Florida. But most of the time it was just us.

"Then one day I was out alone and I saw Fouad's pilot friend. I didn't have anything else to do so I had lunch with him. I'm pretty sure he was interested in going back to the apartment with me. They seem to assume the worst about Western women. I suppose it's because we don't hide our faces, though that no longer seems so common in Baghdad. Anyway, he said more than he should have. About Fouad. I asked him why Fouad hadn't ever taken me to meet his family. Then he told me that it would have been an insult to Fouad's wife and an embarrassment to his parents!

"This man, the pilot, just assumed I knew that Fouad already had another wife! Well, dumb as he was, even he could see I was astonished! So he explained that many of the upper-class men kept mistresses. It wasn't anything unusual!

The Guitar and a Death in Baghdad ▪ 225

"That evening—it must have been a day before yesterday—Fouad came back to the apartment and I confronted him with it. I told him that he would have to divorce his wife. Fouad said he couldn't do that because he had two children! And because his family would disinherit him!

"Well! I asked my husband where that left me! He told me that I could continue living in Baghdad as his other wife, but I could never have anything to do with his family!

"So I told Fouad that he couldn't have it that way and that I was going to his family to settle things. That's when he pulled out the knife. We were sitting on the bed and he reached for me. I realized what he was going to do," she said very quietly. "I got his wrist in both my hands and twisted the knife. I'm quite strong." She said that as a simple statement of fact, not a boast.

"I slid off the bed and he fell where I had been sitting. The knife went right through him." Ilse stubbed out her cigarette, jabbing it into the ashtray as though it were the knife going into Fouad.

"I pushed him off the bed before he bled very much and got him under the bed. Then I changed the bed sheets."

"Did you call a doctor or anybody?" asked Teo.

"No. I didn't have a telephone. But he was dead, I'm sure of that. So I took the money he had on him and all the money I had, and went out to buy an airplane ticket. I had enough to get to Vienna. But the next flight I could get didn't go until the following day—that's yesterday."

"Did you check into a hotel?" asked I, who had visions of the blood-soaked corpse under the bed.

"I didn't have enough money for that. I went back to the apartment and went to bed."

"Good God!"

"It was all right. I said I had changed the sheets. Anyway, now I have gotten this far and I need to know what to do."

"You should have informed the Iraqui police," I suggested.

"I would have been put to death. His family would have insisted on it."

"But it was an accident," I protested.

"I—" said Teo, "I hardly think the question of guilt would be given much consideration in a case like this. Even in Austria she might have had some problems. I think she should go to America at once."

"Wouldn't it make more sense for her to stay in Austria with her mother?"

"No, the problem is to defend against any request for extradition. Austrian law would likely take the position that her nationality should be that of her husband and tend not to interfere. The courts might not view her as an Austrian at all, for extradition purposes. American courts, I believe, would always protect an American woman from foreign justice, even Austrian, but particularly some non-Western country such as Iraq."

"I would have to get money from somewhere if I go to America," said Ilse.

"Can your mother help?" asked Teo.

"The Iraquis may know about her. I took Fouad to meet her when we left the U.S. It might be dangerous for me to go there now."

"We could ask the State Department to approve a repatriation loan, but that might take several weeks. If Teo is right, you might not want to risk waiting around that long. If your mother can afford to help, we could get you on a plane immediately."

We agreed that Teo would put her up overnight and call her mother. I did not ask Teo whether he hid the steak knives. Teo survived the night and Ilse's mother did provide a pre-paid air ticket. Ilse was soon on her way, back to Texas and presumably to safety.

Epilogue: We had almost forgotten about Ilse Schmidt Mahmoud when we got an inquiry from a Texas sheriff's office asking for information about her. The message said that she had been found dead from carbon monoxide poisoning in the garage of her house, and there were apparently reasons, not stated, why the authorities were investigating the possibility that it was not suicide. I wrote back to the Texans giving what little information we knew, but we never heard from them again.

18

The Teenager, Two Swedes, a German Named Herzog, an Englishman Named Charlie, as Well as a Cardinal and an American Lady, Fit to Be Tied

Superintendent Mayerhofer, the officer in charge at the Fremdenpolizei, called Teo directly. Ordinarily, the Viennese police had no problem locking up foreigners, and made little distinction among the various nationalities, but this one bothered them.

Bothered them and irritated them. Two Swedes; no problem with them. A German named Herzog; despite his name, he probably held no title or he would already have waved it at the police soon enough. An Englishman named Charlie; well they had seen his like before and when the British consul came along to bail him out and hurry him on his way, it would be soon enough. For centuries Austrians had been putting up with English tourists (read, for example, Dr. Charles Burney's *Continental Travels, 1770–1772*).

But then there was the teenage American girl. Claimed to be sixteen, but unless her passport was lying, she wouldn't be for almost a year. She also was in an expensive school near Lausanne, Switzerland, or was supposed to be, and that spelled money and money spelled trouble.

Teo and I both went around to the First District police station, where they were holding her. Precious Little. With a name like that, it was easy enough to understand why she would already be in a peck of trouble.

Before the girl was brought up from the jail cell, Mayerhofer filled us in regarding the details of the case. It seems strange noises had been heard at night coming from a derelict palace once owned by the Esterhazy family.

As everybody knows, the Esterhazys were aristocrats of the old Austro-Hungarian Empire. They were quite wealthy until the extravagant Prince Nicholas IV and his successors spent the family into bankruptcy in the nineteenth century. An earlier Prince Nikolaus Esterhazy II was a music lover and amateur musician (the baryton, an instrument with two sets of strings, six above that are bowed and ten or more below that are plucked) and was for almost thirty years (1761 to 1790) Haydn's patron. (The conservatively styled keyboard sonatas 36 through 41 were dedicated to the prince.) Haydn spent many winter seasons living in Vienna at the Esterhazy Palais on Wallnerstrasse.

My story loses some of its piquancy in that the building where Precious Little and her ménage were ensconced was not the Wallnerstrasse building. They should have come to me for advice.

To continue with the police account of the matter, officers went to the palace in response to the reported noises, investigated, and found blankets, clothing, and other evidence of people camping on an upper floor. The noises came from further above and there was the unmistakable sound of nails being pulled out. Reaching the roof, the police found the young people prying loose sheets of copper, and immediately took them into custody, charged with a number of offenses.

The prisoners ranged in age from Miss Little at hardly fifteen to Herr Herzog, who at thirty-one was by a good bit the oldest. Investigation the next day of the nearby *Abfallstationen*, revealed that for some days these young (and not-so-young) people had been bringing in for sale large quantities of copper and lead.

The police were going to prosecute the young men but were prepared to release the girl into the custody of the American consul provided she would immediately depart from Austria. It was suggested that she would not be welcome in Austria until such time as she had grown up and mended her ways.

I said I would be happy to take responsibility for Miss Little, and Teo rolled his eyes in that expressive way that seems to come naturally to Austrians. Teo, I, and a sullen and hostile Precious Little got out of the police station before the Austrians could change their minds. Miss Little's baggage was just a knapsack with an extra sweater stuffed under the lid.

"Well, now what?" demanded Miss Little.

"Lunch, maybe." Bedamned if I was going to miss lunch again because of problems with young, female Americans. That was the way I felt at the time, but looking back upon it now, I think I was unfair to the sex. There had been that young man in Switzerland, when I served there. He had tried to work some sort of auto insurance fraud, the details of which now escape me, except that he was arrested for making a false claim. In that case, too, the police released him to me with the proviso that I get him out of Switzerland before dark, and that he would never, ever, come back to Switzerland.

I gave the young man enough money from our welfare fund to get over the border into Austria, so things have a way of evening out. But the thing about him was, when I was driving him to the train station, he said something like this: "You've got a real cushy job; how do I go about applying for the Foreign Service?" I intended to send a note to Washington warning them about his intention, but I don't believe I ever did. By now, he's probably an ambassador somewhere. Which may explain a lot.

Anyway, as we waited for lunch at Martinovic's hasenpfeffer palace (a delicate Kalbschnitzel that day, as I recall) I asked Miss Precious how she got mixed up in all this. She explained it was her spring break at school in Lausanne, and she didn't want to go home for some reason that seemed to have something to do with her parents' divorces, so she got on a train and went as far as she could without a visa, and that naturally meant Vienna.

"How come you got mixed up with those boys?"

"Oh, I just met them at the Twelve Apostles. They go there all the time."

I knew the place, it was a popular Weinstube, and hangout for students, which, apparently, these boys weren't. "I should think you could have met some nice college boys there," I suggested, assuming her interest in anybody younger would be nil.

"It's full of them. But you never can tell whether they're queer."

Well! That sort of stopped the conversation. I thought about asking her why it mattered what their sexual preferences were, but decided I would rather not know the answer to that one. I hunted around for another topic while Teo ordered ein *viertel* of wine. When it arrived with two glasses, Miss Precious told Martinovic to bring another glass. I shook my head and Martinovic looked a bit flustered and went away. Precious swiped my glass and filled it, managing to do so while briefly sticking out her tongue at me, but not spilling a drop.

I ordered a beer and tried again. "Why did you decide to move into the palace?"

"Why not? I asked them what they did and they told me about scavenging roofing. I'd never heard of anybody doing that. It sounded like fun."

"Why did they do it?"

"To get money so we could get something to drink, of course." Precious drained my wineglass.

"Of course," I agreed. Teo smiled benignly.

"Well, we've got to get you out of town. Do you have any money?"

"Enough. I'll get by."

I'll bet. I asked, "Where do you want to go? Back to school?"

"Prague."

"Prague?" Even Teo started.

"There's going to be a youth conference there. Ought to be fun."

"You'll need to get a visa," I said, hoping this would be a sufficient impossibility to convince her to return to Switzerland.

"No, they give students visas at the border."

Well, what the hell, I thought. After we finished eating, Teo and I took Precious Little to the Franz Josefs Bahnhof and put her on a train for Prague.

I sometimes wonder what's become of Precious. It's been thirty-five years now, so she must be fifty. Probably plays bridge at a country club in White Plains and is upset about the way her daughter is bringing up her grandchildren.

• • •

Now, the next account concerns a trademark dispute deposition. That is something consuls do, taking depositions of witnesses for litigation in U.S. courts. It is not something we do very often because in many cases, witnesses just hop on a plane and go to the States to give their testimony. No more expensive than sending a bunch of American lawyers abroad.

But in this instance, the East German government was mortally afraid their witness might seek asylum in the West, and their claim to an important trademark (known around the world since the beginning of the century) lay in this one witness, Dr. Frömbling.

During the Second World War, the company, which I will call Deutschwerk, was heavily damaged by bombing, and lay in an area occupied by the Soviet forces. Almost all of the company's managerial and technical personnel gathered up what they could and fled to the West.

One lone minor official, Dr. Frömbling stayed at the ruins of the old plant. Then the Soviets picked up all the machine tools that were worth anything and sent them back to the Soviet Union. Small reparations for the damage of the war.

In the meantime, those who had fled to the West reconstituted the company and were soon in business, leading their industry again. They were using the famous old trademark known the world over.

East Germany was envious. They rebuilt the old plant and went back into business, but with much less success. If only they had exclusive use of the trademark! They went to court in New York, the major sales area for the new West German Deutschwerk.

Everything hinged on poor old Dr. Frömbling, as he was the one official who stayed at the old plant even after the rest of the staff went west and the machinery went east. Dr. Frömbling was the continuity.

The East Germans agreed to come to Vienna for the deposition because Austria was neutral under the terms of the State Treaty. It was the one country not in the Soviet bloc where Frömbling would probably not be able to seek asylum.

The two forces were aligned, East German lawyers and plant officials on one side and New York lawyers and West German plant officials on the other side of my long table. At one end, I sat with my stenographers, and at the other end sat an East German Stasi security agent.

After Dr. Frömbling was questioned for days, the New York lawyer said, "And now, Dr. Frömbling, you are a free man." The lawyer paused. An offer to defect? Everybody at the table froze except for the Stasi man who, reflexively, thrust his hand into his jacket for his gun. Then the lawyer continued, cool as could be, "I have no further questions for now."

Hearts started beating again. In a few days we wound up the deposition and I signed my name about four hundred times to the pages of the transcript.

I later heard that the East Germans won that round, but the

West German company continued to prosper, somehow, and with reunification of the two Germanies, my bit of drama just became history.

• • •

It is a little hard, after all these years, to keep the chronology of all these things straight in my mind. But I suppose it was at about this point that the great White Owl affair blew up. This was a matter concerning which I had only a peripheral involvement but it needs mentioning if only that it shows what a peculiar world the Foreign Service inhabits.

It had to do with Hungary's Cardinal Jozsef Mindszenty, who was arrested by the Communists in 1948. After a show trial, the cardinal was convicted of treason and was sentenced to life imprisonment. During the short-lived Hungarian revolution of late 1956, the cardinal was briefly freed, but as the revolution collapsed, he avoided rearrest by seeking asylum in the United States legation in Budapest. Legations have something less than the full diplomatic status of embassies, but something more than the constituent standing of posts like consulates.

The Legation in Budapest did have what we call extraterritorial status, which meant that it was able to provide a sanctuary for the cardinal. During the fifteen years he was confined in the legation, he taught a generation of our diplomats how to speak proper Hungarian and he continually smoked White Owl cigars.

The cardinal should not have been smoking at all because he was afflicted with tuberculosis. From Vienna we sent by diplomatic pouch the components for X-ray equipment needed to monitor his condition and the medicines needed to cure his affliction. All would have been well had he not, without giving us advance warning, run out of White Owl cigars.

In all of Budapest there were no White Owl cigars. The frantic legation telephoned us in Vienna pleading for help. The cardinal was climbing the walls and driving them all crazy. We combed Vienna; no White Owl cigars. In desperation, our military attaché called the U.S. military forces in what was then West Germany. White Owls were finally located, if my memory serves, in our U.S. military post exchange in Munich, though it could have been in either Stuttgart or Frankfurt.

Our air attaché cranked up his C-47 (military version of the DC-3) and flew to Germany for the cigars. Waste of taxpayer money, you say? Well, the air attaché did have to have a certain number of hours flying time to keep his pilot's certification, and besides, it was an errand of mercy. The operations of a legation were being hobbled by the deprived smoker.

In the meantime, I had to figure out a way to get the cigars to Budapest immediately, once we got them from the U.S. military. There was a problem and it had to do with quid pro quo. Whenever a Hungarian diplomat wished to enter the United States, Washington insisted that the visa request be referred to the Department of State for approval. This generally took about two weeks, if only because Washington did not wish to make it any easier for them than that.

So the Hungarians built in a similar delay in their processing of visas for American diplomats going to Budapest, or for our legation staff returning there. Having a nondiplomatic agent carry the cigars—a number of boxes of them—into Hungary would get us into import customs delays. It began to look like it was going to take at least two weeks to get the cigars to Budapest, willy-nilly. Too long.

We finally decided that an officer from our embassy in Vienna would take the cigars to the border and hand the cigars across to someone who had come from the Budapest legation. Thereafter, the legation (which was elevated to an embassy several years later) kept an ample supply of White Owls on hand so that replenishment by regular pouch service would suffice. The cardinal would continue to live in our legation until the Hungarian government at last allowed him to leave Hungary in 1971.

• • •

I was at my office door and saw her coming.

The lady brushed aside Frau Monika Renner up front at the counter. Monika turned, speechless, and watched the American as she steamed toward my office. From her desk Helga Brand looked up at the American. "Can we help you, mada—" But the American was already through my door. Helga got to her feet. She stood just outside my door and shrugged her shoulders in that exaggerated way the Viennese have perfected through centuries of encounters with incomprehensible foreigners of one sort or another.

Without much confidence, I gave Helga an I-can-handle-it smile and retreated to the far side of my office and behind my desk.

Crash! The American threw down her pocketbook on the desk. Perhaps pocketbook was not the proper name for it. Carryall might suit it better. Smaller than a two-suiter, barely, now that I think about it. All sorts of things erupted from a long gash in the side. Cosmetic pouch, various ladies unmentionables (I supposed), guidebooks, comb, brush, Dr. Scholl's emergency products, folders on this and that, Altoids "curiously strong" peppermints (the can now open and gushing peppermints like a sudden hailstorm), a diary with attached ballpoint, a bulging billfold, a passport—it all looked quite familiar. Anybody could tell she was an American.

I reached gingerly into the pile and retrieved the passport, then I looked at the picture and looked at her. They bore a slight resemblance, but unless she was aging faster than usual, she had made the Passport Office use her wedding picture. One of those. I sighed.

"Mrs. Barnes?"

"Yes. I want him arrested."

"Mr. Barnes?"

The woman collapsed in one of my heavy wooden armchairs, one left over from Cleveland's second administration, or if it came from Vienna, from the time of the old emperor. "No, of course not. My husband is in Dayton." She paused a minute and turned her attention inward. With some suspicion, I thought. "At least he's supposed to be," she continued. "He better be."

"Someone else, then?" This was not as uncommon a request as the layman might suppose. Americans are all the time assuming that consuls have the power to arrest people, especially foreigners. They also think consuls can protect Americans from arrest. That can be even more of a problem.

"That man. The one in the limousine. Mercedes, I think it was."

I felt a certain sympathy. I didn't like Austrian drivers very much, either, but you can't very well arrest them all. "That isn't much to go on," I said.

"I got his license number." With that, she lunged from her chair and with both hands tore into the heap of things on my desk, heedless that the pile was now almost as much my stuff as it was hers. More, even, counting my unanswered or unfiled correspondence. I don't keep a tidy desk. After some searching, she found a hotel brochure. "Here it is! Have you got a pencil?"

I looked doubtfully at my desk. "If I can find it." I did. She read me a number; I wrote it down. I didn't yet know why. But that's another rule in this business. If an American tells you to write something down, you do it. Anything less guarantees a letter of complaint to a congressman. "What did he do?" I asked.

"He tried to run me down. Or his driver did, but he probably told him to." She slipped into her idea of an Austrian man's voice, complete with accent. " 'Get the American, Klaus! See? The one with the bag!' He would have been speaking German, of course. I doubt they run us down in English. This isn't London, you know."

I knew. I had never served in England, but I knew she was right. It had been that way in British Honduras when I was posted there. "Yes ma'am," I said.

"I had to jump for my life. See?" She reared back in her chair and hoisted one of her legs up on my desk. There was a hole coming in her shoe. She had walked too much; no wonder she was out of sorts.

"Not my foot! My knee! I fell on it."

Indeed, her stocking would have been ruined, had she been wearing any. Her knee was obviously bruised and scraped. I thought it would probably grow back. "Wash it with plenty of soap and keep it clean. It ought to be all right. Does it hurt?" It likely did, but it is always good to ask even when you're sure you know the answer. Makes the taxpayers think you are concerned.

"That's not why I'm here. The man insulted me. An American. I mean, I am. He can't be allowed to do that; he's not even an American."

This clearly wasn't going to go away. "Just a minute, I want to call in the embassy lawyer." Her face took on a now-we're-getting-somewhere expression. I fled from my office to the one next door, intending to get Teo. I peered in. Teo was there and looked reasonably conscious, thank God. I was in luck. "Come into my office a moment, will you, Teo?" I turned and bumped into Mrs. Barnes. "Uh—come in, ma'am." But she was already in.

Teo rose, and I introduced him to Mrs. Barnes. Her nose wrinkled suspiciously, but only briefly. Her suspicions were wiped away by his Austrian deferential good manners. *"Gnädige Frau,"* he said as he took several steps forward and took her hand. He bowed a precise centimeter toward the symbolic kiss of the hand. Had she been Austrian, he might even have murmured, *"Kuss die Hand."*

I relaxed a bit. Long ago I had found that schnapps was a close enough relative of gin to be mistaken for aftershave. "Dr. Schlitter has just come back from vacation," I said. "Looks like you got a lot of sun, Teo." I thought that might explain away his flush. Teo looked at me, confused, but before he could protest that he had gotten his glow at the little bar in the cellar of our building, I hurried on. "Mrs. Barnes was practically run down by a car."

"Did he hit you?" Teo asked, all business now.

"No. Of course not," she explained. "But it was close. He hit my bag. See? Ripped it open." She held it up; some more things dropped out on Teo's desk. A gash no bigger than that had sunk the *Titanic.*

"He didn't stop, but Mrs. Barnes got his license number."

"I didn't say that," she protested. "He stopped. That's what made me so mad."

"I don't understand," Teo and I said more or less together.

"He stopped, further down the block. Then he sent his driver back to look at me."

"And you were—?" Teo was thinking clearly, I was happy to see. Asking all the right questions.

"Sprawled on the curb. My things were scattered all over. At least with the driver standing there in the middle of the street, the traffic stopped."

"What did he say?"

"Nothing. He just looked at me and went back to the car. After a minute or two, the gentleman got out of the car—no not gentleman. He was just dressed like one but there the resemblance ended. Anyway, he came back. He didn't say anything to me."

"Nothing at all?"

"No, but he bent over and picked up my bag. I thought he was going to gather up all my stuff. But he just examined my bag and said something in German."

"Did you understand it?"

"Of course. Anybody knows that much German. He said 'Es ist nur Plastik,' then he dropped my bag back in the street and returned to his car. They drove away, but I got their number. I want to sue—"

Teo didn't hear the last thing she said. He had gone to beet red and was on the point of exploding with laughter.

"Poor Dr. Schlitter was seriously wounded on the Russian front, and then imprisoned during the war. When he hears about terrible injustice, he sometimes has a fit," I explained.

It took a while, but sure enough, using the license number Teo was able to track down the owner of the Mercedes 600 that had almost run Mrs. Barnes down. A big and expensive car; Mrs. Barnes is lucky to have gotten out of its way. The prominent architect who owned the car didn't deny anything, but referred Teo to his lawyer.

The incident happened on Augustinerstrasse, just behind the old imperial palace, near the Spanish Riding School, where the famous Lippizaner horses perform and practically in front of the Augustinerkirche, the early Gothic church where a few months earlier a praying American woman had been knifed.

Among the things missing from this neighborhood, however, were a traffic light and pedestrian crossing. And though the Viennese, and visitors alike, crossed the street day and night, Austrian justice held that Mrs. Barnes had crossed the street at her own risk. So there was nothing Mrs. Barnes could do to get restitution from the architect who was so offended by her plastic bag. Had it been Gucci leather, who knows? He might have taken her to dinner and perhaps the opera.

All this points a moral, as you might expect. When traveling abroad, always outfit yourself as the person you wish others to take you to be, unless you're concerned about thieves, of course.

And there's something else to remember. Don't expect consuls to call out the marines when you are insulted by a *Diplomarchitekt*. Remember, you probably came to Vienna to look at old buildings by dead architects, not new ones by *Architekts* who ride around in limousines.

19

Disorganized Crime

$\mathcal{I}$ will try to describe Virginia to you. Ordinarily, I don't presume to tell what women look like, at least not in any detail. Maybe young, old, or in-between, but it has been my observation that interesting women are continually changing their appearance from moment to moment, anyhow. For those who aren't interesting, descriptions hardly seem to matter.

I know that people are always saying that some women are pretty and others not, but it is impossible not to be subjective about these things. To avoid making useless judgments, I sometimes try to imagine that women are something like lobsters or maybe caterpillars. The possibilities for this morphosis are limited, however. For instance, only men can manage to be toads.

But it doesn't matter how I transfigure women, just as long as I am thinking about something that is not human and has not been loaded down with sentimental baggage. That rules out dogs and cats, of course. Bad business to call a woman a dog. Or a cat, for that matter. When is a comparison invidious and when is it not? Don't know about goldfish; I never had one and don't feel one way or the other about such critters.

Steyr, another weekend retreat

The whole purpose of trying to deculturize (don't know whether that's a real word, but it'll have to do) women is so I can see what they are, not what anybody might imagine them to be. Take a nose, for instance. There is nothing intrinsically good or bad about a long nose, a big one, or even a little bitsy one so long as it functions properly and will support a pair of glasses. If required. And about those organs that precede a woman into the room. Unless you are a hungry infant or maybe looking to produce one, they shouldn't matter, either.

I've heard tell that the male ideal of feminine beauty has to do with a subtle selection of desirable, and maybe even vital, genetic attributes of a prospective mate. I don't know, maybe so. But that hardly accounts for some of the marriages that seem to be made in Heaven.

I knew a lady once who might have been mistaken for Olive Oyl. You know, the cartoon character. And her husband, he wasn't a bad-looking fellow considering he had red hair. Well, this couple met during prohibition days when she was a student nurse and he was an engineering student. They had this particular thing in common; they both liked to drink a little bit. So they went out of town (Knoxville, Tennessee) to visit a moonshiner and they bought a gallon jug of some kind of spirits.

Don't know which moonshiner it was, because this was before my time. But I can say this, there were some unusual ones in that town. I recall one family of moonshiners who about twenty-five years later did business on this particular road between Knoxville and Maryville. The uncle has his place where the road turned off of Old Maryville Pike, and he had a little café next to his house. He could press a button and the wall behind the counter would slowly swing around and present shelves stocked with liquor, just about anything you'd want, like a real liquor store. And down the road a mile or so there were two identical houses, one on either side of the road. His identical twin nephews plied their liquor trade in these two houses. Whenever the uncle saw the law come down the road, he would push his button to hide his liquor and telephone his nephews. Quick as could be, they would switch houses so whenever they were arrested, they were misidentified and got off scot-free.

But to get back to the nurse and the engineering student of an earlier time, they brought back a gallon jug of moonshine. On the way back into town, Red had to drive a bit fast to get to Fort Sanders Hospital because there was a curfew for nursing students. As luck would have it, the police chased them down. The lady was quick thinking, as befits a nurse, and she slipped the jug under her coat and told Red to tell the policeman that she was in labor and they were speeding to get to the hospital in time. Well, the police car led the way and they were in the emergency room before eleven, or whatever time the curfew was supposed to be. And the other nurses, they also being quick, they wheeled their colleague into the delivery room. No policemen allowed, sorry.

What I am really getting to is their dog. The couple had been married many years, maybe more than twenty, and they got this little dog that looked like it might have been rejected by the pound. The dog had hardly any name at all, just Des. The lady claimed she first named him Des-a-little-bit, but that was longer than the dog so she had to shorten it. Whatever his shortcomings (I suppose that can be taken as a joke), Des fit into the household perfectly, because the couple often had cocktail parties (as you might expect) and Des would make the rounds after the guests left and finish up any of the drinks left over. Odd family, a cartoon wife, a redheaded husband, and a runt of a dog, but perfectly suited to one another.

I mention all this because I am preparing myself to try, at least, to describe one of the more famous, or perhaps infamous, women of our time, who rose from rural Alabama, to hiring the fanciest nightclubs of New York and Miami and Los Angeles for her exclusive parties. Very exclusive; I was never invited.

But back to the present, that is, the present as it was in the latter part of 1965. I was sitting one afternoon at my desk, trying to keep my eyelids from obeying the law of gravity. It had been a good lunch, over at the restaurant in the Rathaus. A *Bauern-*

schmaus, a huge platter with everything on it, chops, beef roast, ham, sausages, dumplings, sauerkraut, and I don't remember what all. As I recall, the menu had claimed the platter was *reich garniert* and that meant a couple of pieces of carrot. And we had beer, of course. We had to have a pitcher of beer to wash it all down. A big pitcher. I turned down the *Kaiserchmarren* for dessert because I thought there were better places and times to die than right in the middle of a busy restaurant.

If the reader will forgive me a further digression about Viennese cuisine, I would like to mention again my old friend Franz Bader. Franz had grown up in Vienna and when I knew him, during the last twenty-five years of his life, he had been away from Austria since before the war. That, as much as anything, accounted for his survival. During his last years, when he was around ninety, we used to have lunch about once a week. In addition to being rather old, Franz was a round dumpling, a *Semmelknödel* of a man, and he smoked, of course. For lunch we usually had cheese and cold cuts, often salami, and all that with rye bread or something of the sort. I would sit there and watch while Franz would during the course of the meal spread a whole quarter of a pound of butter on his bread, to go with the cheese and salami.

Franz never ate vegetables. He claimed they disagreed with him. He once said to me, "When I came to America, everybody tells me to eat vegetables. But when I was young, in Vienna, nobody ever said you were supposed to eat vegetables."

Anyway, you can see why it was that after a proper Viennese lunch, when she, this woman I'm really supposed to be telling you about, came into my office, it took a pretty powerful jolt to wake me up that summer afternoon. No, it had to be early fall. It must have been cool, but not cold (sorry, but unlike George

Washington, I don't keep notes on the weather). I remember she didn't have a coat but she was wearing a wool skirt and a light-weight sweater. Funny color, a light gray-brown mixture. She knew what she was doing. Her hair was an ash blond, maybe showing a little gray, but you really couldn't tell.

The skirt and the sweater were not loose; they followed her, from up here to down there. I would call her a nicely rounded lady, no trace of anything constraining her natural outlines. Not tall, not short, maybe five feet four, and with good posture. A healthy woman, a strong one, by the look of her.

It was her skin that really caught—and held—my eye. Unblemished, and if she wore makeup, you couldn't tell it. The same with her lipstick. It was probably there, but I couldn't be sure. No, it had to be, but she had a lot of natural color. Healthy, like I said. No telltale wrinkles showing too much sun. No sign of bones trying to assert themselves. No sign of fat trying to leave the premises.

She looked familiar, her face did, but I have to admit I couldn't at the time place her. She tossed a passport down on my desk, an Austrian one. "I want you to draft my son into the American army."

For the first time, I noticed that a young man—a boy, really—had followed the woman into my office. I asked them to sit down and picked up the Austrian passport.

On the page for such things, the description of the bearer, there was a photo of the lady and her name was listed as Virginia Hill Hauser. Her place of birth was simply shown as U.S.A. and the date of her birth, 26/8/1916. She saw my expression change as I realized who she was.

"Everybody knows me. Knows who I am. Thinks they know me."

"I know about Bugsy Siegel." Everybody knew about flamboyant mobster Siegel. It was only twenty years earlier that he had been shot through the window of this woman's living room and fifteen years since she had been called to testify before the Senate's hearings on organized crime.

"Ben."

"Ben?"

"People who knew him called him Ben. That other thing— that name—that was just the lousy press. They called him that. And maybe some cops, I suppose."

"Oh."

"Now, I want you to draft my son and make a man of him."

"I'm not empowered to draft anybody. I suppose he could go to one of our military installations in Germany and maybe they could enlist him. How old is he?"

"Fifteen." We were talking about him as though he wasn't there. And in a manner of speaking, he probably wasn't. He sat there, sullen, with his mind far away. "Peter's barely fifteen and he's got something going with one of the maids at the hotel. A Spanish bitch."

"Hotel?"

"We have a hotel. Near Salzburg. My husband's family owns it. I told my son he had to break it off, and I fired her. She's twenty-one, for heaven's sake. But Peter thinks he's going to go back to Spain with her. I certainly named him right."

"I take it your husband's Austrian," I said, looking again at the tan-colored passport. "What about your son?"

"We were still in the States when he was born. That makes him an American, doesn't it?"

"Usually." I tried to think of a reason why it might not. I wasn't sure about children born to foreign diplomats, but that surely wasn't the case here. "But he probably is a dual national. He's probably Austrian as well as American."

Mrs. Hauser began to look bored. I suspected she didn't have a long attention span. "Well, he likely is, but I don't see what that's got to do with anything."

"It has a lot. As an American, even if he stays away from the United States, he's supposed to register for the draft when he turns eighteen. I think he can volunteer at seventeen if he's got your permission, but that's still more than a year away. And I don't know anything about Austrian military service. In the meantime, he might try the Boy Scouts."

Mrs. Hauser started to say something, but didn't. "Well, I'm sorry to have taken up your time." She got up, motioned to her son, and left. I watched her on the way out. Nicely made, too. I wondered if she worked out; she didn't seem to be the type. I sniffed the air. A nice clean smell, but not an obvious perfume.

I wrote down her birthdate. Pretty good for just turned forty-nine. Hoped I would look as good in a dozen years. But I would certainly be able to manage a smile. Smiles don't cost that much. Maybe she didn't think I was important enough to favor me with one. Or maybe just being in the same room with her son got her out of the smiling mood.

• • •

It was a few weeks before I saw her again. This time there wasn't any nonsense about her son. I don't know, even now, whether she really wanted me to draft her son. I suspect he was just a handy prop, something wheeled onto the stage between scenes to provide some excuse for the dialogue. Nothing about Virginia Hill that I knew then, or learned subsequently, gave me any reason to suspect she was a dumb blonde. Far from it. She had been in waters with some pretty dangerous fish and had managed to avoid becoming either bait or a sacrifice for any of the serious players. She had, at that time, been living by her wits for thirty years, aided by nothing but some good brains in a splendid carrying case.

The second time, she came right to the point. "I want to go home," she said.

"Back to the United States? You want to be repatriated?" I looked at her clothes again. Nothing cheap. Nothing even ready-made. Expensive stuff. I'm not a good judge of women's fashion, but it seemed to me she was wearing my year's salary (but maybe after taxes) on her back. I thought about her back. Well, hell, what better place to put it.

She ignored the suggestion that she needed a loan to pay for a cut-rate flight to New York. "Treasury. I want you to get them off my back."

Now, the thought of the Treasury on her back was not as appealing, and as a measure of the cost of her clothing, the U.S. Treasury was probably a bit excessive. A bit. "Tell me about it," I suggested, and over the course of maybe a half dozen meetings, she did just that.

Because unlike Virginia Hill, I wasn't born smart, I did not record it. We didn't have cassette recorders in those days, and used mostly reel-to-reel machines. At my previous post in Belize, roaches had eaten the drive belts of my Grundig recording machine, and besides I couldn't very well take a machine as big as a suitcase and set it to running every time Virginia came into the office. She wasn't big on giving advance notice. And the limited notes I made at the time probably didn't survive.

There has been so much nonsense written or filmed about her in recent years that it would have been nice to have been able to say, "That's not the way Virginia used to tell it when we were alone together." Nobody, except maybe my wife, would have had to know that "alone" simply meant none of my Austrian staff happened to be looking in the open door.

But, alas, all I have is my cloudy memory that collected thoughts under distracting circumstances. (On these later visits, she smiled, occasionally—good teeth. I kept my own mouth shut. Wouldn't want all that amalgam to get out.)

Virginia—I addressed her as Miss Hill because it was hard to think of her as Mrs. Hauser—But since she's dead and gone, let's call her Virginia—told me a lot of things, not always in any particular order. Not that she didn't have an orderly mind, but I believe she was still trying to decide how much to tell me. I represented the government, after all. That first time, the visit with her son, she had not yet decided to tell me anything. But it may have helped that I'm Southern, and under the right circumstances a little bit of my accent (Georgia-Tennessee state line) creeps in. So, little by little, visit by visit, she told me her story, or at least a story. Some I remember; some I've forgotten.

Virginia hated the press. Despite that, or maybe because of it, during the thirties and forties a subspeciality within the newspaper business, that of reporting Virginia's exploits, seems to have grown up. She was a very public person from about 1935 until she left the United States in 1951.

However, accurate information is hard to come by, partly because reporters, as they wrote things down at the scene, were frequently being attacked by Virginia with her spike heels or anything else handy. But perhaps more to the point, Virginia told outlandish stories on herself. She once claimed she was born in the Netherlands of an American mother and a half-Indian father, when the truth (probably) was that she was one of ten children of a wife-beating Lipscomb, Alabama, mule trader.

Her mother took the children and left for Marietta, Georgia, where Virginia grew up. Quickly, apparently.

The essential outlines of her life are fairly well agreed upon. When she turned seventeen, she went to Chicago to make her fortune at the Chicago centennial fair, the Century of Progress. Sally Rand had opened there at the end of May 1933, in the Streets of Paris attraction, dressed (it is said) in nothing but her fans and dancing to Debussy's *Clair de Lune*, a particularly icky piece that mysteriously survived its birth in 1890, but which nevertheless had the advantage of leaving the audience free to concentrate on the dancer instead of the music. Miss Rand, therefore, was an instant success.

Virginia seems to have settled down to being a waitress at a fairground restaurant in what was known as the San Carlo Italian Village. Some say that Chicago's organized crime (which we will call the "mob" for want of a better name) had bankrolled the restaurant. Whether Virginia ever worked at the fair as a dancer is in some dispute.

At this point, it is clear that Joe Epstein came upon the scene. However, there is some disagreement between what Virginia told me about him and what others have written about this seminal event in Virginia's life. The conventional view is that Joe Epstein was linked to the mob as a money manager as early as 1930 and that he was a free-spending customer at the San Carlo Italian Village when he encountered Virginia there.

Virginia's story was quite different. She and Epstein were, she said, staying in a cheap boardinghouse and Epstein was studying accounting and was practically starving. She brought home food for him from where she worked, thus sustaining him. Soon thereafter, the grateful Epstein went to work for the mob.

Whichever story you accept, there is substantial agreement

upon the next phase of their relationship. Epstein started throwing a little work to Virginia. She acted first as a runner and placed racing bets for the Mob around Chicago, doing various things necessary for the laundering of Mob money. Later, when she had earned their trust and shown herself resistant to skimming from the cash she was handling, she took on other duties. It was my understanding that she did a little banking, holding money for people who might need it in a hurry.

It is not possible to talk about Virginia without including her long running affair with Benjamin Siegel, who, as I mentioned above, was known to the public as "Bugsy." A recent biography of Virginia claims that Virginia was first introduced to Siegel by a New York gangster, Joe Adonis. That story goes that Virginia was sent to New York by the Chicago Mob to keep an eye on Adonis and the expansionist plans of the New York Mob. Virginia is supposed to have begun an affair with Adonis, who introduced her to Siegel. And they say Siegel had a one-night stand with Virginia, just to spite Adonis. Virginia and Siegel later resumed the affair after both of them had moved, separately, to Los Angeles.

Virginia's version of the meeting was that one day Joe Epstein (not Adonis) came to her and said (and I quote what Virginia said Epstein said): "Virginia, there is somebody here I want you to meet. You two have got something in common. They can't print enough money for either of you." This account does not preclude the possibility that Adonis might have brought them together subsequently, after Virginia was sent by the Chicago Mob to live in New York, but it doesn't support it, either.

However it happened, Virginia and Siegel spent most of the war years in Los Angeles, and after the end of the war, Siegel began developing the Flamingo Hotel in Las Vegas. He was shot to death in the living room of Virginia's rented mansion on June

10, 1947. By lucky chance (or careful planning) Virginia was in France at the time looking into the possibility of importing champagne. Columnist Drew Pearson wrote that it was a good idea seeing as how she ran up a champagne bill of seven thousand dollars one night at Ciro's.

Virginia had been right in the middle of the business of organized crime for over ten years. While some say she slept with many of the principal crime leaders, most people attribute her long survival, in a business where bullets are usually substituted for pink slips, to the careful diary she kept of the financial transactions of the Chicago and New York mobs and later their operations in Los Angeles.

Following Siegel's assassination, she was interviewed in France by the press. She said Siegel was one of the finest men she had ever met, and he had the greatest respect for her. She was asked about the gold house key found in the pocket of his bathrobe after he was murdered. She said, "Why shouldn't he have a key? What's wrong with that? It was a big house."

She remained at the La Reserve Hotel in Beaulieu, on the French Riviera, until the French urged her to depart. Then she returned in August 1947 to the house she and Siegel had at Sunset Island on Miami Beach.

For the four remaining years that she stayed in the United States, she was hounded by the Internal Revenue Service, which had agents following her wherever she went. At some point the State Department must have revoked her passport, though I have no specific information about that. Such was a common practice in those days for persons subject to ongoing investigations. Then on February 19, 1950, she married an Austrian citizen, Hermann (Hans) Hauser, a ski instructor whom she had met at Sun Valley.

Virginia had possibly been married three times before, once when she was very young (before going to Chicago), once to a football player ("I sometimes wonder why I ever married him, though. I guess it was because all the other girls were crazy about him. He was a football star"), and when she was spending a lot of time in Mexico on mob business, she was briefly married to a Mexican (she said later that she divorced him because he was so jealous: "It bothered my friends").

Hauser had been interned during the war as a possible enemy alien. Some say that prior to their marriage, Virginia had Hauser checked out by the mob in Chicago. I believe that Virginia was mainly concerned with being able to leave the United States if she perceived any danger of being forced to testify against the mob. It was at the time believed by Treasury agents that Virginia knew all about the financial transactions of the mob, particularly money stashed in Havana, and there may have been some truth in that, as I will explain later. The legal advice she probably got from her Chicago friends was that should she marry an Austrian man, she would immediately receive Austrian citizenship and be free to travel abroad on an Austrian passport. Then, short of arresting her, there would be nothing the United States government could do to prevent it.

Virginia's son, Peter, was born in late November 1950, and she was called to testify before the Kefauver committee on organized crime in March of 1951. I can only speculate that she expected to receive advance information about any prospective judicial proceedings, and was caught by surprise by the Senate Crime Committee.

But she brazened it out, providing choice material for press coverage. At the time, Virginia, who had no visible means of support, was living at Bar Harbor, Maine. When asked by the crime committee where she got her money, she said she won it betting on horse races. In a sense, that was probably true. She was often paid by the Mob to launder money by betting at the racetracks. Leaving the hearings, Virginia was true to form and socked a female reporter in the jaw.

After the Senate hearings, she and her husband and small son returned to the house they had bought in Spokane, Washington. Based on her testimony before the Kefauver committee, the IRS was actively investigating her income and net worth. And the Immigration and Naturalization Service was preparing to move to force the departure from the United States of her husband, who had apparently entered the country in 1940 on a visitor's visa and, of course, stayed here many years too long.

Virginia started making inquiries about taking her husband to Chile, where he had last resided abroad, but was told she would not be permitted to leave, her newly acquired Austrian citizenship apparently being overlooked.

She and her husband and infant son were shadowed by the IRS wherever they went. A few months after her Kefauver committee hearing appearance, they set forth in their white Cadillac, pulling a one-wheeled trailer loaded with baggage. IRS agents were close behind.

Virginia finally lost the pursuers about seventy miles west of Minneapolis. Weeks later, the car was found abandoned in California. In July 1951, Virginia turned up in Denver, alone, and claiming that her husband and son had left for Chile. When she returned to the house in Spokane, she found the IRS had taken the house and its contents on a tax lien and were preparing to auction everything.

Virginia compared the IRS to the Gestapo and said, "I never worked in my life. All of the money I got was given to me by men friends. I would have been better off if I had robbed a bank. I've done nothing wrong. I can't understand why everyone keeps hounding me." In October 1951, Virginia finally left the United States, through Mexico, traveling on her Austrian passport.

She is quoted as saying as soon as she was safely across the border, "I will never return," and then it is said that she yelled, "Fuck you, America." Maybe so, but that report reminds me of a thirties radio show in which this one character was always telling wild tales and his straight man asks with a mock German accent, *"Vas you dare, Sharley?"*

By mid-1952 the Hauser family was living in Europe, with Hans at his old trade as a ski instructor, and Virginia living in style. It was soon pretty obvious that she was getting an allowance from someone, probably from her old associates, the money likely being made available by Joe Epstein and disbursed through the Mob in Italy.

Her paymaster might have been Lucky Luciano, who had been deported to Sicily in 1949, but he died in 1962. Joe Adonis fled to Italy in 1956 to avoid arrest, and lived there until his death in 1972, so he could have passed on Virginia's allowance for the rest of the time. My understanding from Virginia was that she received regular payments through these two until the beginning of 1965, when they ceased.

If Virginia knew why the payments stopped, she didn't tell me. It is my guess that in the beginning the payments were made to keep her happy and out of the country. Remember, Epstein had said years earlier (according to Virginia) that they couldn't print money fast enough for either Virginia or Siegel. But now (1965), fourteen years after she left the country, something had changed. Maybe several things. If there had ever been anything she could have revealed about Mob assets in Cuba, as some had speculated, Castro's revolution may well have taken care of that.

And surely, as each year went by, statutes of limitations ran out on various naughty things the Mob had done, and potential witnesses died, or any number of other things. So the danger of Virginia's return lessened. It was probably always a balance between the cost of keeping her abroad and any loss that might be occasioned by her return.

So came that day in early fall, 1965 when Virginia decided it was time to go home. Oddly enough, one of the deciding reasons, in addition to the loss of her income, was her mother-in-law. The Hauser family owned a ski chalet, or small ski-hotel. And the mother-in-law insisted that Virginia do her fair share of the work of running the place. "She tries to treat me like a maid," Virginia complained to me. So Virginia was ready to go home, if only the IRS would be willing to drop the charges of income tax evasion.

I took the question up with the American legal attaché residing in Bern, Switzerland, who also handled such matters for Austria. My last contact with Virginia was shortly before I was transferred back to Washington in early 1966, so I don't know how things turned out regarding arrangements for her return.

Epilogue: I had just finished my home leave and returned to Washington when I read a press account that on March 24, 1966, Virginia Hill Hauser's body had been found on a path near Koppl, a tiny village in low mountains, at about two thousand feet. Austrian police ruled the death a suicide by poison. The fact that Virginia had made a number of halfhearted suicide attempts with sleeping pills in France at the time of Siegel's murder weighed heavily upon the Austrian conclusion. There was also a report that much later she had been hospitalized in Salzburg because of some sort of overdose.

I have since read a report that said that during the medical examination, bruises were noted on her neck, but that this notation was deleted from the final report. Whether this is true, or if true, what it might mean, I have no idea.

It seems to me not outside the bounds of possibility that:

- Virginia was unable to reach any sort of agreement with IRS so she decided to hell with it; or
- the mob decided, after all, that they did not wish to take a chance on having her return, and having her tell what she knew to keep out of jail.

Now and then I used to read about the mob having informants placed inside such organizations as the IRS, so it would not surprise me if the mob was kept current about Virginia's intentions. As for myself, I never breathed a word. Until now, of course.

One of the unexpected things about what I have since read about Virginia, is the frequent reference to her drinking binges and the effects upon her health. Senator Kefauver was quoted as saying after the 1951 crime hearings, "I found Virginia Hill to be a sad and very mixed-up lady. The strain of the life she has led has taken its toll. The fading underworld queen is now a ravaged woman."

Virginia was at the time about thirty-five, and when I saw her fourteen years later, she had made a miraculous recovery. Not only was that comment at odds with my impression of her, it was also unexpected from Senator Kefauver, who, of all people, enjoyed a drink now and then.

In 1957, or 1958 (I don't remember which) my wife and I invited the senator and his lovely wife to a press club dinner. There was a cash bar (an invention of the devil, I don't mind telling you) and on the way into the banquet room Senator Kefauver bought bourbon highballs for each of the eight sitting at our table. Once seated, the senator downed his drink and swapped the empty glass for the full one in front of my wife. During the course of the dinner and the speeches thereafter, he drank his way around the table, always appearing to have a full, untouched drink in front of himself. Whether he thought he was fooling any stray photographers or just enjoyed staring at a full bourbon and water, I don't know. But as the evening wore on and the speeches went on and on, I began to envy him his hobby. Unfortunately, by then my drink was long gone, whisked away in the shuffle, and there was nothing left but wine to drink. Slow and not as sure.

One other thing: Years later when Imelda Marcos was ousted from the Philippines, much was made about her pairs of shoes. The figure of two hundred pairs sticks in my mind. But when Virginia was in her glory, living it up in New York before the war, press reports described her clothes thus: one hundred dresses and two hundred pairs shoes and hats. Five full-length fur coats—ermine, silver fox, blue fox, white fox, and mink— plus four fur jackets. At the time she was quoted: "I've got a pile of jewels. Star sapphires and whatnot. You can't stop men from giving them to you. But I'm not much on wearing the things."

20

Potpourri and Culture Shock

Vienna concluded my seven years of consular work and I was about to be thrust into something I liked much less, science liaison with the Atomic Energy Commission, which to my mind was mostly dogs' work without doing much good for anybody. But Washington probably thought it was doing me a favor, trying to make me into something better than I was. I had not forgotten the Deputy Chief of Mission's condescending attitude toward consuls when he remarked, in the heat of a chess game, that my boss, Trudgeon, was a pretty good man for a consular type.

Looking back over my own experiences, I concluded that the DCM was not entirely incorrect (to borrow a misapplied phrase from the Baroness Margrit). In those years I had had all sorts of chiefs. There was the wonderful good-hearted consul in Zurich who had come into the Foreign Service three years before I was born. He was followed by the ridiculous consul who, morbidly fearful of being blamed for something and to protect himself,

The Viennese home of John and Virginia Devine

insisted that every bit of correspondence be put into the passive voice. Once, when another vice consul (not I) could not please him with a letter, the consul prepared a draft to show the young man just how it should be done. The vice consul studied the draft every time he had a free moment. Being a reasonable fellow, if not intended by nature to be a consular officer, he was utterly bewildered. After a week or so, he dropped the draft letter back on the consul's desk without comment. The consul thought his draft was the vice consul's work and immediately edited it to shreds. Of course, this was the same man I had to defy to get my Egyptian-Sudanese-Armenians into the United States.

In Belize I had two consuls that required a whole book to describe. When I arrived in Vienna, I worked under two excellent consul generals, Trudgeon and Townsend. I had my reservations about Lehar, who, I thought, was unwilling to get out from behind the regulations. And the consul who replaced him, Rose Jones, lived in a world with far too many absolutes for the likes of me.

There are enough consuls (about 50 percent in my experience) who seem unconcerned about the consequences of their actions to make me forgive the DCM for his jaundiced view, and suspect that the Department of State puts such people into consular work by grand design. Maybe if consuls thought too much about their work there would be more burnouts. Alcoholism and other problems get to some of the best officers, but I never met a true knuckle head with a serious drinking problem in this business.

This is a roundabout way to introduce the saddest visa case I ever experienced, and it took place in Switzerland during my first tour abroad. Appenzell is a small town east of Zurich, in the mountains before the grassy upland valleys drop down into the valley of the River Rhein at Liechtenstein. It is known for its dairying, especially for its cheese and for its quaint costumes. There are probably more cows in the Appenzell area than people, though I have never made an actual count. When the winter snows recede to the very tops of the mountains, herdsmen lead their cows up into the uppermost highland valleys to feed on the new grass.

There are huts in the mountains where the herdsmen can shelter during the cold nights and sudden squalls of the summer months. Some of these huts are very crude but sturdy, often set partly into the hillside and using the abundant stone and covering the roofs with sod so the huts seem to grow out of the soil itself. As winter comes, the herdsmen bring the cows down again, with their bells ringing, to the lower valleys. Though I have not seen them for almost forty years, there are doubtless still farmhouses that share roofs with barns so that during the severe winters the cattle can be tended without venturing out in the weather and so the heat of the cows can be contained for the comfort of the herdsmen and their families.

This sort of life breeds an uncommon rapport between men and animals, and some of these people may seem rather primitive to city dwellers and to consuls from other lands.

There was a large family from the Appenzell area that decided in the fifties to immigrate to America. They found an American dairy farmer who wanted such sturdy people to live and work on his farm and he provided the necessary financial guarantees, because the Swiss family was not wealthy as we count such things.

Before the visas could be issued, our law required that each of the family members undergo a medical examination. For visa medical examinations the consulate general in Zurich had a Swiss physician on retainer. The doctor gave a clean bill of health to the family, all save one. And that was one of the sons who was hardly yet a grown man. This young man was found to have a mental defect; to be, in fact, feebleminded.

Since the family was at this point committed to taking up their new life, they went to America leaving the young man behind. He stayed with farmers near his old home, but he was nearly inconsolable. As the years passed, he missed his family more and more and the people in Appenzell feared for him. From time to time they approached our consulate general, asking us to reconsider, but all of our consuls said it was impossible, that a mental defect was a mental defect and the law was the law.

After I arrived in Zurich, someone brought him in to see us again. He had been working hard to achieve some level of literacy, but little else had changed. I was from the mountains, myself, albeit East Tennessee, and it seemed to me that the young Swiss had almost no schooling, but he knew what he needed to know for the sort of life he led, and as such he was different only in degree from some of the people I knew when I used to be a Social Security field representative in the mountains. However, I had to admit that if he was speaking German, it was a form I could not recognize.

I had two local Swiss employees who were familiar with the mountain cantons of Switzerland, one of them coming from St. Gallen, the main city of the area. They spoke to him and said, indeed, he spoke a language, though a dialect that could be understood by others, and certainly by his family. They agreed with me (I was a new vice consul and was not sure of anything, especially not myself) that this no longer quite so young herdsman might not be truly retarded.

The convincing thing was the character of the physician who had examined the man. He was a German-Swiss, and a cousin of a famous German musician who had stayed in Germany during the Hitler times and whose attitude toward the *Führer* might charitably have been called ambivalent. I heard from others that during the war, our physician though a Swiss citizen, had volunteered for military service (as a doctor) in the German army, but for reasons I never learned, was turned down, though possibly for demonstrated irrationality. He had spent some years in Japan and while there had ordered some beautiful cabinets made. When I admired them in his house, I noticed that the metal work was ornamented with neat swastikas.

Perhaps it was unwarranted of me to assume the physician might have rigid views about matters of human inferiority (possibly a weakness for eugenics), but it seemed reason enough to ask the United States Public Health Service doctor in Munich, on his next visit to Zurich, to examine the young man. With the aid of an interpreter, the USPHS exam went as we had hoped. The herdsman was ill-educated and was in fact a country bumpkin, but he did not have a mental defect. The USPHS man said that on the contrary, about things within his experience, he seemed quite clever.

So with a great deal of satisfaction, I issued the visa, for the man at long last following-to-join (regulations phraseology) his family in America.

Some time later we heard about his reunion with his family. They had arranged to go out to the airplane when it arrived, and were all gathered around when the steps were pushed up to the plane. The door to the plane opened and the young man stepped out and saw all his family waiting for him. The excitement was too much. He had a heart attack and died on the spot.

• • •

You know how highly I regarded Trudgeon, my first consul general in Vienna. But I don't wish to make any invidious comparison about my second boss—Townsend. It was a matter of drawing two aces from a deck with too many duces. Townsend knew more about consular work than anybody I ever encountered—what documents could be waived, just how far a consul's authority could be stretched. You would assume he would be a laid-back type of man, but he wasn't; he was a very tense man. Wired, you might almost say. It was evident in the way he moved, the way he paced around. But there was something else there, as well.

One evening he got several of us together to attend a dinner of some British group, the name of which I have forgotten. All I recall about it was that it was very much bound up with ritual, the sort of thing I couldn't imagine Townsend having any patience with. For instance, until the Queen was toasted, and the host gave the command, "Gentlemen, you may smoke," no one dared do so.

I tried to imagine a similar American affair where any smoking would be preceded by a toast to the President, or even the First Lady, who by that time was First Lady Bird. Impossible. Maybe we should, but we never would, at least in those years before smoking was prohibited in public places.

But I seem to have lost the thread. I intended to tell you about Townsend. On the way to the dinner, Townsend and I and maybe a couple of vice consuls were walking up Kaerntnerstrasse, the main shopping street leading away from the Graben and St. Stephan's Cathedral. In those days, on nice evenings it remained a shopping street even after the stores closed. It was there, on a different evening, that I had seen an elegantly attired lady wearing something that looked like black mesh or perhaps it was painted on. It could have been a tattoo, I suppose. And maybe she also had on shoes, but my eyes refused to stray that far to find out.

On the evening of the British dinner, it was chilly. The lady in the mesh was probably at home by the fire, or perhaps she was out there on the street but totally transformed by something furry. For myself, I was wearing a sort of blue-gray overcoat of Austrian manufacture. Very heavy and warm, it was also ungainly, like being wrapped in a blanket. No, a better simile would be a carpet. But Townsend had on a tan camel's hair coat with a black velvet collar.

As we walked along Kaerntnerstrasse, the demimonde along the way flocked around Townsend. They didn't actually push the rest of us out of the way, me and the two vice consuls, but it was clear they did not notice us. They saw only Townsend. At the time, I thought it was probably his camel's hair coat that made him look like a rich industrialist. I just assumed that; nobody likes to feel unattractive to women.

But then a few weeks later an American died in Vienna. He had been an official of a great corporation, and in his retirement he decided he wanted to live in Vienna. I could tell he had hoped his declining Viennese years would last for a long time, because in his effects there were many pairs of expensive shoes that had never been worn. We got in touch with the next of kin and asked where we should send his stuff. His relatives instructed us to sell everything and just send the money.

We auctioned everything. But two coats didn't sell, both expensive and British made, but old with the linings badly worn. One was a tweed, the other a camel's hair coat. To avoid just throwing them away, I made a token payment and took them home. One day I put on the camel's hair coat. If you didn't look at the torn lining, or if I didn't raise my arms so you could see how inexpertly the seams had been repaired, it looked every bit as classy as Townsend's coat. At worst, it made me look like old money, I thought.

Then I walked up Kärntnerstrasse. Not to do anything improper, mind you, but just in the spirit of scientific inquiry and maybe a little bit to enjoy the attention. Not a single hooker stopped to pass the time of the evening. So it hadn't been Townsend's coat that had attracted all the attention, you see, it had been Townsend himself. I suppose it would have been the same if he had worn just black mesh. I slunk home.

• • •

First Townsend's aura, and then there was Erna's bottom. You never quite know what is going to make the difference.

I was painting quite a bit in those days, working in oils. I had done pictures of the towns of Weissenkirchen and Steyr, and had worked up sketches I had made of Amalfi in Italy and Antigua in Guatemala when I used to go up there from Belize. Then I thought I would try some abstracts.

I don't know what I think about abstract painting. On the one hand, I know all the arguments against abstracts. All art is interpretation. The artist has this vision and uses his craft to make it possible for others to share it, too. But what if the subject the artist is interpreting never existed at all? Is it enough for the source to lie entirely in the artist's own imagination? I don't know. Maybe not; maybe that's just decoration.

The most damning condemnation of abstract art, in my experience, is what Carl Bowen, the ambassador's deputy (and my consul-condescending chess partner) once said. There was a big new exhibition of the works of Franz Kline at Vienna's Museum of the Twentieth Century. Much of Kline's work consists of large white-painted canvas with smears of black paint that look like someone has been cleaning a four-inch brush. It is called abstract expressionism, and what it interprets, what it expresses, I haven't a clue.

The museum is housed in a modern building with large exterior glass areas. My wife and I entered the building, and there was Bowen, standing with his hands clasped behind his back, his toes splayed out, and looking out a window. I asked, "What's the matter? Don't you like Franz Kline?"

"I turn my back on abstract expressionism," he replied.

On the other hand, I rather enjoy painting abstractions with lots of colors. When they work, they take on a life of their own. Many realistic paintings (and certainly some of mine) never quite make it. Anyway, despite Mr. Bowen and Franz Kline, I had taken an abstract painting spell (maybe fit is the word) and had set up my easel at home. I had to do my painting in our front hall, a tiny space requiring either short brushes or, better yet, painting knives (*spachtel*, as the Austrians call them). Small though the hall was, it at least didn't have three grand pianos and a harpsichord crammed into it.

But my painting was not coming out right. I was painting an Alma Thomas at the time, though I didn't know it because I had not yet seen any of her paintings. Splotches of color such as a duck might make by walking around in circles with paint on its feet. Then, one day, Erna, our *Haustochter*, was getting coats on the children to take them out somewhere, and she backed into the wet oil painting. In an instant it was transformed. I could see it immediately; the painting was exactly right and there was nothing that I could do to it to make it any better. I hung it up to dry.

● ● ●

Not all encounters with parts of young ladies' anatomy are happy ones. Our town house was one of a half dozen in a row at the American embassy housing. One evening there was a knock on our door and I opened it, as one did in those days, fearing nothing. The wife of a neighbor walked in. She was a young, pretty child. I doubt that she was more than twenty. Skin like a baby and large, limpid eyes, except that one was badly bruised and swollen shut. Parisian blue, I would call the shade of her shiner. One of my favorite colors when in a different context.

My wife asked what happened. The young woman said she ran into a door. It probably felt like it. We offered to get her some help, but she declined, said she only wanted to sit for a few minutes. After a bit, she got herself under control and went back home. It wasn't long before she and her husband, a code clerk, left the embassy without any further disturbance. One day they were there, then they were gone.

It was like any other place, like suburbia, I suppose.

• • •

State Department rules in force thirty-odd years ago prevented my wife from working at her profession, that of a journalist. In those days the State Department thought that anything a Foreign Service officer's spouse (and back then the spouses were almost all wives) did while abroad would be taken as a reflection of the husband's views toward the host country. And as everybody knew, journalists were an unruly lot who could not be trusted not to undermine U.S. policies. So there was set up in Washington a committee on unofficial publications with the power to review any copy produced by a Foreign Service wife for deviant views and other heresies. The review process was slow, to the point of making it just about impossible for the wife to work as a newspaper correspondent. Not that the State Department intended it to have that effect; it just happened. Ha ha.

Perhaps as an offshoot of this official attitude, few State Department people working abroad thought my wife had lost anything important. They did not understand that my wife defined herself as a journalist before she ever met me.

So it was as a breath of fresh air that my wife met Virginia Devine. I use Virginia's real name because she is important to this book and deserves proper recognition. (Yes, Santa Claus, there are two real Virginias in this book, Virginia Hill and Virginia Devine, but the similarities end with the given names.)

On first meeting, Virginia asked my wife what she did, assuming she did something besides sit in a chair designated for a woman in the seating plans of dinner parties. My wife said she was a journalist. (I wasn't present, but I'm sure this was said wistfully.)

Virginia said she used to do a bit of writing, too, freelance for the *Georgetowner*, a neighborhood weekly in Washington. "What sort of writing have you done?" she asked.

"I was a reporter for the *Washington Post*," my wife answered.

"You got me there," said Virginia. But she was being a bit modest. She was and is a painter and in later years became an art restorer.

If the reader wonders why I bring this up, it is not to explain that my wife is a journalist. All the world knows that. It is that Virginia was one of the few senior wives (her husband was political counselor) to treat my wife with a modicum of the respect a professional deserves. In Zurich, there was the consul general who ordered my wife to work for the American Club newsletter and take her editorial direction from a group of not necessarily well-meaning ladies who could barely read. Well, most of them could sort of read, anyway.

In Belize, there were the principal officer and his wife who dressed down my wife for presuming to introduce them to persons above our station. This did not go over well with my little woman, who had stared down a governor who demanded the photo negative of the governor's wife dancing barefoot on a Sunday morning, had breakfasted with President Harry Truman, and interviewed a European queen in the ladies' room.

So when Virginia treated my wife as an equal, it created an enduring friendship. I won't tell you much about Virginia, perhaps just a thing or two. Virginia edited a booklet telling Americans how to get along in Vienna. It was she who told us how to place bids at the Dorotheum, the state-owned pawnshop and auction house founded by the Empress Maria Theresa. From her we learned that Austrians, with crowded housing after the war, often hocked their winter coats and skis in the summer and their summer gear in the winter. The Dorotheum had better cold storage for furs than did most commercial storage facilities, and the fees were cheaper, just so long as you didn't forget to redeem your furs before they were sold.

Virginia acquired odd lots of silver, often as small as settings for four. She liked to have dinner parties with little tables set for four, recognizing that at large parties, guests are often not very good about doing the switch, where you quit talking to the person on your right and shift to the person on your left. I can't tell you how many dinner parties I have gone to where I would have had no one to talk to, had I not discovered the art of engaging my inner self with transcendental meditation.

One of Virginia's particularly memorable dinner parties had several of the guests arrive upside down. While waiting for everyone to report in, we heard the sound of auto horns, protesting tires, and several thumps followed by silence. Virginia went to the door. Her last guests had arrived, albeit with their car upside down in the middle of the intersection. Virginia helped the guests disembark from their car. They were surprised but not damaged. She brought them into the house, called the police, seated the guests, and served dinner. It was a delightful meal, as I recall.

After retirement, Virginia and her husband settled in Vienna. It was cheap, the food was wonderful, and above all, they loved the city. But with the economic recovery of Austria, prices began rising. When the cost of her husband's pajamas increased to $125 (a lot of money thirty years ago), she decided it was time to come home. A good thing, too, my wife was at the time editing a section of the *Washington Post* and needed a good freelance writer with a knowledge of antiques and things European. What goes around comes around.

• • •

"Alf, it's all yours. You know what to do, I take it?"

"Sure, no problem." Alfred Sheltie sat down at my desk, now his desk, and looked perplexed.

I knew Alf's background. He had been at the embassy for some time—refugee and migration affairs. Not much of a leg up for the sort of things he'd be doing now. "I left the safe open because I thought you might like to look through it before you go home. Here's the combination to the lock." I handed him a piece of paper. "Memorize it and eat the paper. Or you could just pass it to the locals. Save them the trouble of figuring it out. If you forget the combination, it's Millard Fillmore's birthdate. Remember, the fooler is I didn't use 00 for the year, I just used the 18. Took them weeks to catch on." Alf was plainly bewildered. "Just kidding of course."

I went over to the safe and extracted Mr. Timmer's file. "This is the money for the Cowardly Lion. He is our own remittance man. The amount you give him is noted on the ledger sheet. Be sure you get his paw print."

"Paw print?"

"Signature. But don't let him use our fountain pen; give him something sturdy."

"Why do we pay him?"

"Ballet. He's learning to dance."

"He's a lion?"

"Yeah. The joke's on us if he turns out to be Nijinsky. Then there's this guy in Chicago. He lives with his mother; she's a schoolteacher. He was over here for a long time, until it got too expensive for his mother, so we repatriated him last year. However, he's lonesome for Vienna and calls us about once a month. Likes to talk and talk. I'd hate to have his mother's phone bill, but we help all we can."

"Pay her phone bill?"

"No, we can't do that. What you have to do is to keep talking while you put down the phone on your desk. Then you move across the room and keep raising your voice. Make sure the last thing he hears before you go out the door is you shouting what a terrible connection it is. Then tiptoe back and hang up. With practice you can get rid of him in less than two minutes. His mother will thank you for it."

I went on down the list of things he needed to know so he wouldn't be as bad off as I was when Buddy retired without telling me anything. "And if you have any questions, ask Helga Brand, she'll tell it to you straight.

"I've got to go by the embassy and then home to see to the packing up of my stuff. I'm still arguing with Admin about my shipping allowance. Remember, lock up before you leave." So off I went to see about packing up my pianos, my paintings, our collection of books, my wife's collection of antiques—oh, yes, and the children—for our move back to Washington and my next assignment, the detail to the Atomic Energy Commission. Everything went without a hitch except that my household effects shipping allowance was cut to the bone or maybe slightly past and we had to throw away the pianos and most everything else that we owned.

It was all due to a change in the regulations that is too complicated to explain here, but the result was that while we had left Washington with a full shipment of effects to unfurnished housing, we were being brought home with a limited shipment from furnished housing. We were expected to dispose of anything that would not fit within a relatively small shipping container.

Two pianos could easily go. The Bechstein was a piece of junk anyway, and the Schrimpf, well it came to me free and I could give it to my daughter's wonderful teacher. It was doubtful that the opera singer would ever come back to claim it. But there was no room for the Luna, the little grand I still dream about. I sold it to the musical wife of a CIA agent. It (the piano) later died under suspicious circumstances. Probably abandonment. It was a very sensitive instrument.

My paintings had to be approved for export. That really set me up. Important at last. Frau Doktor Ganz came out from the Kunsthistoriches Museum to say which could go and which had to be kept in Austria as national treasures. She looked at my canvases and refused to approve any for export. "That's not fair," I protested. "This is my life's work. I won't be able to take any of them home with me." "There's no problem. You can take all of them; they aren't artworks." My face fell; I tried to decide whether to protest. The Frau Doktor saw my distress. "They're not the sort of art governed by the law." Oh.

My wife and I sat on the floor of the moving company's office, sorting through our books. How many novels had to go to make room for our *Webster*'s second edition (the one that still had reasonable standards)? Too many. Too bad. The Knoll cabinets, out. The art nouveau furniture, in. Aalto chairs? Hmm, well, in. They don't weigh much and will stack. The ziricote tabletop, out. Too damn heavy. It was a heart-wrenching day.

We had bought a small station wagon, and we overloaded it with everything else, including the harpsichord, and we headed for England and the boat. If the boat didn't sink (it didn't) we might just make it to Washington.

...

Culture shock!

Back in Washington we bought an old row house on Capitol Hill. Probably built in the 1820s. Next to a Chinese laundry. My wife apologized to a journalist friend about the laundry. The friend said, "But, Sarah, it's chichi to live next to a Chinese laundry." The friend now has a mansion in an exclusive section in Dallas. There are some things better than chichi.

Twenty-foot-wide lot, fourteen-foot-wide house. One big two-level room and a kitchen on the first floor, three bedrooms and a bath on the second. A partially excavated basement where the rats lived. Across the back of the lot was a two-story garage that would be my painting studio. Not art, humph!

Our advance shipment of effects, a few wooden boxes, went into the second floor of the garage, waiting to be unpacked. The light over the back door was shot out the first night. As we were hanging up clothes and stuff in the house, thieves were chopping a hole in the roof of the garage to get at the shipping boxes. There went my camera; there went I don't know what all else.

We stuck it out in the house for two years, assuming that there was no direction the neighborhood could go but up. We were wrong. There was a liquor store across the street. Every other night the burglar alarm went off, and because the store owner apparently lived in Nome, Alaska, and traveled only by dogsled, it always took him a while to come down to the store to turn off the alarm and board up the smashed window.

We bricked up all the windows of the garage except those facing our house, but thieves unbricked them. Our younger daughter, then age six, chased a housebreaker out of her bedroom. I caught him in the living room and sat on him (he wasn't very large). We called the police. They said they didn't know when they could get a squad car to come by. The housebreaker squirmed; I sat on him harder. "What should I do?" I asked the police over the phone, "Should I just kill him?" They found a police car they could send over.

Drunks were throwing their empties at our garage and littering the alley with glass, then passing out leaning against the alley door. It was getting dicey for the girls to go to the park. A friend, one who happened to be a non-littering sort of alcoholic, collapsed all bloodied on our front doorstep. He had been mobbed by a swarm of preteen children who had stripped him of everything that could be sold.

We put the house on the market. One day we had a hot prospect, a fearless young couple who were sure they could live on the edge. We were showing them the little yard in between the house and the garage, where I had bricked everything over (no grass to cut) and built a brick sandbox. Just the place for children if the need should arise, we explained. Very secure with seven-foot concrete block walls (and not leaning too terribly much) separating the little courtyard from the neighbors on either side, the laundry (whose elderly Chinese owner had recently been beaten up and robbed) and on the other side, the nice, quiet labor union local headquarters.

Just at the moment when the prospective buyers were ready to decide our house was the one for them, there was a loud commotion on the labor union side, many people whacking at something. Then a large rat as big as a full-grown opossum leaped over the slightly leaning wall and landed in the sandbox. The rat was stunned for a moment but rapidly recovered and scampered dizzily toward our basement and its safe burrow. While everybody was hypnotized by the rat, several heads and torsos appeared at the top of the wall with hardworking men's arms holding a selection of brooms, sticks, and a board or two. One of the heads spoke, "Did you see him? He wuz a big'un."

Eventually another buyer came along and we sold the house. We moved out ten days before the Martin Luther King assassination and the riots that burned a swath down Eighth Street, two doors away. From our new house, on a hill three miles north of the center of the city, we watched as the smoke from the burning drew closer by the hour. It stopped before it got to us.

21

Green Peas and Gulf Wars

*W*e had just moved into the Capitol Hill house, the one with the rats, when Sam Miller did me another favor. Sam was this friend in the State Department's Office of Personnel—you met him in my previous memoir, the one about Belize—who was always trying to do his best for me. Patch things up when I screwed up, that sort of thing. For instance, when our household goods left Vienna, the shipment still exceeded my piddling little authorization. I had made the embassy administrative officer an offer to burn my belongings on the embassy steps, saving only my draft card. (At the time people were making a big thing of the illegality of burning draft cards, but I was overage, anyway.) The admin officer was not amused. On the other hand, Sam was the one who advised and helped me in my two-year fight to get an exception made. Ultimately, Sam and I were successful, probably through sheer persistence. I won, but with a split decision. It was a lesson for me that it was not safe to assume that one's colleagues in the State Department are necessarily going to be sympathetic just because they have to put up with the same sort of nonsense.

But this is straying from what I wanted to tell you about, which is the first Gulf War, one that came a long time before the one we had with the Iraquis. We are going to have to call the country concerned by a made-up name, the Sultanate of Shebai. The reason for the made-up name is, we aren't currently at war with this particular country, and I don't wish to be the person responsible for starting one.

It was all Sam's idea. There wasn't enough zip in my personnel file. Just run-of-the-mill consular work, and much of that was without the usual exaggerated luster that decorates files of officers on the fast track to the top. In Zurich I had not shown myself particularly adept at framing all my letters in the passive voice, as required by my chief, and I had flat out disobeyed him by getting the department to approve the immigration of the Armenian-Egyptian-Sudanese. I got no accolades there.

And in Belize there was the little matter of the hurricane and my assuming charge of the consulate just because my new chief ran away. Not only did that not get me any superior service awards, but it took years to get any kind of efficiency report at all out of the man. As Sam put it at the time, how are you going to get along with a bunch of exasperating foreigners if you can't even get along with your own boss? Good question.

And then Vienna. It didn't help my case when that former assistant attorney general tried to get me fired for allowing the Austrian police to lock up his drunken and obstreperous assistants, and even wrote to the Secretary of State and my senator (Kefauver) about me. That is the kind of visibility nobody needs to have in his personnel file.

Anyway, Sam was going to fix all that. Since it was going to be a while before I had to report for duty at the Atomic Energy Commission, he would give me the sort of cushy assignment we only dream about; I was going to be escort officer for Sheikh Abdul Ali Bakhali, the minister of Industrial Development in the fabulously rich Sultanate of Shebai.

Sam's words were, as best I can recall them, "You owe me, buddy. You've got escort duty with an Arab sheikh." One of the rare instances when Sam was ever dead wrong, unless you take that to mean I owed him a swift kick in the pants.

Visiting sheikhs still had a reputation, back then, for covering their State Department hosts with unimaginable delights. An assistant chief of protocol had been handed the keys to a new Oldsmobile, for example. Of course it was a bit unwise of him to accept the gift. Hard to overlook it sitting in his garage. Nevertheless, who could not but speculate on the exotic pleasures of which the State Department host might have to partake to avoid offending the illustrious visitors. Since the visit was to be for all of August, I went out and bought several summer suits, extra roomy for all the weight I would gain feasting on suckling pig. I was ready for anything.

Now, let's make up some names. The Shebai desk officer, I will call Mr. Warden. He was a middle-grade officer, youngish, but older than I, and subordinate to the Director of Arab Gulf Affairs. That makes him fairly far down in the pecking order in the part of the State Department that deals with the Arab world.

The Minister, Sheikh Abdul Ali Bakhali, has an aide. He has gotten a degree (recently) from some university in the American Midwest. He is young, in his twenties. He is somewhat suspended, culturally, between the Middle East and Middle America. But he knows on which side his pita bread is buttered. We will call him Jamil Muhammad Qader.

And there is Harry Moon. Harry is an old hand at preparing junkets for visiting foreigners and he works for an outfit we will call Foreign-American Travel, or F.A.T. That is no sillier than the real name of the organization, and is easily remembered. Harry was something of a wizard in dealing with rich and self-important visitors. And klutzes like me.

Finally, we had better find a name for an oil company. It will figure into the minister's visit in a big way. So let's call it the Bigg Oil Company.

• • •

The Shebai desk officer and I went out to Dulles Airport to meet the Minister. It was an awful, hot morning and even though it was only about nine o'clock the heat radiated off of the tarmac, broiling us so the sweat ran down into our shoes as we waited for the plane to get parked, the stairs to be rolled up, the door to pop open, and passengers to emerge from the first-class section.

A young man in a dark suit was the first out, after a crew member opened the door and checked the position of the stairs. I was expecting someone in Arab robes. The young man stood aside as much as he could, on the small platform at the top of the stairs. Another man came out, tentatively. He was older, perhaps in his late forties and also wearing a dark suit.

The older man stopped and looked down at Warden and myself. His face bordered on impassive; but he was not pleased. No happy-to-see-you smile. The younger man looked around; there seemed to be a frown above his nose. At a sign from the older man, the two of them descended the stairs.

Warden approached them and introduced himself, identifying himself as the Shebai desk officer. I had not been told about the aide, Jamil, but it seemed reasonable that the minister would be accompanied by somebody. I went up to Jamal and told him I was to be their escort. Jamil glanced around and said, "The two of you—are here to meet us?"

I understood when he meant. "Yes, the assistant secretary is preparing to meet you for lunch at the State Department. We are just here to get you settled in your hotel and escort you to the luncheon." Jamil's expression did not change. Perhaps I should have said the Secretary of State or maybe even the President was meeting them for lunch. Then later I could have made excuses. Maybe, "The President sends his apologies—aliens from another planet have landed on the White House lawn." But being only a consular officer I was not accustomed to that sort of creative thinking.

The hotel, one of our better ones but not the best, did not impress the Shebaihin (that is the collective name we will use, like "Americans"). But they eventually came down from their rooms and we scuttled off to the State Department, and up to the executive dining room. The dining room was very nice, but nothing to compare to the reception rooms the State Department was to add later to the eighth floor of the New State Department Building. More than thirty years of collecting Federal period furnishings and decorating the place with gold leaf and fake marble have made this part of the State Department into something that needs to be seen to be believed. Kublai Khan meets Ben Franklin, if you know what I mean.

But the dining room back then was good enough for the Secretary of State. Except that he wasn't there. The regional Assistant Secretary was the best we could do, and there were various people from the next several levels down. Like movie extras, we sat there trying not to seem out of place. Some extras have small speaking parts; I didn't. It wasn't too bad through the soup course. I don't remember what kind of soup, maybe a cold leek soup, or something like that. Harmless enough, bland but acceptable.

Then came the main course. Squab, beautifully roasted, and some sort of starch, rice as I remember. And English peas. I dug in. The air-conditioning, after the heat outdoors, had made me hungry.

I noticed the minister, who had been trading name-drops with the assistant secretary, had become very quiet. I saw he was poking something in his peas with his fork. I examined my peas. Hmmm. Little cubes of ham, just the sort of thing to give peas some character.

It was at that point, I suppose, that everything went horribly wrong, though the visit had certainly not started out particularly well. Not being a Middle East specialist, I was not even aware how generally pork is looked down upon as unclean in that part of the world, so my sympathies are with the cook. The minister was rather quiet for the rest of the luncheon. Good manners? Natural reserve? Mad as hell? I couldn't tell.

The next step was to have a meeting with Harry Moon at F.A.T., where traveler's checks would be issued to the minister and all would be explained—what the checks were for and receipts, stuff like that. I was to call at the hotel first thing the next morning to pick them up and get things started.

When I came to the hotel, they were not waiting out front, needless to say, so I left the driver and went in to look for them. Not in the lobby, either, and nobody responded when I called their rooms. So I started looking in all the possible places, coffee shop, restaurant, barbershop, newsstand, out by the pool, where, who knows, they might be selecting their hearts' desires for their evening's sport. Nobody anywhere. I called Harry and told him we might be late, I had lost them already.

When I left the phone, Jamil walked into the lobby. I was overcome with relief. "Where is the minister?" I asked.

"In the hospital." Jamil's manner was matter-of-fact, like the minister was getting his shoes shined or some such.

I was overcome. Maybe it was a heart attack or diabetic coma. All sorts of specters came whizzing through. Maybe he was allergic to the ham? God help us. Or maybe Allah. "Is he very sick?" I asked.

"Just a checkup. The minister believes this is a good time to get a checkup."

"Oh." After I digested that, I reminded Jamil as tactfully as I could that we were expected this morning at F.A.T. to receive the expense money.

"The minister asked me to take care of such things. Shall we go now?"

Harry Moon took it all very calmly, I thought. He went methodically through everything, about how F.A.T. would take care of all the transportation and set up meetings and make hotel reservations, but the minister and Jamil were expected to pay for the hotel accommodations and their meals from the traveler's checks being issued to the minister. Harry patted the pile of checks to show just how adequate the money would be. "As soon as the minister is out of the hospital, he can come here and sign the checks and you can be on your way."

Jamil looked uncomfortable. He glanced at me and then met Harry straight on. "I do not believe the minister will be coming here. He wishes for me to take care of the expenses. I will sign the checks."

Harry paled. This just wasn't done, he explained; it had something to do with accountability and the agreement F.A.T. had with the State Department. Some discussion followed, and it became apparent Jamil was not going to budge from his position. After a time Harry sighed, barely audibly, and left the room to call the State Department. I could hear arguing in the next office, but couldn't make out the words except for an occasional "I know that!"

Eventually, Harry came back and pushed the checks across the table to Jamil. "Sign them. I'm giving you power of attorney."

The rest of the day we were scheduled to tour the city and the next morning, fly to New York. Jamil enjoyed his Washington sight-seeing, though he had seen it all before during his college days. Next day, I turned up at the hotel and waited for the visitors to check out. Eventually, I found Jamil having breakfast. "The minister is still in the hospital," he said.

"When will he be out?"

"In a day or two."

I called Harry. No travel today. Harry fumed. He said it looked like there was going to be a general strike of the airlines. It could come at any moment. "He may have to walk to New York."

Next morning's *Washington Post* said the strike was on for the major airlines. I called Harry again. Yes, he said, it was true, but come over, anyway. He wanted somebody to complain to, and besides, he had a new problem.

At the F.A.T. offices I found Harry sitting at his desk, staring into space. I sat down. As usual, I found twiddling my thumbs unhelpful, so I put my hands on the arms of the chair and imagined a Bach two-part invention. It had been far too long since I had touched a piano. Weeks.

"You got to get him out of that hospital."

"How?" I asked.

"How do I know? You're supposed to be the diplomat."

"Consular." He looked blank. "I'm a consular officer. We only deal with people who want to do things. Not like governments. Or government officials."

"You're a diplomat now. You know the Bigg Oil Company?"

"Not personally, no. But I've used the stuff that comes out of pumps with a big oval BIGG on them."

"They're big."

"Yeah."

"I mean they're huge. And they called the Secretary of State or somebody. They want to invite the minister to dinner tomorrow night."

"Maybe the hospital could provide an extra tray." I knew the moment I said that, Harry would think I was being a smart-ass.

"In Pittsburgh."

I made an effort to be constructive. "So we've got to get him there, with the strike on. I could drive him there, I suppose. Or maybe send him in an ambulance." Damn! There I went again.

"They will come after him in an executive jet. You just get him out of the hospital. Why's he there, anyway?"

"Donno. Maybe getting his oil changed?"

It was easier than I thought. Good thing, too. If I couldn't have gotten the minister to come out of the hospital, Bigg Oil just might have been moved to acquire the State Department. You know, to get things running right. I would have been the first to go.

I told Jamil about the dinner and how the executive jet was going to take him up to Pittsburgh. He could have a nice dinner with all those rich oil men and the jet would bring him back afterward. Just the minister and Jamil in the plane. I didn't see why I had to mention the pilot and me, of course.

A magical cure, better than penicillin. The minister returned to the hotel within hours and looking perfectly fit for someone who had been so near death.

It was late when we left Washington. Already by most people's standards dinnertime. The jet was small, with maybe seats for a dozen or so people. Never saw the pilot, though there had to have been one, I suppose. Nobody said fasten your seat belts or no smoking. We just took our seats and took off. When we were in the air, a youngish man in a sort of uniform wandered into the cabin and asked if we wanted anything to drink. The minister declined. Jamil did too, but it looked as though he was sorry he had to. I ordered Scotch on the rocks, but resisted asking for a double. A double came anyway. Maybe oil company drinks are always doubles; I wouldn't be surprised.

The steward disappeared up front. I sipped my whiskey and wondered if he was also the pilot. Probably just the copilot, I decided.

As I write this now, I have the advantage of knowing more about private jet aircraft, how common they can be some places. A few years after the Shebaihin adventure our journalist friend, the very same one who assured us that living next to a Chinese laundry was chichi, married her own oil man. She and her husband visited us afterward. She told how they were married on one of those huge Texas ranches. It had its own airport, of course, and she said all the guests arrived on their LBJs. We looked blank. "Little bitty jets," she explained.

Rugged country around Pittsburgh. The sun was still on the high ground but downtown was pretty much in shadow. On top of a tall building (everything looks tall compared to Washington) I saw a large illuminated oval sign saying BIGG. Sort of reminded you of a Bigg gas pump.

That wasn't the building. Bigg Oil had an even taller building and we had dinner on the top floor, with a glass wall looking out over the smaller building with the sign. When we arrived, Bigg executives were all lined up at the glass, looking down at their sign and admiring it. Just as though it were something beautiful like the Washington Monument or maybe the Capitol dome. I concluded that the sign was new, or maybe many of the executives attending the dinner didn't get much chance to see the world from the top of Bigg Oil.

Mostly it was just dinner, but there were some speeches, the welcoming sort, and things like that, and how Bigg Oil would be sending people over to Shebai to work out ways the sheikhdom and Bigg Oil could get really rich. What may have been said at the head table, between Bigg's president and the minister, I couldn't hear. I was working on my lamb chops at a table far in the back with some other people whose exact functions were hard to divine.

No ham in the peas. In fact, no peas at all. Bigg Oil would never make a mistake like that.

It was late when I finally made it back to my little embattled house on Capitol Hill. A few hours' sleep and I would be off to New York, unless the minister found something else that needed to be checked out at the hospital.

The airline strike was still on and it didn't seem as though either side was weakening. So we drove to New York in a limo. Not my favorite way to travel, but at least, since I was not driving, I could look out the window and enjoy the scenery along the Jersey Turnpike. (That is supposed to be a joke.)

Our hotel in New York was the Pierre. A nice expensive place and not too large. We got the government rate. There was one dinner party but otherwise I didn't have much to do, since the minister was mostly calling on Arab groups and doing a little shopping. My main concern was to be sure he was at Idlewild in time for his flight. I still thought of it as Idlewild even though it had been renamed Kennedy International more than two years earlier. No, the airline strike had not been settled; Harry Moon had managed to get us on an airline that was still flying into Miami. I don't know how come. I told you Harry was a magician.

The morning of our departure I watched as Jamil and the minister went to the cashier's window. Well, thank heavens they got something right. At least they're paying their hotel bill. (Wrong.)

The flight to Miami was tourist class, but at least we were traveling by air so it was quick. I knew a little about Miami Beach. During the late forties I lived there one summer, when I was working for a company installing communications equipment at the Miami airport. It was a time when almost nobody came to Miami Beach during the summer except for Cubans. My roommate and I were able to rent a room with a bath in a small Miami Beach hotel for a dollar a day, each.

We worked on the night shift on the mainland at the airport and would return to the beach just about dawn. Every other morning we were stopped en transit by the Miami Beach police, who were convinced we were young punks up to no good. The bars would still be open for an hour or so, so once we got past the cops we could get a drink and maybe a sandwich or something. When the bar closed, we would go out and lie on the beach. Eventually, girls would come by and we could talk to them, but there weren't many except for the Cuban girls, who kept pretty much to themselves.

I only remember one American girl very well. I can still remember her name, oddly enough, after fifty years have passed. She had come down to Miami to wait out a divorce and she had her little daughter along, a child maybe four years old. The young woman was all the time asking us whether we thought she was pretty, thought she was sexy, thought she had a good figure.

Well, she qualified in all those categories and even her daughter was pretty. Even as dumb as I was at nineteen, it all made me wonder what had happened to make her so unsure of herself. After a few days on the beach, she and her daughter disappeared, having, I suppose, found someone willing to provide the reassurances she needed.

As the day would wear on and the sun would get hot enough to burn off your skin, we would go back to our hotel, the Monroe Towers, and sleep until we got hungry (better than an alarm clock), have a meal, and go across to the mainland to work. Police never stopped us from going to the mainland.

This time, eighteen years later, when I arrived with the Shebaihin, Miami had changed. There were a lot more American tourists, and no Cuban tourists—just the Cuban refugees driven out by Castro. We were booked into a first-class hotel. I believe my old place, the Monroe Towers, was still there, but small and forlorn looking. I looked around for Elaine, the uncertain young woman who had been getting her first divorce my first summer in Miami. Thought she might be on her third or fourth divorce by now. Saw no sign of her. Probably in Reno now. She'd be too old for Las Vegas.

When we checked in, there was a frantic message to telephone Harry. When I called, Harry was furious. The minister and his aide had left the Pierre without paying their bill. I told

Harry I had seen them at the cashier and maybe there was some mistake. Harry said he would ask the Pierre to check.

In a bit Harry called again. The hotel said the minister had just cashed some traveler's checks. They particularly remembered the gentlemen because there was some question who was supposed to countersign the checks. Harry growled at me that he just knew there was going to be trouble when the minister never showed for his briefing and we had had to do everything through Jamil.

I asked Harry whether he wanted me to wring the money out of the minister, and he said, no, there was enough trouble already. The State Department seemed to think the minister was important, so he would see if they would pay the Pierre. But I was to make damn sure it didn't happen again.

Later I saw Jamil and he said he and the minister wanted to go off on their own for dinner, and I said okay, but I that wanted to meet Jamil for a drink when he returned to the hotel.

As I suspected, Jamil had picked up bad habits and was glad enough to bend an elbow in the bar when he was away from the minister. That also suggested it was by no means certain that Jamil would lay down the law to the minister about handling the money advanced by F.A.T. Determined to try anyway, I explained how much trouble it would cause for me if they didn't pay their bills. Then I was sorry I brought that up. Maybe causing me trouble was not unattractive. Jamil and I finished up the evening discussing how we were going to take a day trip down to Key West.

The next morning I saw just how much Miami Beach had changed from the sleepy place it once was. With a little whispering noise, a sheet of paper was slipped under the door to my room. I picked it up.

The newsletter had all the news you could want if you were Jewish and from New York City. It told about various social activities at the hotel and which rabbis were staying at the hotel. Mentioned whose children had come of age since last year through bar mitzvah or bat mitzvah. And the newsletter reassured visitors that the hotel could provide proper kosher meals on request.

On my way down to breakfast I walked apprehensively by the rooms of the minister and his aide. All was quiet. I could see just the corner of one of the newsletters peeking under the door. Perhaps they hadn't seen it yet. I pulled it back, folded it up, and stuck it in my pocket. Couldn't tell about the other door. Perhaps the newsletters were only delivered one to a customer. Or perhaps they had already picked it up. I didn't know what to do. So I went downstairs for breakfast.

Jamil and the minister were already in the dining room. They looked normal. I relaxed. A bit.

We traveled to Key West in a light, four seat plane. We traveled so low I found myself looking for stop signs at intersections. The narrow, two-lane bridges south from the mainland seemed to go on forever.

Key West was (and I suppose still is) a tiny place, everything in walking distance. Saw Hemingway's house; ate conch. Did not seem to me that the minister was impressed. Oh, well.

We were back in Miami by sundown and the next day, at nine in the morning, it was laid on for us to pay a call on the mayor. There was some reason for it, but I can't recall what it was. Probably program filler, but my vague recollection was that it had something to do with sewage disposal. I went to bed worrying about that newsletter, the one I had been unable to retrieve. Maybe the maid threw it in the trash when she cleaned up.

The next morning I went down early and had breakfast. My favorite hotel breakfast in those days was two eggs poached with the yellows still soft, and rye toast. There was sausage. I didn't ask if it was made with beef or whether they kept it special for the goyim.

By eight-thirty my Shebaihin had not appeared and I was nervous. I called Jamil's room.

"The minister is praying."

"Oh." I couldn't very well ask him to stop it and come on down. "When do you believe he will be finished?"

"It is not possible to tell."

Long silence while I thought. "Why don't I call the mayor's office and ask if they can postpone our visit until ten? Wouldn't that be a good idea?" Jamil agreed that it would. The mayor's office did not sound pleased, but they said ten o'clock would be possible.

At nine-thirty I couldn't stand it any longer and I called Jamil again. "The minister is on the phone to Shebai."

"Will he be long?"

"It is impossible to say. He has important matters to discuss."

"Perhaps I can call the mayor and postpone things until eleven."

"Good idea."

The mayor's office was distinctly testy. "Call us when the minister is available, and then if the mayor can work it into his schedule, you can come over."

I got comfortable in the lobby where I could see whoever came out of the elevators. Somewhat after eleven, the minister and Jamil emerged, followed by a porter carrying their luggage. The minister went to the cashier and seemed to be cashing a lot of checks. Then the minister headed for the gift shop and Jamil came over to speak to me.

"We are ready to go."

"But not to see the mayor."

"No, the minister has decided not. We have checked out and paid our bill as you instructed."

"Our flight to New Orleans does not leave until tomorrow."

"The minister wishes to go today."

"I'll see what I can do, but the airline strike is still on and I understand it is particularly hard to get flights out of south Florida. You'll have to give me some time to make arrangements." I returned to my room. There was little packing to do, because I had left stuff in my bags for just such an emergency. It is better to be wrinkled than left behind.

Harry was fit to be tied. I won't even try to replicate what he said over the phone. Couldn't, anyway, because I pretty much tuned out until he ran down. "I could drive them to New Orleans," I said by way of making amends for my many failings.

"You just may have to do that. But even that won't be easy. So many tourists are stuck in Florida that rental agency fleets are being depleted by one-way hires. They are refusing to rent to people going north. But I'll see what I can do."

Turned out the minister wasn't pressing me, yet, to get him out of Miami. He spent hours in the hotel gift shop buying examples of everything made from seashells. He was having them packaged up and sent to Shebai. "We have many shells in Shebai. Perhaps we can make such things."

It doesn't matter, I suppose, if the whole population is put to making something useless. They are going to make money, anyhow, as fast as they and Bigg Oil can pump it out of the ground.

The car Harry dug up for me was a junker. Out of alignment, it was hard to keep on the road. But anyway, midafternoon we started off for New Orleans, unimaginably far away.

At the first traffic light I threw the minister and Jamil into the back of the front seat. Not maliciously, though if I had thought about it I might actually have done it. The problem was I had been driving all sorts of sports cars and funny cars for years, often with close gear ratios and as many as six forward speeds. None of these had automatic transmissions so I just naturally, without thinking about it, double-clutched my downshifts, snapping in the clutch pedal as I shifted. That might not have been a problem had it not been for the idiot Detroit engineer who designed a brake pedal that covered the place where the clutch pedal would have been had there been one. And the damn machine had power brakes that, of all the car's various mechanisms, worked just fine.

After I had thrown my passengers out of their seats for the second time, I sat on my left leg to avoid doing it again. It was going to be a long 1,346 miles to New Orleans sitting on my leg. It was getting hot. I rolled up my window and turned on the air-conditioning. Thank God (or Allah, whichever) the AC worked. Jamil told me to turn it off. "The minister does not like air-conditioning." I took off my jacket. I sweated. The minister, who had changed to Arab dress, looked nice and cool. Appropriate to the minister's native dress (Jamil kept to his western suit; he apparently was born without sweat glands) my passengers conversed in Arabic. Probably saying things about me.

Sometime later, the minister touched my shoulder. It was the first time he had touched me. I noticed he used his left hand. "We will stop here."

"Here" was an awful-looking little roadhouse, the sort of

place kept dark so you can't see the beer and food stains on the menus and you can't tell whom your wife is with across the room. "Here?"

"Right here!" he said more insistently. I turned abruptly into the graveled parking area in front of the establishment and snapped in the clutch, only it wasn't the clutch. We rearranged their gravel as we did a one-eighty.

I don't know what the waitresses thought about our tumultuous arrival. They didn't seem surprised; perhaps all their customers were in a hurry. They also paid no attention to what the minister was wearing, which must have appeared to them to be a bedsheet. Maybe it wasn't unusual for the customers to bring their own.

My eyes slowly accommodated the dim light emanating mostly from the neon beer advertisements behind the bar; I looked around. There did seem to be an unusual number of waitresses in the place, considering the few customers, most who were seated at the bar. Doubtless business would pick up as the evening wore on.

As soon as we were seated, there was an exchange in Arabic between my two companions and Jamil said to me, "The minister wishes for you to drive on ahead to the next city and reserve rooms for the night. Then you may return for us."

We were just south of Ocala but it seemed to me we ought to make Gainesville before we stopped for the night. Otherwise, we were never going to get to New Orleans in time to make our onward flight that Harry had managed to book for us to Houston. I did not relish the idea of trying to drive this awful car all the way to Texas. I had once been stranded near DeQuincy with a burned out Austin Healey water pump and the thought of having something like that happen again with my Shebaihin was more than I could bear to think about. "If you don't mind staying here for several hours, I might find a hotel in Gainesville. That's the state capital."

"It is no problem. We will wait for you."

So I took off in the car with all the windows rolled up and the air conditioner full on. It felt wonderful. Oddly enough, the shimmy in the front end of the car smoothed out about seventy. I leaned back in the seat and turned on the radio. It was broken.

The hotel I selected in Gainesville was old and not fancy. I chose it because it seemed the sort of place where my passengers wouldn't wish to linger. I grabbed a carryout cheeseburger, fries, and a chocolate shake on the way back to pick up my charges. The roadhouse was easy to identify, though it looked quite different with dozens of cars parked, mostly in anonymity, along the sides and back. But where we had skidded in, earlier in the day, the tire marks in the gravel pointed right to the front door. I followed them in, but more slowly, this time. Jamil and the minister were seated where I had left them. They seemed content.

We did make New Orleans by the evening of the next day, despite my worst fears. Harry had booked us into a quite decent hotel right on the edge of the Vieux Carré. The Shebaihin made excuses and retired to their rooms. I thanked the Lord and repaired to the hotel restaurant, which was still serving. If they were going out on the town without me, they had my blessing. If they got lost, well, *salaam aleikum.* As I recall, I had quite a decent meal. But just what it was escapes me now. I was concentrating my attention on a nice single malt. A double, actually.

There is no gainsaying it, the next day did not go well. In the first place, they were doing it to me again. Praying, then talking on the phone, and finally missing the flight that meant they stood up the mayor of Houston. What Harry said when I reported back to him would not make proper reading for my gentle public. He also seemed to think I bore some responsibility for the way things were going. Can't say he was wrong there. I could have left them at the roadhouse and the locals would probably eaten them when they ran out of money. If they ever did.

That evening I lured Jamil into the hotel bar. If there was going to be any hope to come out of this, I was going to have to appeal to Jamil's weaker side. That is, keep him drunk.

"The minister does not wish to go to Houston."

"Not much problem there; we missed our last chance for a plane ride and it's a long way to walk. We could, of course, take a bus." I repressed a grin. The vision of the minister on a bus ride across Louisiana and Texas in August trying to get the driver to turn off the AC, and get the other sweating passengers to open all the windows, was quite cheering. Entirely possible one of them would have a lariat and they would hog-tie the minister and drag him along behind. I allowed my smile to burst forth.

"Absolutely no reason why he should go, then." I ordered us another round of drinks while I gave the matter further thought. "It seems to me there are several possibilities. The minister could tell us what he would rather do and I will try to arrange things. This is his visit, not mine. I've seen Texas.

"Or if he wishes to return home, he is free to do so. The transportation might present some problems, but if he doesn't mind staying in New Orleans for a few days, we ought to be able to get him some connection to an international flight." I thought about that one. The State Department wouldn't like that; maybe they would bust me back to a consular assignment. I could hope.

"If the minister likes it here," I continued, "he could just stay. In six months it will be Mardi Gras. I'm sure he would enjoy that."

"Well, see what you can do," said Jamil.

He didn't say do about what, so I took it to mean I was free to come up with something. I slept on that overnight. And the next morning I talked to a seething Harry Moon. "It seems to me," I told him, "that the only part of this trip that has gone well was the trip up to Pittsburgh with Bigg Oil."

Harry was silent so long I was afraid I had lost the connection. "Harry? Harry?"

"I'm here. I'm thinking. I'll call you back."

I had time to wander around a bit. It had been more than ten years since my last visit and it seemed the place had gotten more touristy than it was in the fifties. I looked for some restaurant that looked familiar but didn't see one and all the strange ones looked crowded. I returned and ate in the hotel. It was good enough. A red snapper stuffed with shrimp and crab. I considered a seafood gumbo as well, but the weather was hot so I selected a gazpacho instead. See? I remember my lunches better than my dinners. Maybe I should cut out before-dinner drinks.

It was well into the afternoon when Harry called. I needn't have hurried my lunch (I didn't). One of Bigg Oil's jets was going to pick us up next morning in New Orleans and take us to Houston and then stay with us across the country until we got to California. The only absolute requirement was that the minister was to attend dinner of the Oil Men's Club in Houston. If the minister would agree to that, everything else was on. Harry would shift around the other appointments to allow for the late arrival.

I passed the word to Jamil and he conversed briefly with the minister. The minister said "fine" in an offhand way as though there had never been any problem.

The visit to Houston was uneventful. During the late afternoon, while waiting for the minister to come down from his room to go to the dinner, I had nothing better to do, so I wandered into the hotel's antique shop. The difference between Vienna and Houston prices was breathtaking. I decided Houston was where the money was; the minister should be happy here.

The dinner was just a dinner. On the top floor of a tall building, of course. I was beginning to believe that oil men were trying to keep well away from the unruly peasants who might turn on them if the price of gasoline went up. I felt like a peasant who had gotten off of the elevator on the wrong floor.

The next day we took a limo ride out to a chicken ranch. There may be something less interesting, but I can't think of it. Besides, I am deathly allergic to chicken feathers. Always have been. When I was a child, my grandmother used to wring the heads off of chickens, and when the creatures finally realized they were dead and quit flopping around, Grandmother would pluck out their big feathers and then build a fire to singe off the rest. I would go into asthmatic collapse, at least until dinner was served.

Following our now leisurely schedule with our very own private jet, a size or two up from an LBJ, we wended our way to Phoenix. There, we visited Boulder Dam, the Salt River project, and Frank Lloyd Wright's Taliesin West, near Scottsdale. To my amazement, nothing unfortunate happened. At least until we got to California.

In Los Angeles, as I should have expected, things started downhill again. No more did we have the corporate jet to spread Bigg Oil over the troubled waters, though the minister seemed content during the day we spent at Disneyland. It was probably just me. I know I should have loved Disneyland, but perhaps I'm just un-American. On the way back from Anaheim, the minister told me he would like to have his own Disneyland in his country, and would I please find out what it would cost. I said I would try. Perhaps it would be possible to sell him ours, I mused. I thought about that Austrian architect who ran down the American tourist, then dropped her ripped-open handbag back in the street, saying it was only plastic. I saw the Austrian's point.

By the time we returned from Disneyland I had had it with the Shebaihin and with the whole damn tour, and was thinking about taking up smoking again. I went shopping and I bought a carton of Benson & Hedges. I lit up. They made me sufficiently sick to take my mind off of the magic kingdom or whatever it is called.

The next day was a visit to an aquarium and then an asphalt plant. The fish were nice enough, but I, who have worked in acid plants, ore roasters, and an H-bomb plant, could find nothing of compelling interest in asphalt.

On the way back to the hotel my visitors became unusually talkative, to themselves, in Arabic. I thought about fish, mostly imagining ways to cook them. Back in my hotel room, I tried smoking again. It was neither my hay fever nor my asthma season, so I ought to have been able to do it. While my hotel room was whirling around there was a knock at the door. I groped my way to the door. It was our limo driver.

"I think you ought to know," he said, "that they want me to take them to Las Vegas."

"I suppose it's all right, but I better clear it. How long does it take for a round-trip to Las Vegas? What time tomorrow should we start?"

"They didn't say anything about a round-trip. They want to leave tonight. I don't think they wanted you to know."

"Oh." I thought about that some. "Oh," I repeated. "Well, check it out with your people, and I'll be waiting in the limo when they are ready to leave. They can't very well throw me out."

I started packing up. I broke the filter off of a Benson & Hedges to make it stronger, and lit up. I wished I had a cigar. And a drink.

I got a call just as I was about ready to leave the room. It was from the local visitor programing agency. Most large cities have such groups, usually made up largely of volunteers, who work with organizations like F.A.T. for local visit arrangements. The limo driver was hired by them and they billed F.A.T.

"There's something you should know about your driver," the caller said. "He says you want him to take your visitors out to Las Vegas."

"That's right. The minister asked for it. I can't very well stop him. He would probably just make other arrangements I wouldn't know about. But what's wrong with the driver? He seemed okay to me."

"He is out on bail pending trial for shooting someone. And he has a prior conviction, malicious wounding or something like that. We don't know how much risk there is, but we thought you ought to know. It's a long, lonely road at night. Almost three hundred miles."

"Thanks a lot. What do you suggest?"

"We'll try to get you another driver, but it's late and I don't know whether we can. You may be stuck with the one you've got."

"I could drive the car."

"It isn't ours and it has to be returned."

There was no way I could get help from Harry. With the

time difference between the East and West Coast, he was long gone from his office. Damn! I thought about being stuck at night out on the desert. I looked in the phone book and found a gun shop nearby. I hurried out to see if they had anything I could use.

There was an old pistol that was cheap enough and looked like it might fire a time or two before it blew up. I tried to buy it. For some reason, perhaps because I was a nonresident, or maybe because all I had was State Department identification (who knows what crazies they've got in Washington) or perhaps I looked like I was clean out of my mind, they declined to sell the pistol to me.

I went back to the hotel. I felt the comforting bulk of my Swiss army knife in my pocket. Perhaps I could hold off the crazed chauffeur with the corkscrew.

As I was getting ready to go get in the limo, there was another call from the local programming agency. They had found another driver, a very experienced man with no criminal record.

Considerably relieved, I was sitting in the front passenger seat of the car when Jamil and the minister came out of the hotel. I had introduced myself to the driver, a craggy hulk of a man aged somewhere in excess of seventy. That doesn't seem so old to me now, but back then he seemed like Methuselah. A bit unsettling, but not as bad as it had been. I told the driver he was not to leave without me, regardless of what the other passengers said.

The Shebaihin saw me at once but said nothing. They watched as the porter loaded their luggage in the trunk and climbed in the backseat. We were off. We made the first half of the journey while it was still light. The landscape was like nothing I had seen before in the East. Then night seemed to fall quite suddenly, and the reach of the headlights' illumination appeared to be inadequate for the speed we were traveling. I glanced at the speedometer. Eighty. I made sure my seat belt was tight.

Some distance farther, we came upon the scene of an accident. People were milling about. Pieces of automobiles were on both sides of the road and in between, the road was covered with glass and small debris. Maybe human remains, but we were on it too quickly to tell and were beyond it in an instant. Our driver didn't seem to see the carnage. I turned around and looked at other passengers. They showed no signs they noticed. Perhaps that was the way with the people of Shebai. When the roll is called up yonder, it will be soon enough for them to pay attention to the trip.

In Las Vegas, I stayed close to the lobby of the hotel, watching. My charges disappeared into the dubious delights of the place. I spent the time trying to reconcile what was around me with the Las Vegas that Virginia Hill had described to me and which she had hated so much. I didn't like it very much either.

It has now been thirty-odd years since my visit to Las Vegas, but judging from modern pictures, the Strip has become much more built up. Back then, there weren't too many places a sheikh could go that he couldn't be found. I made arrangements with the hotel desk to tell me if my boys were checking out or anything like that. I was sure that they could cross a few palms and defeat my arrangements, but probably they wouldn't bother.

Besides, there was no easy way to travel east from Las Vegas until the airline strike was settled. I had Harry's word on that. But it shouldn't take long. There were signs the negotiating parties were close, and when flights resumed, Henry promised to use his muscle to get us reservations back to Washington.

Good fortune, who had only been an occasional companion

on this journey, brought the minister and Jamil to the over-whelmed concierge at the same time I got us reservations to Washington through Chicago. I waved the tickets at the Shebaihin.

Unfortunately, since there was a tremendous backlog of peo-ple waiting to get onward flights, we had a considerable layover in Chicago. I brooded about that as we flew along at 30,000 feet, looking out the window at the parched late-August land-scape. We crossed the Grand Canyon. I glanced across the aisle at the minister. Thank God, he hadn't noticed it, or I would have been instructed to buy him one like it.

We had not quite four hours in Chicago. At O'Hare I rented a car. I didn't want to, but the minister insisted that he be driven into the city, where I was to leave him and Jamil. Taxi, perhaps? No, they wanted me to drive. They assured me they would be back at the airport in time for the flight. Yeah, right. I gave them their tickets. If they missed the plane, they could jolly well be on their own.

But I was still so nervous returning to O'Hare that I missed a turn and got hopelessly lost. You would think that as big an air-port as O'Hare is, it would be impossible to miss. But not for me; I could be heading west and miss the Mississippi River. My navigation was not helped by images of the minister and Jamil arriving in Washington without me.

Nevertheless, I was able to turn the car in and make it to the gate in time to board. My Shebaihin strolled leisurely up in time for the last boarding call.

The limo in Washington dropped me off at my little dilapi-dated house on Capitol Hill, the fourteen-foot-wide house next to the Chinese laundry. The visitors stared at it the way you would a mud hut in some primitive place. I got my bags out of the car and walked toward the laundry next door. I turned and waved good-bye, scrootching up my eyes, trying to look Oriental.

• • •

Sam Miller asked me, "How did it go, Conroy?"

"Just wonderfully, Sam. You wouldn't believe it if I told you."

"You got that right. Harry's been calling me just about every day."

"Oh."

"But I think we can get it hushed up. Nobody but Bigg Oil cares about Shebai."

"Very comforting."

"Not so sure what we can do about that other thing."

"Other thing? What other thing?"

"Your security violation."

"What security violation?"

"When you left Vienna, you left your safe open."

"I turned it over to my successor. I gave him the lock combination and left him looking through the classified files. What was I supposed to do, lock him up inside?"

"Might have been a good idea."

ABOUT THE AUTHOR

Richard Timothy Conroy was born in a mining town in the Tennessee mountains. After a time making H-bombs in Oak Ridge, he joined the U.S. Foreign Service and served in Zurich, Belize, and Vienna. He then transferred to the Smithsonian Institution, where he worked as an international liaison until he retired to write and play the piano.